THE LAST FORTRESS OF CONGRESS DOMINANCE

Thank you for choosing a SAGE product!
If you have any comment, observation or feedback,
I would like to personally hear from you.

Please write to me at **contactceo@sagepub.in**

Vivek Mehra, Managing Director and CEO, SAGE India.

Bulk Sales

SAGE India offers special discounts
for purchase of books in bulk.
We also make available special imprints
and excerpts from our books on demand.

For orders and enquiries, write to us at

Marketing Department
SAGE Publications India Pvt Ltd
B1/I-1, Mohan Cooperative Industrial Area
Mathura Road, Post Bag 7
New Delhi 110044, India

E-mail us at **marketing@sagepub.in**

Subscribe to our mailing list
Write to **marketing@sagepub.in**

This book is also available as an e-book.

THE LAST FORTRESS OF CONGRESS DOMINANCE

MAHARASHTRA SINCE THE 1990s

SUHAS PALSHIKAR
RAJESHWARI DESHPANDE

SAGE SERIES ON POLITICS IN INDIAN STATES
VOLUME 5

SERIES EDITORS
SUHAS PALSHIKAR
RAJESHWARI DESHPANDE

Los Angeles | London | New Delhi
Singapore | Washington DC | Melbourne

First published in 2021 by

SAGE Publications India Pvt Ltd
B1/I-1 Mohan Cooperative Industrial Area
Mathura Road, New Delhi 110 044, India
www.sagepub.in

SAGE Publications Inc
2455 Teller Road
Thousand Oaks, California 91320, USA

SAGE Publications Ltd
1 Oliver's Yard, 55 City Road
London EC1Y 1SP, United Kingdom

SAGE Publications Asia-Pacific Pte Ltd
18 Cross Street #10-10/11/12
China Square Central
Singapore 048423

Published by Vivek Mehra for SAGE Publications India Pvt Ltd. Typeset in 10.5/13 pt Berkeley by Zaza Eunice, Hosur, Tamil Nadu, India.

Library of Congress Control Number: 2020948212

ISBN: 978-93-5388-679-0 (HB)

SAGE Team: Rajesh Dey, Shivani Anupkumar Damle, Neena Ganjoo and Rajinder Kaur
Cover image: Shailesh D. Jadhav

CONTENTS

LIST OF TABLES

LIST OF ABBREVIATIONS

AIMIM	All India Majlis-e-Ittehad-ul-Muslimeen
BBM	Bharipa Bahujan Mahasangh
BJP	Bharatiya Janata Party
BPCC	Bombay Pradesh Congress Committee
BRP	Bharatiya Republican Party
BSP	Bahujan Samaj Party
BSS	Bahujan Shramik Samiti
BVA	Bahujan Vikas Aghadi
CAG	Comptroller and Auditor General
CM	Chief minister
CPI(M)	Communist Party of India (Marxist)
CPI	Communist Party of India
CPPDG	Centre for Public Policy and Democratic Governance
CSDS	Centre for the Study of Developing Societies
DMIC	Delhi–Mumbai Industrial Corridor
DNT	Denotified Tribe
DPDCs	District Planning and Development Committees
EGS	Employment Guarantee Scheme
ENP	Effective number of parties
FDI	Foreign direct investment
GSDP	Gross state domestic product
HMS	Hind Mazdoor Sabha
ICS	Indian Congress (Socialist)

IHDS	Indian Human Development Survey
INC	Indian National Congress
INCU	Indian National Congress (Urs)
IND	Independents
IT	Information technology
JD(S)	Janata Dal (Secular)
JD	Janata Dal
JP	Janata Party
JSS	Jan Surajya Shakti
KKP	Kamgar Kisan Paksha
KTSTP	Krantikari Shetkari Party
LKD	Lok Dal
LS	Lok Sabha
MIDC	Maharashtra Industrial Development Corporation
MIHAN	Multi-modal International Cargo Hub and Airport at Nagpur
MLAs	Members of Legislative Assembly
MNS	Maharashtra Navnirman Sena
MP	Member of Parliament
MPCC	Maharashtra Pradesh Congress Committee
MVA	Maha Vikas Aghadi
NCAER	National Council of Applied Economic Research
NCP	Nationalist Congress Party
NDA	National Democratic Alliance
NES	National Election Studies
NPCIL	Nuclear Power Corporation of India Limited
NT	Nomadic Tribe
NVPP	Native People's Party
OBCs	Other Backward Classes
PCC	Pradesh Congress Committee
PDA	Progressive Democratic Alliance
PDF	Progressive Democratic Front
PM	Prime minister

PSP	Praja Socialist Party
PWP	Peasants and Workers Party
RPI(A)	Republican Party of India (Athawale)
RPI(K)	Republican Party of India (Kamble)
RPI	Republican Party of India
RPK	Republican Party of India (Khobragade)
RRP	Ram Rajya Parishad
RSP	Rashtriya Samaj Paksh
RSS	Rashtriya Swayamsevak Sangh
RUSA	Rashtriya Uchchatar Shiksha Abhiyan
SCF	Scheduled Castes Federation
SCs	Scheduled Castes
SEZ	Special economic zone
SHS	Shiv Sena
SJP(M)	Samajwadi Janata Party (Maharashtra)
SMS	Samyukta Maharashtra Samiti
SP	Samajwadi Party (post-1990 period)
SP	Socialist Party
SPPU	Savitribai Phule Pune University
SSP	Samyukta Socialist Party
STs	Scheduled Tribes
SWP	Swabhimani Paksha
UGC	University Grants Commission
UP	Uttar Pradesh
UPA	United Progressive Alliance
VBA	Vanchit Bahujan Aghadi
VS	Vidhan Sabha
WUA	Water Users Associations
ZP	Zilla Parishad

SERIES NOTE

The Sage Series on Politics in Indian States aims at developing comprehensive, contemporary political histories of Indian states looking at the past two and a half decades. The series consists of volumes covering important trends in the politics of major states of India. Each volume, devoted to one particular state, situates the politics of that state in the larger socio-historical context and presents a detailed analysis of the significant patterns of competitive politics in the state with a focus on framework of party competition, rise of new social forces, role of leadership and the context of regional political economy. Going beyond state-specificity, each volume also attempts to situate the politics of the state in the larger all-India context.

Besides analysing the state-specific trends in party politics that have led to the rise of many state parties, these volumes also carefully look at the social bases of parties and their electoral fortunes in the backdrop of fluctuations in voter choices during elections of past quarter of a century, making use of the rich data archives of Lokniti.

The unfolding dynamics of politics since the 1990s, which manifested at the state level at slightly different moments and sometimes even preceded the 1990s, have forcefully brought back the states in the consciousness of students of Indian politics. It has also led to a renewed interest among sociologists and economists about the political processes at state level and their interconnections with socio-economic developments in India. At the same time, there is a glaring absence of detailed documentations of the state-specific political processes during past two decades. The series addresses this gap in the literature on Indian politics. The series also propels more informed cross-state comparisons as a starting point to truly grasp 'all-India' politics.

ACKNOWLEDGEMENTS

During the past more than two decades, we have been fortunate to have two colleagues from whom we have benefitted, both through their collaboration and their understanding of Maharashtra's politics. They are Nitin Birmal and Vivek Ghotale. They have been co-authors of many writings on Maharashtra politics that we undertook and have used those writings in this book; they have been collaborators in many research projects we took up together or individually and have also been leaders of many field surveys we did in Maharashtra. Above all, we acknowledge our debt also for their long and steadfast friendship.

Many of our past students and other student friends participated in the surveys from which we have culled the data presented in this book. We would like to thank them. We are also thankful to the Lokniti, Programme for Comparative Democracy at the Centre for the Study of Developing Societies (CSDS), Delhi, for access to the valuable data from its Data Unit and especially to Himanshu Bhattacharya for untiringly supporting our requests for data. Shivaji Motegaonkar, Rohini Wani, Manoj Pandkar and Radha Kulkarni helped us with the references. We thank them all.

We acknowledge the financial support of Lokniti—CSDS; University Grants Commission (UGC); the Indian Council of Social Science Research; Rashtriya Uchchatar Shiksha Abhiyan (RUSA), Maharashtra; and Savitribai Phule Pune University (SPPU) to our various research projects over the years which have contributed to the argument in this book.

We also wish to sincerely acknowledge the critical encouragement received from two anonymous referees through their detailed and substantive reviews and suggestions for improvement in the draft manuscript.

Finally, we thank Abhijit Baroi, Rajesh Dey, Neena Ganjoo and colleagues from the editorial and production teams of SAGE.

NOTES ON SOURCES

1. All election results tabulated in the book are based on tables compiled by CSDS Data Unit from ECI results.
2. Unless otherwise mentioned and referenced, all tables using survey data are based on data made available by CSDS Data Unit.
3. All references to newspapers, periodicals, etc., are given in the footnotes.
4. All other references are given by using the in-text method and listed in the references at the end of the book.

INTRODUCTION

Writing this book proved deceptively tough. Having been following politics of Maharashtra over past three decades and also soiling our hands with using much survey data to understand electoral trends, we thought that we had a finger on the core of this book, namely how Maharashtra's politics arrived at the present juncture and what that means for the future of Maharashtra's politics. Weaving through different chapters, we realized that Maharashtra's politics keeps eluding us! As a result, and as a coincidence, this book finally shaped during the 'diamond jubilee' of the State.[1]

Just before Maharashtra completed 60 years of its existence, an early morning intrigue was effected by Devendra Fadnavis of Bharatiya Janata Party (BJP) and Ajit Pawar of the Nationalist Congress Party (NCP) followed by a counter-coup by Sharad Pawar resulting into a rather unlikely political alliance called the Maha Vikas Aghadi (MVA) in November 2019.[2] As we witnessed those rapidly evolving events, momentarily we thought that we perhaps needed to completely reframe our analysis. Of course, the politics of coalitions that evolved

[1] In this book, we use capital 'S' when referring to States of the Indian Union.

[2] After the Assembly election of 2019, SHS parted company with BJP breaking their pre-election alliance and in a surprise move, BJP forged an alliance with Ajit Pawar with Devendra Fadnavis as chief minister (CM) and Pawar as deputy CM (23 November 2019). But following the Supreme Court directive for holding an immediate vote of confidence, they both resigned on 26 November and, subsequently, with support from NCP and Congress, SHS's Uddhav Thackeray became the CM (28 November 2019).

in India since 1989 had ensured that observers and students of party politics would cease to be stirred, leave aside shocked, by any configuration taking shape in the political arena. And yet, Shiv Sena (SHS) coming together with Congress and NCP, after three decades of assiduous attempts to carve out a non-congress space in the politics of the State, did deserve adequate amount of surprise. Having overcome that surprise, as we went into finalizing this manuscript, we decided that we could certainly situate that latest development within the broader framework of this book.[3]

As is often the case, things change despite appearing not to be changing much. In fact, throughout the period that this book deals with, Maharashtra displays this tendency of appearing as if it were not changing much and then, in retrospect, making us realize how politics in the State has indeed changed. Even at the time of writing this, the jury is still out if the formation of MVA indeed stalled the changes the 2014 elections had brought about or simply slowed them a bit.

While someone following the deterioration of the Congress party in Maharashtra might wonder what this book is doing when it still talks about Maharashtra as the 'fortress' of the Congress, a reader reading this book in a relative temporal proximity to 2019 might be querulous about our continued reiteration that the Congress party in the State is indeed on its endless downslide—throughout the period that this book focuses on. In all humility, we would argue that both these stories—the fact that Congress refuses to completely give way to a new party system and also the fact that a new party system is knocking at the doors of the State—are together true and summarize the politics of the State. We also hope that this assessment might resonate when someone is looking at the State's politics five years down the line.

---

[3] Even then, a trenchant criticism of the draft manuscript on this issue by one of the two reviewers spurred us into taking this question head-on, which we had otherwise tucked into the last parts of Chapter 6. We gratefully acknowledge our debt to the anonymous reviewer for this.

The book focuses on the politics of Maharashtra since the 1990s. The reasons why we identify the 1990s as the crucial moment inaugurating a different phase in the State's politics are explained through Chapters 1–3. These chapters also explain our claim that Maharashtra was, for a considerably long time, a stronghold of the Congress. This claim is not merely about the electoral trajectory of the State; as we argue through the initial chapters, politics of Maharashtra was more characterized by the successful preponderance of the 'congress system' rather than mere electoral dominance of the party. Parenthetically, it is this factor of the congress system that probably has delayed the complete marginalization of the Congress party in spite of the party dipping below the mark of 25 per cent vote share for a long period. With such a disastrous string of electoral setbacks, the party would have been a forgotten force, as indeed it did in many other States. But in Maharashtra, that dismal future has continued to get postponed since 1995!

This congress system in Maharashtra was as much a product of the skilful management of power and social forces by Yashwantrao Chavan as it was an extension of the all-India congress system. We believe that this aspect holds a rich potential for those interested in the field of comparative politics of India's States. At the same time, this more 'State-specific' feature of congress system in Maharashtra also allows us to understand both the dilemma faced by Sharad Pawar and his NCP in deciding not to join hands with the BJP and the longevity of his politics despite repeated setbacks during the post-1990 period. As we shall briefly mention in Chapter 4, while he has been at the centre of State's politics, Pawar's politics has been the target of sharp criticisms by both his political adversaries and other activists. However, stepping back from his continued contemporaneity, one cannot but escape the connection his politics has with the congress system and the way in which he appropriated that system and in the process also modified it.[4] Transcending personalities, this implicitly poses a challenge for the students of State's politics.

---

[4] For an assessment on these lines, see Palshikar (2017a).

As we discuss in Chapter 4, the Congress party was defeated in 1995. That election, as we argue, constitutes a critical moment in the politics of the State because since then, a new era of coalition politics emerged in the State and along with it, experiments of new social equations to sustain the politics beyond the old congress system also emerged. Chapters 5 and 6 chronicle the exciting tussle between the emergent sociopolitical forces and the Congress parties (since then, there have been two Congress parties in Maharashtra) and the inability of the SHS–BJP coalition to retain the advantage they had got in 1995. Since 2014, that began to change.

By the end of 2014, it appeared as if, finally, a new party system had emerged. In Chapter 6, we discuss this shaky dominance of the BJP—shaky not just in retrospect, but we know that it could not retain power in the Assembly[5] elections of 2014. The emergent order was shaky for two other reasons. One is its dependence on a partner. Throughout the five years of the BJP–SHS government of 2014, the State witnessed not just the bickering between the two allies but also an extraordinary situation where the coalition partner was a more strident opponent than the opposition parties. Other reason why we call BJP's domination shaky is that even after handsome victories in 2014, the BJP was unable to forge a durable winning social coalition. As we discuss in the book, the BJP has often experimented with a dual strategy—on the one hand, presenting itself as the authentic representative of the Other Backward Classes (OBCs) in the State and, on the other hand, making every effort to win over the Maratha community. This strategy means an uncertainty about social bases of the party, something that comes to the forefront in Assembly elections of 2019.

Two very important processes intervene in electoral politics, and we argue that these two not only help us understand election outcomes but also comprehend broader political processes. These are the identity–materiality dimension of caste politics and the political

---

[5] We interchangeably use the terms Legislative Assembly, State Assembly, Assembly and Vidhan Sabha (VS).

economy. Chapters 7 and 8 connect the electoral narrative and discussions of party politics to these two, respectively. In Chapter 7, we
discuss the long-term crisis of the Maratha community in the context
of its claims to be the natural leader of other caste groups in the State.
Here again, we encounter a 'State-specificity' of Maharashtra. While
many other dominant castes have also manifested similar symptoms
of crisis leading to demands for reservations, in Maharashtra, the
Maratha community, historically bound with the Congress, has only
fragmented so far. At the same time, no alternative to the power of
that community has shaped. As mentioned above, the BJP always
attempted to bring together 'OBCs' as an alternative to the might of
the Marathas, but in spite of having popular leaders from the OBC
communities, such a sociopolitical consolidation of OBCs has eluded
the party. In this backdrop, when it came to power in 2014, the BJP
saw an opportunity to woo the Marathas—both the Maratha elite
and the masses—on account of the agitation over separate reservations for Marathas (by recognizing that they are backward). Electoral
fluctuations and shifts are contingent and as we complete the writing
of this book, we cannot say for sure that the Marathas have shifted
towards the BJP. This complex interplay of ambition to hold on to
power, an imminent loss of hegemony and the pressures of aligning with different parties for temporary political gains, has led to
what we call the 'crisis of the Marathas', which is distinct from what
the Lingayats or Patels or Jats have faced respectively in Karnataka,
Gujarat or Haryana.

The reasons are not merely historical; they have deep roots in the
political economy of the State too. The compulsions of adjusting to
industrial and service sector interests along with the necessity to maintain electoral winnability on the basis of large mass of voters from the
agrarian–rural sectors have produced many distortions in the field of
policymaking in the State, connecting the question of caste politics
to the political economy on the one hand and linking questions of
economic policies to the ability of political parties to sell those policies
to the voters on the other. We discuss these in Chapter 8. In other
words, the book seeks to traverse the four fields of Maharashtra's

politics—political history prior to the 1990s, the trajectory of Maratha hegemony during the period of political shifts, distortions of political economy and the party-political arena.

Writing in the early 1980s, Lele drew attention to the 'resilience' of the Congress (Lele, 1984). Looking at the smart coup staged by the NCP and Congress in agreeing to have an SHS CM must, therefore, look like a leaf from that book of resilience. However, more than three decades later, today, the Congress (and NCP) would not find a national political context for their healthy survival. Moreover, the ideological space that the BJP has carved out for itself might be more than what the two Congress parties can negotiate today. In all probability, the ideas associated with Hindutva are likely to replace the idea of *Bahujan Samaj* (see Chapter 1 for this idea)—and even subsume that idea. Therefore, we argue that despite the humiliation faced by the BJP in not being able to form the government in 2019, the political arena is much more likely to be ideologically dominated by the BJP and possibly ensuring the sustenance of the BJP as a single major player in State politics. The coming couple of years are going to be crucial in the journey of State's politics. The governance record of the MVA, their internal equations and, above all, their interventions in the field of societal relations and the political economy will be the deciding factors whether the 'shaky' dominance of the BJP is consolidated or halted. It is useful to keep in mind that the BJP in Maharashtra does not have a strong prior existence as in the case of Gujarat or a long history of social roots as in MP or Rajasthan. That makes the party vulnerable in Maharashtra and gives a fair chance to other competitors. All the same, this also alerts us to the possibility that as the BJP expands its influence, the pattern of its dominance may vary from State to State. So far, the BJP in Maharashtra, though on the rise since 2014, has not thrown up any such Maharashtra-specific pattern of dominance.

But if one thing is certain, it is this: Maharashtra has moved away from the rather comfortable resilience of the Congress. Whether this shift finally gives way to a new party system and whether it allows the shaping of newer bases of dominance are the questions that we discuss in the last chapter. It is hoped that even if the prognostications of this book do not come to fruition, to the extent this book generates debate about State's politics and throws up new ideas for comparing political processes across different States, the book would serve an important purpose.

Framework of Congress Dominance

Known for being a textbook example of one-party dominance and the famous congress system, Maharashtra began moving away from both these characteristics around the late 1980s. In fact, the beginning of this shift had taken place even earlier, in the mid-1970s, but the actual impact of that beginning was felt only during the 1980s, and the political character of the State manifested some alterations only by the late 1980s. In the 1995 State Assembly elections, the Congress party was roundly defeated and, thus, 1995 is the convenient and clear point of rupture. It is, therefore, commonplace to situate the shift in State politics only around 1990–1995.

This book is, of course, not about the shaping of the congress system in Maharashtra but about politics *after* the decline of that system had set in. When a dominant party declines, it allows sudden political mobilizations on unexpected lines; it facilitates many new forces to enter the arena of competition; it also sharpens pre-existing distortions and thus produces new configuration of party-political competition. A dominant party system also stunts 'normal' articulation of sociopolitical protests and once that dominance is eroded, new social mobilizations appear on the scene. Therefore, it is useful to begin with a brief review of the congress system, though in much of the period under discussion in this book, the congress system was mostly broken and on its way out. This book identifies the point of departure and rupture around the mid-1990s and at the same time links up the post-1995 politics to its predecessor, the congress system.

In this chapter, we summarize the historical evolution of the congress system in Maharashtra. While Rajni Kothari (1964) is rightly credited with the conceptualization of the phenomenon of the congress system, his theorization primarily hinged on the functioning of that 'system' at the all-India level through its evolution since the early 1950s. This system both drew its sustenance from and gave shape to State-specific patterns which have been documented less and celebrated even less. But the real strength of the congress system lies in this horizontal spread across many States (Yadav and Palshikar, 2003). While some States always bucked that trend (Tamil Nadu, West Bengal and Kerala, to name a few), some States often manifested a weak congress system (Odisha, Madhya Pradesh and Uttar Pradesh). On the other hand, States such as Karnataka, Andhra Pradesh and Rajasthan distinguished themselves not only by remaining under Congress rule for long but also by evolving State-specific congress systems that often jelled well with the all-India congress system and gave it concrete existential strength. Among these States, Maharashtra is perhaps the most interesting case where the congress system (a) extended beyond its all-India life, (b) was closely connected to the life and aspirations of one caste-bloc, (c) remained in truncated form almost till the 1990s and (d) was never challenged by any single party successfully. This book, then, while being an analysis of the State's politics since 1995 is simultaneously a narrative of how congress system slowly gave way at the State level and in what ways the post-1995 configuration is different from what it replaced.

Before we turn to the post-1995 political process and the unfolding of the post-congress polity in the State, it is useful to map the nature of society and party system that the State experienced till the 1990s. This overview would enable us to unravel the puzzle of resilience and final collapse of the congress system in the State and also the puzzle of the complex relationship between the congress system and Maratha dominance.

REGION, DEMOGRAPHY AND MEMORY

The State of Maharashtra comprises of different sub-regions (most commonly identified as Mumbai, Konkan, Vidarbh, Marathwada and western Maharashtra), having diverse administrative and socio-historical backgrounds. Mumbai has had long experience of British rule since 1665 (though some areas continued under Portuguese rule for some time after that), and much of western Maharashtra and Vidarbh areas too had come under colonial rule in the early 19th century itself (barring some small 'princely states'). But Marathwada region was under Nizam rule until the new Indian state liquidated the Hyderabad-based Nizam state in 1948. While most of Vidarbh was part of the Central Province since the early 19th century, Bombay, Konkan and western Maharashtra regions were administratively combined with Kannada-speaking northern regions of today's Karnataka and Gujarati-speaking areas of today's Gujarat. Only in 1956, at the time of reorganization of many States on linguistic basis, all Marathi-speaking areas came together in the Bombay State. However, this reorganization was still not complete because although Kannada-speaking areas were merged with the newly created State of Mysore (later Karnataka), the State created in 1956 was a bilingual State of Marathi-speaking and Gujarati-speaking populations.

The State of Maharashtra (as it now exists) consists of a large population that belongs to the Maratha-Kunbi caste cluster. Most accounts agree that this castecluster comprises of nearly 30 per cent of State's population,[1] but it has a much larger share of population in the Marathwada region, while the Vidarbh region has a more diverse population comprising of Scheduled Tribes (STs) and Scheduled Castes (SCs). Besides, this region also has a large 'OBC' population. Thus, beneath the surface of Maratha preponderance, the State does have sub-regional variation in its caste composition (Palshikar, 1998). Overall, the State has 11.8 per cent SC population and 9.4 per cent ST population.[2] As per 2011 Census, Muslims account for 11.5 per cent and Buddhists for 5.8 per cent of the State's population.[3] Although

---

[1] Using 1931 Census, Lele shows that for present-day Maharashtra, Maratha-Kunbi population accounts for 31.19 per cent. He also gives estimated shares of other major communities based on the same (Lele, 1990a; 116–117).

[2] 2011 Census. Retrieved from http://pibmumbai.gov.in/English/PDF/E2013_PR798.PDF

[3] 2011 Census, Retrieved from https://www.census2011.co.in/data/religion/state/27-maharashtra.html

Brahmans once ruled as the Peshwas, their population in the State is less than 4 per cent—something that distinguishes Maharashtra from States of North India. Similarly, the 'backward communities' (until the Marathas were so acknowledged in 2014) consisted of a large number of small castes, each often not accounting for more than 3 or 4 per cent.[4]

All regions of the State are linked together not just by a common language but also by a set of historical memories that constitute an evocative element in contemporary politics around which political mobilizations can easily be shaped. These memories can be broadly divided into three groups—the memories received from pre-British period, the controversies and reconfigurations of social power during the 19th century and, finally, the 20th century political struggles centred on national movement and formal electoral competition. Of course, these memories are much more complex than this schematic narration presents them and are mutually overlapping and sometimes mired in controversy and, above all, often amenable to renovation and redefinition.

At the centre of these memories and continuous redefinition is the iconic figure of Chhatrapati Shivaji (Deshpande, 2007). But beyond Shivaji Maharaj, the historical legacy common to the entire State is that of the Varkari *sampradaya* and the *bhakti* tradition (More, 2013). No wonder, therefore, that these twin historical legacies have played a critical role in mass mobilizations throughout the 19th and 20th centuries (continuing in the 21st century as well), including the movement aimed at the formation of the State. These legacies have also been relevant to politics of the State since its formation in 1960. Similarly, intellectuals during the late 19th and early 20th centuries and the movement for formation of a Marathi-speaking State chose to highlight the historical 'Maharashtrian identity' deriving from the idea of Maharashtra dharma.[5] Through this idea, it was possible to link

---

[4] Both the facts that Brahmans are far less numerous in Maharashtra than in the North and no single 'OBC' caste exists in the State account for the muted response to the Mandal controversy in Maharashtra during the 1990s. We further discuss this in Chapter 3.

[5] There are varying interpretations of 'Maharashtra dharma' and also their varying appropriations through history. According to one interpretation, this concept captures

together a wide range of legacies from Shivaji Maharaj to Sant Ramdas and from Tilak to Ranade.

The other legacy that constitutes historical memory consists of 'reform' movements involving questions of caste, patriarchy and role of state in 'private' matters of the family and subsequently the anti-caste polemic extended by the 19th century radical liberal, Jyotirao Phule. The 'social reform' movement often culminated into a straightforward dichotomy between the moderate liberals and the conservative nationalists. Interestingly, both these camps belonged to Brahman intellectuals and were not inclined to a radical approach to questions of caste and religion.[6] Only with the intervention of Phule did the caste question, as also the gender issue, came to the forefront (Deshpande, 2002). Following Phule's teachings, the non-Brahman movement emerged at the turn of the 19th century, which was strengthened by the royal support and foresight of Shahu Maharaj (O'Hanlon, 1985; Omvedt, 1976). Building up on these initiatives, a powerful critique of caste system emerged in the 20th century through Dr Ambedkar's leadership of the then untouchable communities. Going much beyond merely issues of untouchability, the Ambedkar legacy enriched anti-caste arguments that had initially emerged through the life and work of Phule. In contemporary Maharashtra, the Phule, Shahu and Ambedkar legacies are often seen as constituting a common intellectual heritage in favour of equality and dignity.

In the early 20th century, Maharashtra also witnessed the rise of militant Hindu nationalism mainly with Savarkar as its chief proponent. The 20th century also saw the bitter battle between Tilakites and Gandhi's followers within the national movement. Gradually,

---

the historical complexity of the competition between the Marathas and Brahmans, both belonging to the traditional elite status. For more details, see Vora (1999).

[6] Sumant ([1988] 2006; 18–27) discusses at length how in the 19th century literature on caste there were clearly two traditions, the Brahmanical one and the non-Brahman one, and how the former had a rather narrow understanding of reform and of caste question. Similarly, Pradeep Gokhale ([1988] 2006; 39–47) points to the limitations of anti-caste critique of Lokhitawadi (Gopal Hari Dehsmukh) and Deshpande (2000; 123–128) illustrates how an early reformer like Balshastri Jambhekar's views on caste and gender were marked by 'silence'.

the Gandhian segment of the nationalist movement got an upper hand when it agreed to shed its Brahmanical character, as explained further. These memories and their continuous revival and redefinition during public mobilizations have ensured that the State would have a common sociopolitical identity and ideological anchor.

Through the nationalist movement and Gandhi's leadership, the Congress gained acceptability and organizational clout in the Marathi-speaking regions despite attacks on Gandhi both by Brahmans engaged in the Hindu nationalist movement and Dr Ambedkar. In the early parts of the 20th century, the non-Brahman movement known as Brahmanetar movement gathered momentum in many Marathi-speaking parts (Gore, 1989). More interested in contesting Brahman domination and the caste inequalities, initially, the non-Brahman movement stayed away from the national freedom movement led by the Indian National Congress, claiming that the Congress did not care for the ordinary masses comprising of non-Brahman castes. The Brahmanetar movement dubbed the Congress as a Brahmanical outfit. This was, of course, quite true of the Congress in Maharashtra since Tilak's time and even into the first two decades of the 20th century. However, Gandhi's leadership forced a change of assessment on many non-Brahman leaders. After 1930, sections of the Brahmanetar movement turned to the Congress. Vitthal Ramji Shinde was one of the early non-Brahman intellectuals and activists who persuaded the non-Brahmans, particularly the Marathas, that they must join hands with Gandhi's Congress (Kulkarni, [2010] 2019). The role of Keshavrao Jedhe, an important non-Brahman leader from Pune, was crucial in the entry of large number of rural, agrarian masses from the non-Brahman community into the Congress.[7] The 1930s witnessed the unity of two leaders, Keshavrao Jedhe and N. V. Gadgil (Phadke, 1982). The former was a firebrand critic of Brahman superiority and the latter, a Brahman by caste, was a leader of the Congress who believed that the Congress must accommodate interests of rural (non-Brahman) peasant

---

[7] Jedhe was influenced by Phule and was active in the anti-Tilak camp. But as the Gandhian movement grew, he became convinced that the non-Brahman masses must fight against the British rule. Thus, he joined the national movement through the Congress. For Jedhe's political biography, see Phadke (1982).

masses. The Jedhe–Gadgil alliance also meant a truce in the ongoing battle between Marathas and Brahmans. In a democratic set-up, this alliance ensured electoral majority without actually compromising the interests of the Brahmans. In this sense, the Brahman–Maratha alliance was simultaneously a socially 'integrative' formation and politically a democratic manoeuvre by the dominant classes. This alliance contributed to the Congress party's rise to domination in the Marathi-speaking areas. As a result, other political parties and groups had to be content with a role on the fringe of State's politics. The Congress dominated because it occupied a large social space: the rural non-Brahman sections plus a substantial section among the Brahmans. The Congress also occupied an ideological space which was very crucial: In a caste-ridden society, the rise of Maratha leadership within the Congress represented a progressive aspect, and in a competitive democratic context, this alliance ensured majority.

Jedhe's entry into the Congress meant that by 1931, no major political force existed in Marathi-speaking areas which could effectively challenge the Congress. Both Rashtriya Swayamsevak Sangh (RSS) and Hindu Maha Sabha had only thin popularity and that too only among Brahmans. The Communists were gaining ground, but this was confined only to Bombay city. The Ambedkarite movement was certainly opposed to the Congress, but it too did not have sufficient strength to take on the Congress. Therefore, at the time of independence, the Marathi-speaking areas of Bombay Province were completely under the ideological influence and political control of the Congress.

MOVEMENT FOR LINGUISTIC STATE

It was not surprising in this background that the Congress handsomely won the 1952 elections to legislature of the then Bombay Province. Politics after independence took the shape of Congress dominance, but it also had two other significant dimensions. Within the Congress, in spite of the famous Jedhe–Gadgil alliance, a sense of injustice was felt among the non-Brahman leaders. They continued to be in secondary position when it came to power-sharing. The other aspect that dominated politics was the demand for formation of a Marathi-speaking state with Bombay as its capital. While the former factor contributed to the formation of Peasants and Workers Party (PWP) in 1948 (Bhole, 2010; 8–23), the latter produced a prolonged agitation first under the leadership of a joint committee called Samyukta Maharashtra Parishad (Conference for United Maharashtra) formed in 1946 and later the Samyukta Maharashtra Samiti (SMS; Committee for United Maharashtra) formed in 1956. The SMS consisted of Socialists, Communists and Republican Party of India (RPI; then Scheduled Castes Federation [SCF]) apart from many intellectuals, journalists and literary figures. Since the Samyukta Maharashtra Movement has been the only large-scale agitation witnessed by the Marathi society wherein a broad spectrum of leaders and intellectuals came together to play an important role, this agitation has attained a somewhat mythical status in Maharashtra.[8] It also contributed to the rejuvenation of the memories of the Shivaji legacy and the idea that there is a certain ideological basis to the unity of Marathi people through the memory of Maharashtra dharma.

The State Congress kept away from the SMS. Thus, the SMS virtually became a platform of non-Congress groups and parties. It provided for anti-Congress politics. Anti-Congress politics got a shot in the arms when in 1956, while reorganizing the States, Gujarati- and Marathi-speaking areas were combined into one big bilingual State known as the State of Bombay.

Public resentment over the formation of a bilingual State was very strong in western Maharashtra and Bombay regions. In comparison, the people of the Marathwada area of former Hyderabad State (annexed to Bombay State) were generally supportive of the Congress. In the

---

[8] The struggle for the formation of a State on linguistic basis is not in itself very novel because a large number of regions have witnessed similar popular struggles. While some, like in Punjab, were combined with territorial and religious identities, most such struggles have always combined territory and language, thus invoking history and culture. These movements have often facilitated the rise of a regional elite. In Maharashtra, the movement for a linguistic State assumes importance because it brought together the competing elites from Brahman and Maratha communities, brought together many non-Congress parties which otherwise did not have anything in common and saw the intervention by literary elite and journalists in mass agitation. For a detailed history of the movement and an account of the role of the SMS, see Phadke (1979).

Vidarbh region, many leaders from the erstwhile Central Province and Berar were not very enthusiastic about merging with the Bombay State. In this area, there was considerable support to the idea of a separate State of Vidarbh. The 1957 elections were held in this background and in a surcharged atmosphere. The SMS defeated the Congress in Bombay and western Maharashtra. Out of 26 Lok Sabha (LS) seats from these regions, the Congress could win only 4 seats, while it won only 46 out of the 159 Assembly seats from these areas. Its success in Gujarati-speaking areas and the Marathwada and Vidarbh regions helped it in retaining power in the Bombay State. The Praja Socialist Party (PSP) and PWP emerged as powerful opposition parties with 30 and 26 Assembly seats respectively from western Maharashtra and Bombay. Additionally, they won three and five seats respectively from Marathwada and Vidarbh regions. The SCF and Communist Party of India (CPI) also won 13 seats each to the Assembly from the Marathi-speaking areas of the Bombay State.

Looking at the result of 1957 elections, it appears as if politics in the State had started becoming very competitive. The RPI and PWP looked like having the potential to take on the Congress. This scene was matched by widespread popular resentment against State Congress which was not adequately assertive on the issue of formation of a Marathi-speaking State. But more than the significance of election results, the situation around 1957 threw up factors that dominated State politics for some time to come. In the first place, the agitation for Samyukta Maharashtra bolstered large-scale popularity of communist trade union leaders and helped in their entry into areas which had no trade union politics. Second, the agitation meant an alliance of urban-based leaders with leaders having a rural base. Independently, neither could influence State politics. But the combined leadership made its mark on State politics through the SMS. Third, the agitation was mainly centred in Bombay. It had wide popularity in cities and towns while its rural base was limited. Thus, in the late 1950s, the State saw an urban-based agitation shaping State-level politics for a brief moment. But after receiving a setback in the 1957 elections, the Congress soon regained prominence because it accommodated the claims of elites and also adroitly managed the popular assertion of Marathi identity.

Besides temporarily putting the State Congress on the back foot, the Samyukta Maharashtra agitation is important for shaping a regional sensibility in Maharashtra that kept influencing State's politics from time to time. In this sense, the ideological themes projected by the agitation proved to be very influential. The movement for Samyukta Maharashtra created a strong sense of pride in being Marathi—a 'Maharashtriya' (Maharashtrian). The agitation created a sense of self-awareness and self-respect among the Marathi people. The Marathi *asmita* (pride in identity) played an important role in stirring people into action, although only temporarily. This was boosted by the participation of journalists and literary figures in the movement. The significance of the theme of Marathi identity lies not so much as a force behind the movement but as a real rallying point after the formation of Maharashtra. After 1960, the issue of the Marathi identity was to dominate politics considerably. Identity requires symbols. The Marathi identity relied on the symbol of Shivaji Maharaj. He was seen as a leader who consolidated the Marathi people against an unjust regime of Delhi. On the other hand, Shivaji was also seen as a Marathi ruler with a sense of purpose. The Shivaji symbol expressed the hope that a new Marathi State would emulate Shivaji by ensuring the well-being of all Marathi people. This was not the first time when the symbol of Shivaji was invoked for purposes of political mobilization. During the early nationalist movement, Tilak had also relied on Shivaji as a symbol and, in fact, initiated public celebration of Shivaji's birth anniversary. Tilak attempted to project Shivaji Maharaj as a fighter against outside domination and as a Hindu ruler (Cashman, 1975). During the Samyukta Maharashtra agitation, there was less explicit reference to the Hindu dimension. Shivaji Maharaj was portrayed as a representative of Marathi pride against the Delhi-based rulers (Pendse, [1965] 2010). This shift of emphasis, however, does not mean that the potential of relating Shivaji to Hindu sentiments was totally exhausted. In fact, both Brahman intellectuals and elite Marathas have been very comfortable in portraying a Hindu image of Shivaji Maharaj since this image is supportive of the leadership claims of these sections.[9]

---

[9] While in the 1950s film director Bhalji Pendharkar depicted life and times of Shivaji Maharaj in a decidedly Hinduist manner, similar depictions continued on television

SHAPING OF CONGRESS DOMINATION

In most parts of India, popularity of the Congress stemmed from its role in the national freedom struggle in the immediate post-independence period. Nehru supplemented this popularity by representing the promise of converting freedom into well-being. Thus, in many provinces, the local unit of Congress did not need to have nor did they actually possess a separate popular basis. This was not the case with the Congress party in most Marathi-speaking areas. While the non-Brahmans who had joined the congress movement under the influence of Shinde and Jedhe brought to the Congress considerable social base in rural areas, the Brahman leadership of the Congress ensured urban support and also a strong organization. The popularity and electoral victories of the Congress after independence thus owed their existence to both national character and national role of the Congress party and the local networks that had already shaped during pre-independence period.

These networks were further strengthened when Y. B. Chavan succeeded Morarji Desai as the CM after the formation of bilingual Bombay State. Chavan continued as the CM after the 1957 election and also became the first CM of the newly formed Maharashtra State in 1960. Initially, Chavan relied heavily on Congress high command and Morarji Desai in his efforts to ease out the senior leader Bhausaheb Hiray. But he also evolved autonomous State-level networks that constituted the 'congress system' at the State level. He adopted the strategy of combining ideology with pragmatism. Broadly, the Chavan strategy came to be known as the strategy of accommodation (Lele, 1982a). This strategy was based on the twin aspects of keeping party organization under control and simultaneously evolving a system of satisfying active factional leaders. Chavan not only controlled the government

through serials like *Chhatrapati Shivaji* (Hindi) and *Raja Shiv Chhatrapati* (Marathi) around 2000 and later (see Motegaonkar, 2012). On Shivaji symbol, also see Jasper (2002). In order to contest such interpretations of Shivaji in popular culture, the veteran CPI leader Govind Pansare wrote a forcefully argued tract suggesting that Shivaji Maharaj was a people's king who had well-being of the populace at heart and was a fair and just ruler looking after the interests of peasantry above anything else (Pansare, 1988).

but also assumed the role of an arbitrator as far as local-level intra-party competition was concerned. Under his leadership, the Congress government opened up new democratic avenues of conducting political competition and sharing power.

Initially, he was berated (both within his party and among the opposition parties) as a stooge of the central leadership. But he quietly worked his way towards the formation of the Marathi-speaking state. (His critics would argue that the State was formed due to popular pressure built by the agitation and Chavan merely capitalized on it; Pendse, 2010; 18–19.) The fact that he was the CM at the time when the State of Maharashtra was formed added to his stature.

Immediately after he became the CM of the 'big' bilingual State in 1956, Chavan set out to create a popular, democratic and caring image of Congress government by visiting all areas of the bilingual State. He sought to convince the people about the sincerity of his government in bringing about development in both Marathi-speaking and Gujarati-speaking regions (Phadke, 1979; 201–206). At the same time, Chavan worked assiduously to gain complete control over the party organization (Phadke, 1979; 213–214). When the Central government finally decided to bifurcate the bilingual State and create Maharashtra with Bombay as its capital, Chavan and the State Congress could claim that they, rather than the leaders of the movement for State formation, had brought about this success for the people of Maharashtra. The atmosphere in the State changed quickly in favour of Chavan and Congress, once the State of Maharashtra was formed. The SMS was the first and worst casualty. Its very existence became endangered. The Samiti was the main opposition in the Assembly. But its constituents, who were anyway having a very uneasy co-existence, started falling apart. While Jan Sangh and PSP left the Samiti, the leaders of one faction of the PWP not only left the Samiti but also joined the Congress. They included Yashwantrao Mohite and R. K. Khadilkar. In fact, there was a steady stream of workers, Members of Legislative Assembly (MLAs) and faction leaders towards the Congress. It has been estimated that between 1960 and 1962, about 40 legislators of different parties joined the Congress (Sirsikar,

1965; 32–33). These were not defections in the ordinary sense. Many MLAs and leaders felt that once Maharashtra was formed, there was no contentious issue between them and the Congress. Of course, it is true that the persuasive style of Y. B. Chavan attracted them to the Congress hoping that Congress would be an ideal vehicle for their social and political aspirations. Even after 1962, this attraction for Congress remained and leaders from the socialist party as well as the PWP and RPI continued to move towards the Congress. Thus, throughout the 1960s, the Congress in Maharashtra not only successfully recruited fresh entrants aspiring for political power but also experienced political workers from various political parties.

In its bid to make available new structures of opportunity, the Congress government created the elective Panchayati Raj institutions in 1962. Earlier, village panchayats were created in 1958 based on a new legislation. After 1960, the government decided to create local government bodies at district and taluka levels. An elected council known as Zilla Parishad (ZP) was created for non-urban areas of every district, and at the block level, which was roughly equivalent to talukas, a panchayat samiti was established. This new local government structure meant that over 1,000 elected representatives would be functioning as members of these bodies and every ZP would have a president, which would be an important post at the district level. In the first elections of ZPs held in 1962, the Congress won 827 seats out of a total of 1,271 in 25 ZPs (Joshi, 1968; 210). The Congress won the office of president in 24 ZPs, losing only one (Dhule) due to local factionalism (Kulkarni, 1968; 292) and gained control over 280 of 293 panchayat samitis (Vora, 1982; 11). The Congress continued to hold its local power base by winning 743 seats out of 1,202 in 1967 (with additional 25 to RPI as an ally) and 815 seats in 1972 out of 1,166 seats in the ZPs. The strength of PWP declined from 64 in 1962 to 38 in 1972 (Shinde, 1988; 102–111). This indicates the extent of Congress strength at the local level.

The ZPs were not merely structures giving political aspirants share in power. These were supposed to look after the development projects within the district. As such, control over ZPs meant control over development expenditure and considerable access to patronage distribution. This aspect of the ZPs made them important centres of power. Throughout the period of 1960–1978, the entire ZP structure had remained under Congress's control. Whenever the Congress failed to win chairmanship of a ZP, the post would invariably go to a Congress rebel rather than any non-Congress politician. Studies of local elites by Carras (1972) and Carter (1975) conducted during the 1960s show that often the dominant district leaders preferred to become officials in the ZP rather than being ordinary members of the legislature, since the Panchayati Raj institutions ensured effective access to state resources. In any case, no opposition party was strong enough to gain majority in any ZP. Even after 1978, in the 1979 ZP elections, the Janata Party (JP) could get majority in only two ZPs: Ratnagiri and Alibag (Raigad).

The other important development encouraged by the Congress government in the 1960s was the expansion of the cooperative network. The cooperative movement had already begun before 1960.[10] After 1960, the Maharashtra government actively supported cooperativization of many local rural activities. Maharashtra has become famous for its rich sugar cooperatives. But the network of cooperatives other than in the area of sugar production is very vast. For every district, one central cooperative bank has been created. For every village, there exists a multipurpose cooperative society. Cooperatives in the field of dairy and milk production have also been created.

---

[10] D. R. Gadgil may be seen as an important ideologue of the cooperative movement and supporter of farmers' cooperatives for sugar production. He was actively involved in the foundation of the Pravara Sahakari Sakhar Karkhana in the early 1950s (see Gadgil, 1952, 1975, 2011). In the mid-1950s, the Central government sought to revise the structure of rural credit. The then Bombay government, thus, reorganized the cooperative structure thoroughly after 1955 (Rosenthal, 1977; 11). Scholars as well as political workers look upon the cooperative movement in two different ways. One approach emphasizes the local initiative, democratic dimension and development potential of the movement. This approach puts a premium on the ideological aspect of the cooperative movement. Others treat the movement as a political strategy for developing grassroots structures building political support. The evidence of cooperative movement in the State as it evolved since after 1960 suggests that the former approach is certainly overshadowed by the politicization of the cooperative movement.

Every taluka has a cooperative society which manages the market of agricultural products. The State government has encouraged the establishment of these cooperatives, and large amounts of state funds have gone into these cooperatives by way of aid and subsidy. The State government subsequently almost made a philosophy out of these cooperatives.

What distinguishes the cooperatives in Maharashtra from those from other States, such as Gujarat, where too they have contributed enormously to the local economy, is the political role they have played and were aimed at playing in the state of Maharashtra. They are crucial bodies facilitating access to enormous resources at the local level. After the reorganization of village panchayats on the basis of Village Panchayats Act of 1958, the cooperativization of rural economic institutions began in right earnest. In 1958–1959, there were 24,696 cooperatives. This number rose to 45,840 in 1972–1973. Although the speed with which cooperatives were being formed slackened slightly after 1972–1973, the number still reached the figure of 47,902 in 1974–1975 (GoM, 1972; 73, 1977; 90). This numerical expansion was matched by enormous rise in working capital and turnover of the cooperatives in the State. Between 1959–1960 and 1963–1964, the working capital of all cooperatives in the State together kept rising annually by about 5,000–6,000 lakh (23,790 lakh in 1959 and 48,753 lakh in 1963–1964). Between 1963–1964 and 1969–1970, the working capital kept rising at a greater pace reaching 127,985 lakh in 1969–1970 (GoM, 1972; 73). This almost fivefold increase in turnover in one decade shows the pivotal role of cooperatives in the rural economy of the State. It must be borne in mind that a vast amount of State funds have gone into the cooperative movement. Considering the fact that the majority of the cooperatives have been engaged in rural credit, the role of the political leaders controlling these bodies at local level becomes very significant. Therefore, they exist as both opportunity structures and arenas of political competition. Although Congress workers were in control of the cooperatives, these workers frequently engaged into bitter competition for control of these bodies. Thus, development, politics and intra-party factionalism have been interwoven in the cooperative movement.

While subsequent Congress governments in the State did continue with these initiatives (local government and cooperatives), because of his adroit introduction of these in the initial stage, Chavan can be rightly seen as the architect of these strategies of 'rulership' that involved crafting of legitimacy for Congress rule in the newly created State of Maharashtra. He coupled these strategies with a skilful rhetoric of 'development'. This language of development was in consonance with but independent of the language of national development. Chavan was projecting the promise of a developed State on the basis of the policies of industrial expansion (in certain pockets), strengthening of agriculture and evolution of agro-industries.

Chavan also employed an ideological component along with the language of development. He invoked the term *Bahujan Samaj*[11] which implied two meanings at the same time. Literally, the term means the masses or the general public—the majority in the society. This gave a generalized democratic tinge to the term. On the other hand, in the specific context of Maharashtra, the term also implicitly referred to the toiling, non-Brahman rural masses. Chavan claimed that the Congress was ushering in rule by the Bahujan Samaj. This phraseology skilfully combined modern democratic language with the social reality. Besides, the term in itself avoided any exclusionary reference to any caste group; thus, it avoided to take a confrontationist stance and yet communicated to the non-Brahman masses that the Congress stood for their interests. The Bahujan Samaj ideology was a skilful attempt of appropriating the legacy of non-Brahman movement without involving

---

[11] The term *Bahujan Samaj* literally means a section of community that is in large numbers or in majority; it has been a political term employed in the public rhetoric of Maharashtra since early decades of the 20th century. Deriving inspiration from Jyotirao Phule's argument that the society consisted of *shetjis–bhatjis* (traders–Banias and priestly class, Brahmans, respectively) on the one hand as exploiters and the lay masses comprising of women and persons belonging to Shudra varna as also the Atishudras (traditionally treated as 'untouchables'), the thinker, sociologist, political leader, Vitthal Ramji Shinde coined the term *Bahujan Samaj* when he launched the Bahujan Paksh. His idea of *Bahujan* consisted of all workers, toilers, peasants and broadly followed Phule's ideological criteria mentioned above. Since then, this term was also employed in the public debates in Maharashtra to refer to the majority of non-Brahman castes; for details of Shinde's concept of *Bahujan*, see Kulkarni, 2019; 73–75.

the risk of alienating any particular caste group. The Bahujan Samaj ideology served yet another purpose. It implicitly argued that since the Congress government was one belonging to Bahujan Samaj, its policies were and should be seen as being pro-people. This provided ideological justification to the policies of State government, which aimed at capitalist development, in general, and strengthened the entrenched rural interests through the network of agro-industries. Thus, Bahujan Samaj ideology tried to insulate government policies from opposition criticism for being pro-rich.

The Congress domination over State politics which evolved after 1957 and lasted for almost two decades may be seen as an edifice consisting the following: (a) popularity based on the legacy of freedom struggle, (b) entry of rural, non-Brahman masses and of the leaders of non-Brahman movement into the party, which eventually facilitated change in the social composition of state-level leadership after 1957, (c) the system of accommodating district-level aspirants into the power structure of government and/or party, (d) establishment of new, democratic opportunities for competition and power-sharing, (e) carefully organized electoral strategy for winning elections, (f) capacity to attract workers/leaders from outside the party, (g) introduction of policies balancing the welfare claims of the party and the interests of entrenched social sections and (h) an ideological exercise in the form of Bahujan Samaj ideology which sought to bind together the various strategic aspects of the party's politico-economic domination with the democratic aspirations of people and compulsions of competitive politics. These factors together constituted the regional version of the congress system.

Many of these features were strengthened through electoral politics in the following decades but, as we show, there was a considerable decline of this domination from the 1990s onwards. In the following chapters, we trace that decline and attempt to explain the factors that contributed to that decline. As the State completed six decades of its existence as a linguistic State (2020), it had witnessed many turnovers in the governments of the State and experienced two terms of governments that comprised of non-Congress forces; and while at the time of celebrating its diamond jubilee, a further reshaping of political alliances had taken place, the older 'regime' known as the congress system was clearly becoming a thing of the past. In this sense, the foregoing discussion is mainly a reminder of what sustained that congress system, what might have replaced it and how the shift away from the congress system has been producing a new politics in the State.

Towards Competitive Politics

2

1960s to 1980s

This chapter aims at discussing the historical context in which the congress system in Maharashtra got destabilized and made way for reconfiguration of party competition that took place subsequently. Like Karnataka, Maharashtra presented a picture of an invincible Congress party poised for a long-term dominance around the mid-1960s. But this did not mean that there was something so extraordinary as to buck the normal trend found in party politics, namely internal factionalism. The leadership of Chavan was able to fend off the challenges from both opposition parties and competing factions within the party. Nevertheless, gradually, party factionalism became unmanageable and the capacity of the party to mediate among warring factions and to accommodate new aspirants came under severe strain due to State-level developments and also in the backdrop of the national-level goings-on within the Congress party. If this story continues to centre around the Congress even during the early 1970s, that is because non-Congress parties have a very poor record of being able to alter the nature of political competition in Maharashtra—even in the immediate aftermath of the Emergency and Congress's rout in 1977. Broadly, the slow erosion of the Congress in Maharashtra before its ultimate fall in 1995 can be seen through two phases—the first being 1967 to 1979–1980 and the other being the phase during the 1980s between Pawar's ouster in 1980 and Pawar's shift to national-level politics in 1991. This chapter revisits these two phases.

FACTIONAL ACCOMMODATION

In terms of electoral contest, politics of the State appears to be quite one-sided during the period 1962–1972. As was the case in most States of India, the Marathi-speaking areas of the then Bombay Province were deeply dominated by the Congress party in the immediate post-independence period. Only a concerted opposition and a surcharged political atmosphere over the issue of formation of a separate Marathi-speaking State could partially endanger the domination of the Congress party in 1957 (see Tables 2.1 and 2.2). In contrast to the setback received in 1957 elections, the subsequent dominance of the party was indeed spectacular. The Congress continued to dominate outcomes of parliamentary and State-level elections without any trouble (Tables 2.3 and 2.4). The victory of 1962 certainly belongs to the leadership skills of Chavan, while that of 1971–1972 was because of the rise of Indira Gandhi. As the 1967 outcome indicates, there was more to Congress victories than mere leadership factor coming as it did in the backdrop of national-level crisis that the party faced in 1967. As discussed in the previous chapter, these victories were an outcome of both the national-level nature of the Congress party and the State-level system of dominance and accommodation. This did not however mean the suspension of normal party politics.

Table 2.1 *Assembly Election Results: 1952*

Party	Seats Contested	Seats Won	Votes[a]
Congress	313	269	50.0
Socialist Party (SP)	182	9	12.0
PWP	87	14	6.5
Communist Party of India (CPI)	25	1	1.4
Hindu Maha Sabha	9	0	0.3
Jana Sangh	2	0	0.1
Kamgar Kisan Paksha (KKP)	33	2	2.2
SCF	37	1	3.1
Others	128	1	7.2
Independents (IND)	427	18	17.2
Total	**1,243**	**315**	

Notes: Turnout: 51.1 per cent.

[a]All vote figures in all tables are in percentages.

Table 2.2 *Assembly Election Results: 1957*

Party	Seats Contested	Seats Won	Votes
Congress	396	234	48.7
SP	98	36	9.0
PWP	55	31	6.7
CPI	32	13	3.6
Hindu Maha Sabha	10	1	0.4
Jana Sangh	23	4	1.6
SCF	48	13	6.2
Ram Rajya Parishad (RRP)	10	0	0.1
IND	400	64	23.7
Total	**1,072**	**396**	

Note: Turnout: 53.1 per cent.

Table 2.3 *LS Election Results: 1962–1971*

	1962		1967		1971	
	Seats	Votes	Seats	Votes	Seats	Votes
Congress	41	52.9	37	48.5	—	—
Congress (O)	—	—	—	—	—	2.7
Congress (R)	—	—	—	—	42	63.2
CPI	—	4.1	2	5.1	—	1.9
CPI(M)	—	—	—	—	—	0.5
Jana Sangh	—	4.4	—	7.4	—	5.2
Swatantra	—	0.3	—	1.0	—	—
PWP	—	6.3	2	7.5	—	5.3
PSP	1	5.4	1	2.6	1	1.7
SSP	—	—	2	3.7	—	2.2
Others	—	12.4	—	12.7	2[a]	9.2
IND	2	14.2	1	11.5	—	8.3
Total Seats/Turnout	**44**	**60.1**	**45**	**64.8**	**45**	**59.9**

Note: [a]One seat each for Forward Bloc and RPI (Gawai faction).

Table 2.4 *Assembly Election Results: 1962–1972*

	1962		1967		1972	
	Seats	*Votes*	*Seats*	*Votes*	*Seats*	*Votes*
Congress	215	51.2	203	47.0	—	—
Congress(O)	—	—	—	—	—	1.1
Congress(R)	—	—	—	—	222	56.3
CPI	6	5.9	10	4.9	2	2.7
CPI(M)	—	—	1	1.1	1	0.8
Jana Sangh	—	5.0	4	8.2	5	6.3
Swatantra	—	0.4	—	1.1	—	—
PWP	15	7.5	19	7.8	7	5.9
PSP	9	7.2	8	4.1	—	—
SSP	1	0.5	4	4.6	3	4.6
RPI	3	5.4	5	6.7	2	3.8
Others	—	0.1	—	—	5[a]	5.8
IND	15	16.7	16	14.6	23	12.7
Total Seats/Turnout	**264**	**60.1**	**270**	**65.0**	**270**	**60.1**

Note: [a]SHS, BKD, Muslim League: one each; Forward Bloc: two.

While the State-level congress system continued to operate without interruption until the mid-1970s, politics of the Congress party was not without its own hiccups and challenges at the State level. The influence of Chavan was the key factor in keeping the system running. Even after Chavan moved to the Central cabinet in the aftermath of the Sino-Indian War of 1962, politics in the State continued to be dominated by Chavan and the model developed by him. The crucial test of Chavan's politics took place on the issue of selection of the new CM. As a part of the negotiated settlement with the protagonists of separate Vidarbh, it was assured that the CM's position will rotate among different regions. On the exit of Chavan, M. S. Kannamwar, from Vidarbh region, staked his claim; and Chavan yielded because Kannamwar had considerable grassroots support and also enjoyed the support of sections of the activists of Nagvidarbh agitation.

Kannamwar's tenure was cut short by his death in 1964 and Chavan managed to bring in V. P. Naik. It is notable that in a State famous for Maratha domination, both successors to Chavan, Kannamwar and Naik were non-Marathas. Thus, Chavan could claim that the Congress rule represented *Bahujan Samaj* in the true sense and that it was not merely Maratha rule. On the other hand, selection of a non-Maratha candidate for CM ensured that no other Maratha leader would be in a position to gain control over the party in the State. Chavan continued to be the sole leader and mentor of State Congress. Kannamwar and Naik had to rely on Chavan's leadership in order to get the support of the Congress MLAs, majority of whom were Marathas. In this sense, the choice of non-Maratha CMs from Vidarbh suited Chavan in more than one ways.

During this period, State Congress party did have many factions. There were ambitious leaders from western Maharashtra like Balasaheb Desai, somewhat junior but aspiring leaders like Yashwantrao Mohite and Vasantdada Patil and upcoming leaders from Marathwada like S. B. Chavan. Y.B. Chavan could convince them to defer their ambitions or could neutralize them through a plurality-based competition among them. Different factions struggled for control over the organization, and they could be accommodated at the district level by distributing the ZP and cooperative posts among them. Even in 1967, when factionalism in the party at the national level gained momentum, only two important leaders from Maharashtra deserted the party. They were Dhairyasheel Pawar from Nasik district and Malojirao Naik Nimbalkar from Satara district. They could not muster support from the rank and file. Except this, factional competition was usually conducted within the party and usually the CM and Chavan would play the role of arbitrator.

Another dimension of intra-party factionalism during the 1960s was the strained relationship between the Maharashtra Pradesh Congress Committee (MPCC) and the Bombay Pradesh Congress Committee (BPCC). During the days of Bombay State, a separate Pradesh Congress Committee (PCC) existed for Bombay city. It was generally dominated by Gujarati Congressmen. S. K. Patil, a Maharashtrian from Konkan, had risen to prominence in BPCC in the post-independence period in alliance with Gujarati leaders. Patil was openly opposed to the forma-tion of Samyukta Maharashtra. The MPCC was usually dominated by Maratha leadership belonging to agricultural interests. Patil and BPCC saw this as a threat to their industrial and business interests. Although Chavan struck a cordial relationship with Bombay's business and industrial lobby, the rivalry between MPCC and BPCC did not abate. V. P. Naik inherited this legacy.

Nehru always considered S. K. Patil as belonging to the lobby opposed to him, while Chavan and Naik, though powerful in the State, consistently remained supportive of Central leadership. The rivalry between MPCC and BPCC reached a climax, when in 1969, S. K. Patil along with Morarji Desai and other influential Congress leaders crossed swords with Indira Gandhi. In that historical intra-party fight, Chavan and Naik finally decided to support Indira Gandhi. As a result, in the MPCC, no leader of any significance opposed Indira Gandhi's leadership. The MPCC thus proved to be a major asset to her when S. K. Patil chose to challenge Indira Gandhi's leadership. Although Maharashtra Congress supported the anti-Indira camp in presidential elections, after the split in the Congress following presidential election in 1969, the first session of Indira Gandhi's new Congress was suc-cessfully held in Bombay where Y.B. Chavan pledged his support to Indira Gandhi. However, it may be noted that Chavan had hesitated a bit before finally throwing his weight behind Indira Gandhi (Lele, 2015; 41–42).

The dramatic developments of 1969 sharpened intra-party fac-tionalism in State Congress. Chavan's equivocation and his strong base were perceived by Indira Gandhi as a threat and she set out to make inroads in the Maratha-dominated Maharashtra Congress. This development gave Naik an opportunity both to retain his position as the CM and to distance himself from Chavan. While one side of this entire episode was indeed related to personal ambitions, these devel-opments involved many more issues. Indira Gandhi wanted to evolve a new social base for herself bypassing regionally dominant castes which had thrown up the Congress bosses. Thus, it was not merely a question of reducing Chavan's importance. She was wary of Maratha leadership in general. But the social composition of Maharashtra meant that there was no other major and widespread non-Maratha caste which could form the backbone of her new social base. Therefore, instead of dismantling State-level Maratha domination, she settled only with undermining it. This required creation of dissension within the Maratha lobby and simultaneously reducing its importance. Particularly in the 1972 Assembly elections, with the help of Naik and Antulay, Indira Gandhi managed to introduce new candidates either from non-Maratha castes or persons who were not part of the giant complex of Maratha domination (Lele, 1984; 179–180).

The period after 1972 proved uneasy for Naik. As the State-promoted growth of cooperatives reached its peak by the early 1970s, factionalism superseded the cooperative movement. The tension between local cooperative leaders and State leadership also grew as a consequence. Stagnation of political opportunities accompanied stagnation of the economic clout of cooperatives. In the case of agricultural credit cooperatives, turnover dropped in 1972–1973. There was no appreciable growth for the next couple of years. Similarly, the working capital of agricultural credit cooperatives dropped between 1971–1972 and 1972–1973. Identical trends were witnessed in the case of marketing cooperatives (GoM, 1977; 90–91). Thus, the Green Revolution enriched the rural cooperatives, but the growth pattern remained skewed. This development needs to be noted for a better understanding of intra-party turbulence in the Congress. The leadership of Chavan and Naik was still prominent, but objective conditions at the ground level were creating new hurdles in the implementation of Chavan's model. This was also the period when Naik attempted to evolve his own identity distinct from Chavan and when Indira Gandhi engaged in an uneasy relationship with Chavan (Lele, 1990a; 185–187).

As the economic situation had worsened due to severe droughts, the opposition was on the offensive on the issues of price rise, unemployment and plight of agricultural labourers. At the same time, S. B. Chavan, who hailed from Marathwada, was pressing the demand that after completing 10 years by CM from Vidarbh the post should now go to Marathwada. Conveniently for him, students in

Marathwada became restive, and an agitation for the development of that region took place in 1973–1974. The leaders of Marathwada, who had worked for freedom from Nizam's Hyderabad, supported the agitation which had also the support of the opposition. The Congress circles believed that this agitation was supported (and perhaps started in the first place) by S. B. Chavan to create pressure against V. P. Naik. Naik was finally removed from the position of CM and was replaced by S. B. Chavan in 1975. Although a Maratha by caste, S. B. Chavan did not belong to the Maratha lobby of western Maharashtra and was opposed to Y. B. Chavan. Since he belonged to Marathwada, his appointment signalled further jolt for the Maratha leaders of western Maharashtra.

On the whole, the complex structure of the social support and intra-party competition that had evolved during the 1960s began to crumble after 1972 under the pressure of internal contradictions (both between Maratha and non-Maratha leaders and between leaders from western Maharashtra and other parts) exacerbated by Indira Gandhi's strategy of undermining local power structures and creating a set of loyal supporters within State Congress unit. S. B. Chavan's appointment as the CM hastened this process. Chavan understood his task as undermining the interests and political strength of leaders from western Maharashtra. But he did not actively initiate any regrouping in State politics. By the time S. B. Chavan became the CM, Naik had emerged as an Indira-loyalist, a strongman of Vidarbh, and clearly distanced himself from Y. B. Chavan. He had already attempted to work out a new strategy of selecting non-Maratha candidates from Vidarbh. In western Maharashtra, Vasantdada Patil led his informal group which was not very friendly with Y. B. Chavan. Sharad Pawar, then a young and upcoming leader from Pune district, had the closest links with Y. B. Chavan. Neither of these factions liked the move to have S. B. Chavan as the CM. During the Emergency, they kept quiet but retained their respective spheres of influence. Congress factionalism came onto the surface as the LS elections of 1977 were announced. As we shall discuss further, the Y. B. Chavan faction and Vasantdada Patil faction jointly struck against S. B. Chavan, defeating his candidates approved by Indira Gandhi (Vora et al., 1983). This was not only an example of weakness of Indira Gandhi's strategy in Maharashtra but also had the result of weakening the congress system in the State.

Soon after the LS elections, S. B. Chavan was replaced as CM by Vasantdada Patil. But the split in Congress at the national level in 1978 on the issue of Indira Gandhi's leadership again created confusion in State Congress. Under Y. B. Chavan's leadership, many important factions of State Congress chose to join the Congress opposed to Indira Gandhi. Leaders like A. R. Antulay (Konkan), S. B. Chavan (Marathwada), Babasaheb Bhosale (Bombay), Ramrao Adik (Bombay), Vasant Sathe and Nashikrao Tirpude (Vidarbh) joined Indira Gandhi's Congress (I). Unlike in 1969, this split had a deep impact on State-level intra-party configurations. Thus, intra-party competition spilled over and gave rise to an open confrontation. The period of 1977–1978 marks a major departure from the earlier system of Congress domination because from this time onwards, the Congress could not effectively accommodate factional competition at both all-India and State levels, resulting in many 'Congress parties' with varying names.[1] In the case of Maharashtra, these events suggest that cracks were widening as far as politics of Congress domination was concerned.

---

[1] Brahmanand Reddy was elected as the Congress president following Congress's defeat of 1977. However, Indira Gandhi was unhappy with that arrangement since it did not give her full control over the party. This led to a split in the Congress by the end of that year. Indira Gandhi's faction labelled itself as Congress (I), while for some time, the Reddy-led faction continued as 'Congress' party. In 1979, a further split in Congress (I) occurred following the exit of Devraj Urs, who formed Indian National Congress (Urs)—INCU. The groups opposed to Indira Gandhi thus came together under INCU. In the 1980 elections, there were these two Congress parties—Congress (I) and INCU, and in Maharashtra, most of INCU leaders who did not join Pawar when he left the alliance in 1978 chose to join Congress (I). Thus, in 1980 Assembly elections, the Pawar faction was named by the Election Commission of India (ECI) in its official results as INCU. Subsequently, Urs left the Congress party to form a State-level party and the faction opposed to Indira Gandhi then continued as Indian Congress (Socialist)—ICS. While Chavan joined Congress (I) in 1981, Pawar became one of the key leaders of ICS, but following the 1985 Assembly elections, he also decided to join Congress (I) which was by then recognized as Indian National Congress (INC). While ICS continued to function in Kerala, for purposes of Maharashtra's politics, it became redundant since then.

The dramatic setback to the Congress in 1977 LS elections from Maharashtra and the subsequent splits and regrouping mark the turning point in the trajectory of Congress dominance in the State. While the party did remain in power all through the 1980s, the hegemonic nature of the party was almost over by the late 1970s. This development is almost parallel to the trajectory of Congress dominance and party competition at the all-India level. The only difference perhaps is that in the case of Maharashtra, the severity of Congress's decline was less and speed was slow. While this was partly because of the bulwark of Maratha support to the Congress, this was also due to the weaknesses of opposition politics in the State.

OPPOSITION TO CONGRESS: 1960–1980

Like many Congress-dominated States, the opposition to Congress in Maharashtra was dispersed across the ideological spectrum and was characterized by weak and shaky social constituencies. So long as Congress managed to accommodate different interests and provided a platform for limited competition, the prospects of organizing an opposition party were bound to be weak. Therefore, a number of non-Congress parties continued to exist on the margins of the political process throughout the 1960s and in the first half of the 1970s.

In the 1950s, non-Congress parties got an excellent opportunity to consolidate themselves because of the unwillingness of Central leadership of Congress to create a Marathi-speaking State and the refusal of State Congress leaders to challenge their Central leadership on this question. The issue of State formation had a long history dating back to the pre-independence period. The issue had a strong emotive dimension at least in some parts of the Marathi-speaking areas. The question of Bombay was also equally sensitive. The Marathi-speaking people nursed a sense of injury that they were only of partial consequence in the financial capital of the country. Morarji Desai's insensitive handling of the agitation demanding State formation further strengthened the urban-middle-class opposition. This section was supported by rural population to some extent, which helped the agitation to register impressive victory in western Maharashtra in 1957. Thus, opposition politics in Maharashtra had a good beginning in 1956 when the SMS was established. It consisted of practically all non-Congress parties barring Lohia's Socialist Party (SP). But all the parties tried to outsmart each other and derive maximum benefit for themselves. Therefore, the SMS was always on the brink of split and collapse. Immediately after the decision to form the State of Maharashtra, constituents of the SMS started moving out of it. The CPI, PWP and one faction of RPI (Gaikwad group) continued as the SMS after 1960. Since the Samiti was a platform demanding formation of Maharashtra State, it lost its purpose after 1960. The pending issue of border dispute with Karnataka was not sufficient for popular mobilization. Thus, after 1960, combined opposition to Congress quickly dispersed.

At this point, the PWP was an important party which had some potential of taking on the might of Congress. In fact, it was seen as the main opposition to Congress. Formed in 1948, most of the leaders of the PWP had a Congress background. Two things distinguished the PWP leadership. It belonged to the Maratha caste and many were associated with the non-Brahman movement. Second, the PWP leadership took a strong leftist position, although its base was among rural peasantry. These factors gave the PWP a strong ideological character and class–caste identity. The PWP had wide support in South Maharashtra and parts of Marathwada. But its history from 1948 to 1960 consists of intense intra-party rivalry and threats of decimation due to desertion by leaders.[2] After 1960, many MLAs belonging to the PWP joined the Congress. Since 1960, the PWP remained a weak opposition to the Congress. Although the party had adopted the Marxist–Leninist ideology, it did not work among the landless agricultural labourers. It associated itself with the demands for better prices for agricultural products. After the 1972 drought, the PWP, with its meagre machinery, fought hard for the protection of drought-hit peasantry and agricultural labourers. When the Naik government introduced Employment Guarantee Scheme (EGS) for rural unemployed, the PWP demanded that the scheme should be used for undertaking farming

---

[2] The internal differences within the PWP encompassed many factors, ideological and personal. For early PWP and its problems, see Bhole (2010, especially 74–113). For a later period, Jagan Phadnis (1978) gives a useful account.

activity which would open up possibilities of cooperative farming. It also played an important role in post-Emergency elections by joining the non-Congress parties and contributed to the defeat of the Congress in 1977–1978. Thus, throughout 1960–1978, the PWP functioned as a small but an important anti-Congress party.

The CPI enjoyed considerable support among Bombay labour through its trade union base. It also worked among the tribal communities in Thane district and among agricultural labourers. Apart from Mumbai–Thane, it had some pockets in Ahmednagar and Beed districts. But the party could never spread in the interior of the State. It came into prominence mainly in the course of the agitation for State formation. The party and its leader, Dange, were in the forefront of this agitation. But it was often criticized, particularly by the socialists, for its attempts to hijack the State-formation agitation and taking control over the SMS for its partisan interests. In spite of leadership of the agitation for State formation and popularity through the SMS, the CPI could not strike roots in the rural areas. The nationwide split and the creation of the Communist Party of India (Marxist)—CPI(M)—further weakened the CPI in Maharashtra as the trade union base also split between the two communist parties. The CPI(M) also carried with it the tribal support and that of agricultural labour organizations. As a result, after 1964, the role of CPI and CPI(M) remained only nominal as far as State politics is concerned. After the rise of the SHS, the communist trade union base in Mumbai also eroded considerably, as explained further.

Another factor which contributed to the erosion of 'left' opposition was the intense rivalry between communists and socialists. The latter, particularly under George Fernandes, successfully eroded the communist trade unions. The two socialist parties (first PSP and SP and later Samyukta Socialist Party [SSP] and PSP) also occupied the ideological left terrain. Originally formed in 1948 by socialists who were forced out of the Congress, the SP underwent repeated regrouping and splits mainly involving the ideas, strategy and leadership of Lohia. We need not go into the detailed history of these splits here (for details of these splits, see Shah, 1994). Suffice it to say that the socialists in Maharashtra dutifully split in accordance with the splits in the all-India socialist movement and followed the same ideological arguments. Thus, there is nothing specific to Maharashtra in these developments save perhaps the fact that many national-level actors in these splits such as Madhu Limaye, N. G. Goray and S. M. Joshi were Marathi leaders. The main strength of the socialists was Hind Mazdoor Sabha (HMS), a trade union with wide support in Mumbai. Electorally, however, socialist parties failed to influence State politics. As late as during the 1960s, some socialist leaders joined the Congress, but it was socialist leader Mrinal Gore along with the CPI(M) leader Ahilya Rangnekar who led the opposition during the 1970s, and socialists were in the forefront of the anti-Emergency activities and the anti-Congress oppositional politics thereafter. The intervention of socialist leader S.M. Joshi was instrumental in bringing together all opposition parties to agree on the idea of having Sharad Pawar as the leader of the progressive democratic front government of 1978. During the 1980s, the socialists disappeared into oblivion first through the disintegration of the JP and subsequently by the fragmentation of the Janata Dal (JD).

The RPI generated considerable interest among the political circles in the 1960s. The RPI was formed in 1957, though Dr Ambedkar had planned the creation of the party himself. Ambedkar's death in December 1956 resulted into postponement of party formation. The SCF, predecessor of the RPI, had joined the SMS, and the RPI continued to work as a member of the SMS. This implied cooperation with the communists who were also part of the SMS. Since many followers of Ambedkar were aware of Ambedkar's opposition to the communists, there was resentment among one section of the RPI on the issue of working in the SMS. Dadasaheb Gaikwad, who was then an important leader of the RPI, was seen as being sympathetic to communists. Even his espousal of the cause of the landless agricultural labourers did not go well with diehard sections of the RPI. Gaikwad had initiated *satyagrahas* of the landless in 1959 for redistribution of land. Although most Dalits are landless, Gaikwad had not pitched the issue as merely one pertaining to Dalits. Y. B. Chavan assuaged the protestors by assuring more speedy redistribution of excess land. Chavan also restored reservation benefits (within the State) to Dalits who had converted to Buddhism. These moves considerably softened RPI's sharp anti-Congressism. The history of the RPI is a history of splits and defections. Chavan's deft handling of the Dalit question contributed to this process. The first split occurred in 1959 when B. C. Kamble led one faction to form a separate RPI(Kamble)—RPI(K). His complaint was that Gaikwad was much too sympathetic to communists. Kamble later allied with the PSP. The second split took place in 1964 when R. D. Bhandare formed a separate RPI, which was short-lived since Bhandare and some of his associates joined the Congress party in 1965. Gaikwad had decided to have a limited alliance with the Congress in 1967. This move was supported by R. S. Gavai. In protest of this, Khobragade left the RPI and formed a separate RPI (Khobragade; 1970)—RPK. In 1971, Dadasaheb Rupwate, who was then in Gaikwad faction, joined the Congress (Kshirsagar, 1979; 75–113).

By 1971, there were three major RPI factions respectively led by Gaikwad/Gavai, B. C. Kamble and Khobragade. These factional fights dissipated the energies of Dalit leaders, and the issues of Dalits remained unattended. This situation angered the newly educated and politically aware Dalit youth in particular. The riots in parts of Mumbai between the caste Hindus and Dalits convinced many youth activists of the ineffectiveness of the old RPI leadership. They felt the need of militant Dalit organization. This led to the formation of Dalit Panthers in 1972. At the same time, efforts were made to bring together all RPI factions. These efforts failed. The Dalit Panthers forced the Dalit question to the forefront of Maharashtra politics. They also developed a strong critique of the Brahmanical social order and criticized the futility of parliamentary party politics. But the Panthers movement lacked proper organization. Every leader was left to pursue his programmes independently. Soon, Panthers movement too underwent a split on the old ideological issue of anti-communist versus pro-communist stand. Namdeo Dhasal, a founder leader, was charged for his pro-communist stand by Raja Dhale, another founder (Murugkar, 1991; 72–73). This development made the Dalit Panthers irrelevant to State politics. RPI(K) and some Dalit Panther groups joined the post-Emergency anti-Congress alliance. But that did not resolve the issues of 'Dalit unity'; instead, many more factions of the Republicans kept emerging throughout the 1980s and 1990s (Jagzap, 2010). While the RPI always remained a strategic force in State politics, its fragmentation has often left it with only limited relevance.

The Swatantra and Jana Sangh parties had the most limited role in the 1960s and 1970s as far as Maharashtra politics is concerned. The Swatantra Party was simply non-existent in the State, while the Jana Sangh remained very weak. Although Jana Sangh was formed nationally in 1951, its Maharashtra unit started functioning only in 1952–1953 because the RSS workers were not enthusiastic about taking up political work. Only after the RSS deputed some of its cadres for organizing the State unit of the party, Maharashtra Jana Sangh came into existence (Kulkarni, 1968; 165–166). The Jana Sangh participated in the SMS with a bit of hesitation. After the formation of Maharashtra, the growth of the Jana Sangh stopped. It was seen as a party of the Brahmans. Thus, more than its Hindu nationalism, its Brahmanical character impressed upon the public. As such, the Jana Sangh could not spread to rural parts of Maharashtra. Despite its predominantly Brahmanical image, the Jana Sangh did have important non-Brahman leaders in early days too and systematically cultivated its small base among sections of non-Brahman communities besides its urban con-stituency (Datar, 2007). During the late 1960s, the Jana Sangh joined the anti-Congress grand alliance. This did not help the Jana Sangh in its efforts to strike roots in the State. The lacklustre performance of the Jana Sangh and total absence of Swatantra allowed the Congress to expand its base on the basis of a broad socialist platform while its main opposition initially came from parties which too were following a more or less 'left'-oriented ideological position.

Among the urban opponents of the Congress during the 1960s and 1970s, a major share goes to SHS which was based only in Mumbai–Thane belt during this period. Formed to fight injustice against the Marathi-speaking people of the Mumbai–Thane region, caused by a constant stream of jobseekers from other states, particularly the south, the SHS has had a chequered history (Palshikar, 2004). Although the SHS was founded in 1966, its founder, Bal Thackeray, had already started, in 1961, publication of a Marathi weekly *Marmik*. He used this publication for publicizing the plight of Marathi-speaking people of Mumbai. Thus, immediately following State formation in 1960, the platform of Marathi identity—at least in Mumbai's urban territories—was taken over by the regionalist political expression accompanied by militant—often violent—street action. The SHS soon created terror in the city and became a law unto itself. The Congress government of V. P. Naik allegedly did not seriously attempt to discipline the SHS because SHS activities were useful in maligning the BPCC. In fact, both the BPCC and MPCC used the SHS against each other. While the BPCC could criticize the MPCC-dominated State government for inefficiency, the MPCC charged that this was a result of BPCC's anti-Marathi policies (Gupta, 1982; 162–165). The leaders of the MPCC including MPCC president attended SHS rallies during the early period of 1966–1967 (Morkhandikar, 1967; 1903).

S. K. Patil, a leader of the BPCC, saw the SHS in a different perspective. Very soon after its emergence, the SHS started organizing Marathi workers separately (in 1968, its trade union front, Bharatiya Kamgar Sena was formed). This brought the SHS in direct confrontation with leftist trade unions. Ideologically, too, the SHS took an openly anti-communist stand. In the intense struggle between left unions and SHS, violence occurred frequently. One CPI MLA, Krishna Desai, was murdered allegedly by SHS activists. Thus, the single most significant task performed by the SHS between 1968 and 1972 was to weaken Mumbai's left-led trade union activity. This directly helped the industrial bourgeoisie (Palshikar, 1999). The BPCC and S. K. Patil chose to see the SHS as a convenient outfit for dealing with industrial trade unionism. This character of the SHS endeared it to the BPCC. The SHS could therefore derive tacit support from both factions of the Congress, and the rivalry between the MPCC and BPCC ensured that the SHS would be free to spread its activities without much hindrance either from the law and order machinery or from the political leadership. Since 1967, the SHS started playing an important role in the municipal corporations of Mumbai and Thane. Its supporters in Mumbai included migrants from Konkan and even other parts of Maharashtra. However, the SHS could not spread beyond Mumbai–Thane. It was to resurface as a major force in State politics only at the end of the 1980s.

Nevertheless, the support which the SHS could muster immediately after its establishment is suggestive. First, it indicates that the movement for State formation and the response it received were a complex affair. On the one hand, popular aspiration for assertion of linguistic cultural identity was involved in the movement. But at the same time, the support included ethnic chauvinism and sentimental identification with conveniently distorted images of self and others. Second, we have observed earlier that urban support was very prominent in the movement. Rise of the SHS draws attention to the middle-class nature of this support and the willingness of supporters to caricature all those not involved in the movement. Third, the SMS agitation had frequently relied on Shivaji Maharaj as a reference point. But the SHS could easily transform Shivaji into a narrow regional and Hindu symbol. Right from its inception, the SHS identified with the 'Hindu' cause, criticizing the Muslim community on various grounds but mainly on the ground of suspect nationalism of Muslims. Thus, the response SHS received initially was not merely on issues of Maharashtra's pride and identity; Maharashtrian identity included anti-Muslim position. SHS's initial success in Mumbai–Thane region, therefore, suggests the existence of an anti-left, regionalist and 'Hindu' constituency among the urban population.

EMERGENCY AND POLITICS AFTER 1977

The Emergency and its aftermath mark a departure. As we have noted, the congress system was already under pressure by the early 1970s. But the shock of Emergency, the national-level political party configurations and the opportunity this context provided to Congress factions to reconfigure mark a departure from the narrative of Congress dominance around the moment of the Emergency.

Although compared to North India, the adverse effects of Emergency were not felt strongly in the State; the Emergency brought together many non-Congress political leaders during their imprisonments. While Maharashtra government did not indulge in so-called 'Emergency excesses', public activists were detained on a large-scale. The Emergency also created an overall adverse atmosphere among urban areas. Press censorship produced whispering campaigns giving free run to mouth publicity about excesses. In a rare case, socialist leader N. G. Goray was not arrested, although he continued to address numerous 'closed-door meetings' of people opposed to Emergency. Since a ban was imposed on the RSS, many RSS and Jana Sangh workers were picked up even from small towns and put under preventive detention. The result was that when elections came, people easily remembered the detentions of political workers.

Elections to LS took place in this overall background of Emergency. When censorship restrictions were revoked, the press took its own revenge by criticizing the Emergency post facto. The merger of main non-Congress parties at the national level enthused anti-Congress workers. The move by Jagjivan Ram to leave the Congress proved a shot in the arms for the opposition. The opposition in the State was further bolstered by active support by a section of the intelligentsia. The JP, PWP, CPI(M), RPI(K) and RPK reached an understanding regarding seat sharing, although they also fought against each other in at least four constituencies. The JP had an alliance with the leader of Forward Bloc and Mahavidarbh Rajya Sangharsh Samiti in the Vidarbh region. Some setback to the Congress was generally expected on account of anti-Emergency atmosphere and opposition unity. But the results proved to be more adverse for the Congress than was imagined. It won only 20 out of 48 seats, although managing to poll 47 per cent vote. Compared to 1971, its vote share came down by 16 percentage points. The results were generally seen as a denunciation of Emergency and also the proof of the advantages of opposition unity (Table 2.5).

An earlier study of 1977 LS elections does not support this belief. The LS elections of 1977 undeniably took place in the national context of Emergency. But as far as the State is concerned, elections had a specific State-level context also. In a sense, the 1977 elections can be seen as part of the developments after 1971–1972. As already discussed above, the 1977 elections were seen by Congress factions as a ground for settling internal rivalry. The groups led by Y.B. Chavan and Vasantdada Patil tacitly conspired to defeat candidates not acceptable to them (Vora et al., 1983).

Table 2.5 *LS Election Results: 1977*

Party	Seats Contested	Seats Won	Votes
Congress	47	20	47.0
Bharatiya Lok Dal	31	19	31.4
CPI	4	0	0.7
CPI(M)	3	3	3.6
PWP	6	5	6.1
RPK	5	1	4.3
Others	1	0	0.8
IND	114	0	6.1
Total	**211**	**48**	

Note: Turnout: 60.3 per cent.

Table 2.6 *Region-wise Results: Assembly Elections, 1978*

Region	Seats	Congress (I)	JP	INCU[a]	PWP	RPI	Others[b]	IND
Mumbai–Thane	47	0	36	1	1	0	6	3
Konkan	18	0	13	3	2	0	0	0
North Maharashtra	36	9	12	8	0	0	1	6
Vidarbh	66	46	4	2	2	0	4	8
Marathwada	46	4	15	16	6	0	1	4
Western Maharashtra	75	3	19	39	2	2	3	7
Total	**288**	**62**	**99**	**69**	**13**	**2**	**15**	**28**
Vote Share		18.3	28.0	25.3	5.5	1.1	7.7	14.1

Notes: Turnout: 67.6 per cent.

[a] INCU was listed as INC in ECI reports as mentioned in footnote 1.

[b] Others include CPI (01), CPM (09), Forward Bloc (03) and RPK (02).

This interpretation is further borne out by the developments surrounding 1978 Assembly elections and their outcome (Table 2.6). Following the 1977 debacle, the State unit of the Congress party split between supporters of Indira Gandhi and her opponents within

Congress. Most of those who thus distanced from Indira Gandhi were Maratha leaders mainly from western Maharashtra. In contrast, the Indira loyalists were strong mainly in the Vidarbh region. This is also evident from the region-wise outcome of the results. The 1978 elections took place in the backdrop of the rise of JP, the national-level setback received by Congress and the split in that party. For the first time, two strong factions from the Congress party were contesting separately as two distinct Congress parties. This led to a hung assembly. It is noteworthy that barring the period of 1987–1999, the State has always seen two Congress parties in the electoral arena since 1978. Even when the two parties were united, the factionalism within the party was not manageable. The two Congress parties quickly decided to form a coalition at the State level with Vasantdada Patil (who was then in the anti-Indira Gandhi camp) as CM and Nashikrao Tirpude (a loyal Indira supporter) as deputy CM. This coalition ministry could not last long because the then young leader from the anti-Indira camp, Sharad Pawar, left the cabinet and formed a separate group as mentioned earlier and brought together the JP and the PWP to form a new coalition government. This development further disintegrated both the Maratha lobby and the State Congress. The coming together of these various political forces could not ensure the defeat of the Indira Congress in subsequent LS elections.

Thus, while in the all-India context, 1977 is a major landmark for a variety of reasons, in the case of Maharashtra too, it is a landmark because it signifies a major departure away from the congress system. While national Emergency was surely an important factor in that election, many local Congress leaders saw it as an opportunity to assert their local powers. Rather than intervening in the grand narrative of liberating the country from Indira Gandhi's dominance, they were more interested in ensuring their own position locally (Vora et al., 1983; 65–66, 71–72). And yet, within the larger framework of the congress system, the issue was not confined merely to intra-party factional fight for power. It involved both the strategy of rulership and the manner of conducting political competition. Maharashtra Congress had generally followed the pluralist path of constructing durable support base by sharing (albeit limited) of resources and power among 'legitimate' claimants. Legitimacy of their claims derived from the social character of claimants and capacity to mobilize votes at grassroots level. This type of politics did not necessarily require a universalized popularity of the leader. In this scheme, leaders are basically managers of resources and power. The task of leaders involves the conduct and supervision of political competition.

Indira Gandhi was evolving a different kind of politics in which one leader would claim all popularity and the responsibility of generating political support that remained exclusively with the leader. Her framework implied removal or at least containment of leaders like Y. B. Chavan and of strategies of elaborate construction of support. Since leaders of Maharashtra Congress were endangered by this strategy, they wanted to assert themselves in the 1977 elections. It may be argued that what happened in Maharashtra was the result of the competition between two models of politics being pursued within the Congress. This competition had the side effect of making formal electoral politics more competitive all of a sudden. The all-India context of opposition unity enhanced this new competitive dimension of State politics producing an electoral arena where the Congress was no more invincible. Politics in the State was thus entering the phase of intense electoral competition and challenge to Congress domination.

The rebellion led by Sharad Pawar temporarily strengthened that competitiveness. Pawar's Progressive Democratic Front (PDF) ministry was dismissed by Indira Gandhi when she returned to power in 1980 (Table 2.7), but he chose to remain outside of Indira Congress even after that. Although Pawar could not win a majority in the Assembly in subsequent elections, he remained the focal point of opposition in the State. Pawar's ICS also ensured continued competitiveness of electoral politics in spite of failure of JP to capture much political space either in 1980 or later in that decade (Tables 2.8–2.10).

Both these factors, the increased competitiveness of electoral party politics and the continuing decline of the congress system took shape

Table 2.7 *LS Election Results: 1980*

Party	Seats Contested	Seats Won	Votes
Congress	48	39	53.3
INCU	24	1	11.8
JP	31	8	20.4
CPI	2	0	0.5
CPI(M)	4	0	1.4
PWP	5	0	2.6
RPI	23	0	1.7
Others	32	0	3.3
IND	246	0	5.0
Total	**415**	**48**	

Note: Turnout: 56.08 per cent.

in the context of three State-specific developments during the 10 years between 1977 and 1987.

Shetkari Sanghatana

In the post-Emergency phase, when electoral politics was getting reconfigured, agitations by farmers erupted mainly in western Maharashtra on the issue of support prices for cash crops—starting with onion. A total outsider to State's politics, Sharad Joshi was leading these agitations. Employing the methods of roadblocks and sit-ins, these agitations shook the State. The organizational platform for the farmers' agitation was Shetkari Sanghatana. From the late 1970s, the Shetkari Sanghatana captured the limelight and harassed successive State governments, forcing them to negotiate on its demands (Dhanagare, 1994; Lenneberg, 1988). This development is worth noting because the Congress traditionally claimed to be the representative and protector of agrarian interests and no one could imagine that agrarian mobilization could take place outside of the Congress. This is not the place to go into the arguments and debates generated by the Shetkari Sanghatana. It is relevant here that farmers, mostly

Table 2.8 *Region-wise Results: Assembly Elections, 1980*

Region	Seats	Turnout	Congress		INCU		JP		BJP		Others[a]	
			Won	Vote	Won	Vote	Won	Vote	Won	Vote	Won	Vote
Mumbai–Thane	47	38.4	35	45.6	01	02.7	02	14.7	07	24.6	02	12.4
Konkan	18	50.4	09	41.6	00	04.2	05	24.1	01	08.0	03	22.1
North Maharashtra	36	55.5	22	44.8	06	22.9	04	12.9	00	06.0	04	13.4
Vidarbh	66	55.3	55	49.1	03	15.7	00	02.2	03	12.7	05	20.3
Marathwada	46	55.5	25	41.5	17	29.4	00	05.4	01	04.9	03	18.8
Western Maharashtra	75	60.2	40	42.5	20	29.4	06	08.1	02	03.9	07	16.1
Total	**288**	**53.1**	**186**	**44.5**	**47**	**20.5**	**17**	**08.6**	**14**	**09.4**	**24**	**17.0**

Note: [a]Others include PWP (09), Independents (10), CPI (02), CPI (M) (02) and RPK (01).

Table 2.9 *LS Election Results: 1984*

Party	Seats Contested	Seats Won	Votes
Congress	47	43	51.2
BJP	20	0	10.1
JP	15	1	7.6
CPI	2	0	1.0
CPI(M)	2	0	1.5
Lok Dal (LKD)	13	0	0.4
ICS	15	2	12.1
PWP	3	1	2.1
Others	4	0	0.8
IND	377	1	13.2
Total	498	48	

Note: Turnout: 61.7 per cent.

coming from Maratha caste (but also those from other agrarian castes), could be mobilized not only by an 'outsider' to politics but also a non-Maratha himself. Moreover, young activists from agrarian backgrounds cutting across party lines joined the Shetkari Sanghatana.

This development indicated the exhaustion of Congress's capacity to retain control over the ways in which politics would be conducted in the State. It also indicated the space available for mobilization among rural masses. The Congress, relying on its politics of networks, had for long ignored this mobilizational space, and other parties did not have the base and the imagination to appropriate it. Sharad Joshi was successful in tapping into this space and forcing successive Congress governments through the 1980s to give attention to the demands of the middle peasantry. The long years of success of the Shetkari Sanghatana were the first such politics of middle peasantry outside the Congress fold that sought to change the course of State politics. Sharad Joshi's Shetkari Sanghatana could mobilize the farmers in different parts of the State, starting with Central and western Maharashtra but also entering the Vidarbh region. This made the farmers' agitations a State-wide phenomenon during the 1980s. It is indeed possible that

Table 2.10 *Region-wise Results: Assembly Elections: 1985*

Region	Seats	Turnout	Congress		ICS		JP		BJP		Others[a]	
			Won	*Vote*	*Won*	*Vote*	*Won*	*Vote*	*Won*	*Vote*	*Won*	*Vote*
Mumbai–Thane	47	48.0	34	41.7	01	02.9	03	09.6	04	15.3	05	30.5
Konkan	18	58.8	08	36.9	00	0.1	02	16.8	02	06.1	06	40.1
North Maharashtra	36	59.3	10	42.1	12	20.2	06	14.8	05	07.9	03	15.0
Vidarbh	66	62.7	45	43.5	10	17.9	03	02.5	03	09.3	05	26.8
Marathwada	46	57.7	24	42.4	16	24.3	00	03.4	01	03.4	05	26.5
Western Maharashtra	75	65.7	40	46.6	15	22.8	06	07.5	01	03.2	13	19.9
Total	**288**	**59.2**	**161**	**43.4**	**54**	**17.3**	**20**	**07.4**	**16**	**07.3**	**37**	**24.6**

Notes: Turnout: 59.02 per cent.

[a] Others include IND (20), PWP (13), CPI (02) and CPM (02).

various Congress factions colluded with Sharad Joshi from time to time to settle intra-party factional claims; nevertheless, the objective reality of unfulfilled aspirations of middle peasantry remained an important factor both for the assessment of the congress system and for a critique of the State's political economy.

Rise of 'Neo' Hindutva

Another key development of the 1980s was the emergence of many small-scale organizations of the neo-Hindutva variety. The RSS and its version of Hindutva were never very attractive for rural masses and the non-Brahman sections. However, in the 1980s, a somewhat modified version of Hindutva began to gain acceptance among these sections. We discuss this at greater length in the next chapter. Along with the rise of small organizations espousing the politics of Hindutva, the 1980s saw the transformation of the SHS from a party confined to only Marathi interests to a party combining regionalism with Hindu identity. This development facilitated new patterns of mobilization in the State. The traditional support base of Hindutva, comprising mainly of the urban white-collar and Brahman supporters began to expand to non-Brahman castes. Much of the Hindu mobilization that happened in the 1990s thus had its origins in the previous decade. The spread of Hindutva appeal to small towns and even rural areas indicates that just like in the case of Shetkari Sanghatana, there were multiple disappointments shaping during the 1970s among the rural and semi-urban segments of the population and that the Congress was increasingly becoming incapable of addressing these disappointments. This limitation of the Congress facilitated the slow reconfiguration of party competition.

Unstable CMs

The limitations of Congress were evident in the 1980s despite the large majorities enjoyed by Indira Gandhi's Congress in the State. Thus, unstable governments despite big majorities marked the third feature of the politics of the 1980s. Following her strategy to keep strong Maratha elite away as far as possible, Indira Gandhi brought in Antulay as the CM immediately after the 1980 elections. Antulay made every effort to disempower the Maratha elite, particularly from western Maharashtra. During his tenure, the scandal over cement distribution escalated into misappropriation of official machinery when funds were generated for a trust in the name of Indira Gandhi. While the opposition was active in bringing this scandal to the forefront, the Maratha lobby was alleged to have a hand in leaking information and damaging Antulay's case. Shalinitai Patil, a strong leader in her own right and also the wife of Vasantdada Patil was in the forefront of the internal attack on Antulay. When Antulay had to resign under political pressure and under judicial strictures (January 1982), Babasaheb Bhosale from Mumbai, but not having much base himself, was brought in as the CM who had to quit within a year under the pressure of internal factionalism. This was the time when Indira Gandhi finally yielded to the pressure from the Maratha lobby and brought in Vasantdada Patil as the CM but he was never comfortable with the party's national high command. Finally, he left office in June 1985 and yet another weak Maratha leader from Marathwada, Shivajirao Patil Nilangekar, was made the CM. He too had to soon quit under High Court strictures about alteration of marks of his daughter for the final-year medical examination (March 1986), making room for Shankarrao (S.B.) Chavan. (He was replaced by Sharad Pawar in June 1988 after the latter agreed to return to the Congress winding up his ICS party.)

This chain of events leading to frequent change of the CM suggests the difficulty of retaining power without involving the strong Maratha lobby. Although finally the Central leadership of the Congress was forced to concede CM's position to Pawar, by then, the State Congress was completely in disarray and the Maratha lobby was humiliated to a great extent. Thus, the decade between 1976–1977 and 1987–1988 constitutes the critical period as far as the congress system and nature of party competition in the State are concerned. Most of the features of the congress system on which dominance of the Congress party hinged were corroded during this period, giving rise to mobilizations like Shetkari Sanghatana and various neo-Hinduist organizations and, finally, made room for the entry of the SHS in the hinterland of the State. The churning and reconfiguration were however marked by the inability of the PWP or JP to seize the opportunity and occupy the space being vacated by the Congress. At the same time, the BJP was yet not as strong and able as to become a major force in the State, although the agitation on the issue of Ram Janmabhoomi was already under way and attracting fair amount of support in the State. This was also the phase during which new and non-Brahman leadership from within the BJP was becoming prominent.

Much is often speculated about possible consequences if Pawar had not returned to the Congress. These speculations were relevant because of reports of many young activists from Marathwada choosing to join the SHS in the event of dissolution of ICS. Nevertheless, what is more important, and perhaps a crucial reason why he returned to the Congress, is that during the decade that he was outside the Congress, Pawar could not fully win the Maratha lobby nor was he able to bring victory to his party defeating the Congress. In this sense, the resilience of the Congress was not fully lost even after a consistent attack on State-level leadership by Congress's high command. Once ICS merged with the Congress, the decade-long space for non-Congress parties, cultivated since 1977, was thrown open and the JD, SHS and BJP rushed to claim that space.

Since 1989, the BJP in the State allied with the SHS, an experiment that was to shape the politics of the State for next almost 25 years. In 1989, when Rajiv Gandhi's popularity was on the wane, the State witnessed a triangular contest among the Congress, JD (mainly comprising the sections of previous JP from the State) with its allies and the alliance of the BJP and SHS. In spite of the three-way contest, the LS elections from the State strengthened the non-Congress parties (Table 2.11). Although the Congress found itself in a much better situation compared to 1977, the outcome signalled the beginning of its decline as elsewhere in the country. In 1990–91, the SHS and BJP continued their coalition and posed a serious threat to the Congress, although the Congress had almost reached the half-way mark and comfortably formed the government (Table 2.12 and 2.13). The 1990 election outcome also

Table 2.11 *LS Election Results: 1989*

Party	Seats Contested	Seats Won	Votes
Congress	48	28	45.4
BJP	33	10	23.7
SHS	3	1	1.2
JD	23	5	11.0
CPI	3	1	1.9
CPI(M)	2	0	1.2
JP	1	0	—
PWP	5	0	2.3
Others	123	0	5.1
IND	352	3	8.2
Total	**593**	**48**	

Note: Turnout: 59.9 per cent.

indicates an emerging regional variation in the electoral outcomes. The Congress retained its strength in western Maharashtra but lost considerably in Marathwada and Vidarbh and more so in Bombay–Konkan regions. This was to replicate in most of the later elections from the State. The ability of the Congress to ward off the challenges of internal factionalism and of a new formidable alliance of two opposition parties indicated that unlike in the States of North India, the Congress could not be written off easily from politics of Maharashtra. This was further evidenced in the LS elections of 1991 when State Congress posted a handsome victory with 38 seats out of 48. In other words, the BJP and SHS could emerge as the main challengers to the Congress, but the Congress was yet to be roundly defeated or ousted.

THE TURBULENT 1980S

The resilience of the Congress party in Maharashtra thus meant that in spite of the adverse circumstances obtained throughout the entire decade of the 1980s, the party was not easily to be dislodged from the position of power.

Table 2.12 *Region-wise Results: Assembly Elections, 1990*

Region	Seats	Turnout	Congress[a] Won	Congress[a] Vote	BJP Won	BJP Vote	SHS Won	SHS Vote	JD Won	JD Vote	Others[b] Won	Others[b] Vote
Mumbai–Thane	47	54.3	14	34.7	11	15.9	19	25.5	01	13.9	02	10.0
Konkan	18	66.0	04	35.0	03	8.3	07	25.1	01	11.8	03	19.8
North Maharashtra	36	60.7	21	39.3	08	14.6	02	12.4	03	15.2	02	18.5
Vidarbh	66	63.4	25	30.6	13	11.9	09	12.6	10	13.1	09	31.8
Marathwada	46	62.5	23	34.8	05	9.0	11	18.2	02	9.9	05	28.1
Western Maharashtra	75	66.7	54	48.7	02	6.2	04	10.7	07	12.5	08	21.9
Total	**288**	**62.1**	**141**	**38.1**	**42**	**10.7**	**52**	**15.9**	**24**	**12.7**	**29**	**22.6**

Notes: Turnout: 62.1 per cent.

[a] By this time, Pawar's ICS had merged with the Congress party.

[b] Others include IND (13), PWP (08), CPI (02), CPM (03), Muslim League (01), ICS (01) and RPI(K) (01).

Table 2.13 *LS Election Results: 1991*

Party	Seats Contested	Seats Won	Votes
Congress	48	38	48.4
BJP	31	5	20.2
SHS	17	4	9.5
JD	33	0	10.5
CPI	3	0	1.0
CPI(M)	2	1	1.3
JP	23	0	0.7
PWP	6	0	1.3
Others	142	0	2.9
IND	557	0	4.2
Total	**862**	**48**	

Note: Turnout: 48.8 per cent.

The mid-1980s produced an unforeseen vacuum in party politics in the State. As mentioned above, the Maratha lobby was busy fighting its internal battle within the Congress party over the issue of its dominant role. Therefore, in spite of being in power throughout the decade since 1980, the Congress party was not only a divided house but a party having lost the capacity to mobilize or aggregate. It could neither mobilize new entrants eager to occupy positions of power, nor could it provide a basis to the new aspirations shaping among the OBCs of the State. As the congress system too was on the decline, the Congress party in particular and the party system, in general, were unable to bring together different social sections and their sectional interests under the umbrella of an acceptable policy framework. The JP was a non-starter and by the early 1980s, it had lost all initiative. The JD that comprised of many of the JP elements too had a very weak base in the State. It was at this juncture that Pawar's ICS merged with the Congress party, thus dissolving one of the existing platforms for mobilization and around the same time, the Shetkari Sanghatana also lost its early attraction.

The BJP was yet to become a force in the State, but the SHS seized this moment and began spreading across Marathwada. In 1985, the SHS held its party conference at Bhivandi, a town that had witnessed Hindu–Muslim riots the previous year around the time of Shiv Jayanti. Even before that, SHS chief Bal Thackeray had mooted a suggestion that all Hindutva organizations should come together and form a Hindu Mahasangh. At the Bhivandi conference, the party officially signalled its move towards Hindutva and also declared that it would now spread across the State by opening its *shakhas* (branches) in every village (Palshikar, [2007] 2010; 94). This development facilitated the rise of a new political configuration in the State, particularly when in 1989 the BJP and SHS decided to form an alliance. In both LS elections of 1989 and later in 1990 Assembly elections, this alliance posted an impressive electoral performance. Although Pawar's tactics and his organizational ability saved the Congress party in 1990, the victory in 1990 Assembly elections was only nominal. The Congress was not sure how to respond to the emerging political sensibilities among the non-Maratha communities and the SHS and BJP were not sure how to capitalize on those. But for all practical purposes, it can be said in hindsight that 1990 marked an important stage in the ongoing decline of the Congress and the overall pre-eminence of the Maratha leadership in the State.

The 1990s were to further sharpen this trend and erode the bases of both the Congress party and Maratha leadership, thus paving the way for a new phase in the politics of the State. This new configuration was to happen in 1995. However, for that to happen, the narrative of State politics was also to undergo changes in that decade.

Politics in the Times of Congress Decline

Key Themes

As we saw in the preceding chapter, the 1980s witnessed the silent collapse of the congress system. Yet, electoral outcomes did not throw any dramatic results and the Congress party remained central to the politics of the State. It even continued to rule the State till the mid-1990s. Only in the 1990s, the first signals of political change indicated possibility of new configuration of competitive politics. In retrospect, the numerous electoral battles between 1990 and 2014 present us with a long-term picture of this transformation. A lacklustre performance in the LS election of 1989 (28 seats) and a near loss of majority in the Assembly election that followed in 1990 mark the alignment of Maharashtra with the all-India trend of Congress's 'decline' in the electoral arena. In 1995, the party squarely lost State elections, making way for a coalition government of the SHS and BJP. This transformation was contemporarily seen as 'a moment of realignment' (Palshikar, 1996; Vora, 1996) and a possible shift to a new party system (Palshikar and Birmal, 2009). The residual power of the Congress party and its support base, however, was reflected in the subsequent elections—the party posted a handsome victory in 1998 parliamentary elections, taking along with it a number of smaller parties. This performance within one year from its dismal defeat in the State Assembly elections did not fully symbolize the recovery of the party. But Congress (and NCP which was formed later in 1999 following Sharad Pawar's exit from the Congress party) did manage to keep the opposition out of power for a long spell of 15 years from 1999.

Two factors always shadowed the changes that were happening during the interregnum between decline of Congress party and the rise of BJP in 2014. One was the continued importance of the Congress (and its breakaway faction, NCP) in terms of government formation and the other was the inability of non-Congress parties to produce a consistent alternative to the Congress. Since these two factors dominated the realm of formal competitive politics, not much attention was given to the larger transformation taking place in the realm of political process in the post-1990 period. Nevertheless, as we have argued earlier, there was no doubt about the decline of the Congress during this entire period (Palshikar et al., 2014). As such, the long period of more than two decades since 1990 marked a slow transition away from the congress system and subsequently also from domination of the Congress party, albeit without producing any single alternative to that party. Thus, one witnesses both, the continued decline of the Congress and the halting transition to a new configuration of party competition during the eventful period of 1990–2014.

Except for the defeat of the Congress party in 1995, the political process in the State did not have any dramatic rupture. Also, the routine political manoeuvres and ups and downs create an impression of transient tendencies or, alternatively, tempt one to argue how politics in the State is so very different from the all-India processes. However, when we take a long-term view, in more than one sense, this moment of transformation coincides with the major transformations shaping at the all-India level and indeed in many States of India. The 1990s marked a transformation in India's politics mainly because the decade opened with a yawning absence of towering leadership at the national level and also a remarkable decline in the ability of the Congress party to retain power. This changed the structure of political competition. Along with that change, this period marked the rise of State-level parties as both State-level players and key players at the national level. This change was more dramatically reflected in the politics of some North Indian States. Karnataka and Andhra Pradesh, which had witnessed tumultuous transformations a little earlier in the 1980s, were less explicitly affected by the national-level changes which occurred around the turn of the decade. The 1990s also witnessed changes in the nature of politics because of the emergence of a new set of issues around which political mobilizations shaped.

In Maharashtra, initially, it appeared that nothing much was going to change because Sharad Pawar ensured that the Congress party retained power at the State level in 1990. But as the decade of the 1990s unfolded, it became clear that like the all-India level, the State too was poised for changes. Also, there were unmistakable echoes of national-level political rhetoric, though the actual text and texture of the State-level rhetoric was quite different at times. As we shall see further, although changes happened in the shadow of the political transformation at the all-India level, Maharashtra did have its own independent trajectory, logic and narrative as regards the transformation of the 1990s. Therefore, in this chapter, we shall review the larger and more general themes that not only dominated public discourse but also had a deep impact on the way electoral politics was shaping in the State during this period. These themes are not different from the ones that dominated all-India politics during the same period, though their specific expression in Maharashtra and their relative relevance to the politics in the State do deserve a detailed discussion in order to not only understand the outcome of 1995 but also appreciate the change that later occurred in 2014. These themes consisted of economic liberalization, implementation of Mandal recommendations and the agitation over the issue of Ram Janmabhoomi.

In case of each of these three themes, Maharashtra has had similarities and differences in the trajectory of politics around them. Like most other parts of the country, Maharashtra too did not witness any major agitation or movement on the question of liberalization. But unlike Andhra Pradesh, it also did not have an aggressive rhetoric and policy of liberalization (Suri, 2003). The pace of liberalization was moderate, often halting. At the same time, unlike North Indian States of Uttar Pradesh (UP) and Bihar, Maharashtra did not wait till the late 1990s for the policy of liberalization to unfold. So also was in the case of Mandal. There were neither vociferous pro-Mandal mobilizations that marked politics in the State nor was there a strong anti-Mandal political mobilization. No major party in the State represented itself as the mascot of Mandal (though the JD tried that and the Bharipa Bahujan Mahasangh [BBM] that emerged during the 1990s hoped to benefit from OBC mobilization that it engaged in), and also, no party could be eventually maligned as being anti-Mandal.

In fact, full-fledged 'Mandalization' of politics in the sense that a key community (Marathas) began demanding reservations, happened much later—in the early 21st century, almost a decade and half after this issue gained traction in North India and also much after the Lingayats of Karnataka sought and gained OBC status. But as we shall see further in the chapter, Mandalization in the sense of changed composition of the political elite did commence as early as the late 1980s and constituted the major feature of State politics by the mid-1990s.

Finally, the frenzied pro-Hindutva mobilization that the North witnessed was absent in the State; the BJP was not the key factor in appropriating Hindutva initially, but Maharashtra was not as distant to Hindutva politics as the States of Andhra Pradesh or Tamil Nadu. Apart from communal conflagration, new political alignments also took shape in the State on account of Hindutva. The BJP nevertheless did not benefit much from it in the 1990s. That was to happen almost after a decade. We discuss these commonalities and State-specificities of these key all-India themes further.

LIBERALIZATION

Even before the 'new economic policy' began to formally take shape with the Union Budget of 1991, the first steps in that direction were taken in the State under the leadership of Sharad Pawar when he became the CM in 1988. Much earlier, Indira Gandhi had initially tried to tame the trade unions of Mumbai by ensuring that the textile mill workers' strike of the early 1980s would fizzle out (Wersch, 1992). So, by the time liberalization came about, Mumbai's trade unions were already weakened. In particular, the unions led by communists and socialists were replaced by professional, economistic and non-ideological unions under the leadership of R. J. Mehta and Datta Samant. With the failure of the textile mill workers' strike, Datta Samant too had lost critical power in the trade union politics of

Mumbai and Thane. So, in the industrial bastion of Mumbai–Thane, resistance to new policies was at best nominal. This was also partly due to the strategy of slow and selective liberalization that the State adopted.

By the late 1980s, except the strong unions of bank employees and government employees, the tradition of mass mobilization itself was also on the decline. In the hinterland of the State, the farmers' movement led by Sharad Joshi had lost steam by the mid-1980s. In this sense, politics of mass mobilization had already witnessed a shrinking of mobilizational space by the late 1980s. This situation made it easy for governments to take small steps in the direction of limited and selective liberalization.

Pawar's initial efforts to liberalize were, of course, cautious and his departure to Delhi in 1991 and the subsequent communal riots deflected attention away from the issues of economic policy. Also, around 1989–1990, the erstwhile socialists, then in the JD, were more concerned with issues of social justice. So, their emphasis too was less on economic issues when policies of economic liberalization commenced. Once he returned to State politics in 1993, Pawar began to more speedily bring about various changes in the economy. The centrepiece of this was the 'Enron project' (Kale, 2014).[1] Just as the Enron project became the symbol of privatization and 'economic reforms' that the State government aimed at, this project also became the rallying point for those opposed to foreign investments, privatization and new economic policy. It ran into severe opposition on a number of grounds—environmental, issues of displacement and resettlement,

---

[1] The Enron project was to take place at Dabhol in Ratnagiri district of Konkan region. It was an ambitious power project that aimed at responding to the increasing demand for electricity for both consumer use and industrial use that the State was finding difficult to meet. Apart from the many technical issues involved in the design of the project, the key sociopolitical issues were environmental hazard for the ecology of Konkan, questions of land acquisition, allegations of corruption and, above all, the question of the investment and ownership model that was visualized. This model included a large share from non-India-based multinational corporations along with investment by Indian state—the State government in particular. This led to controversies regarding the principle of partnership between public-owned entities and privately-owned entities as also questions about control over assets and profits besides the issue of rates of power generated from the plant.

corruption charges and, of course, entry of a foreign multinational corporation in the power sector. In the run up to the 1995 Assembly elections, 'Enron' became one of the key issues—not just in Konkan where the project was to take place but elsewhere in the State too, where it became a symbol of alleged kickbacks and adverse effects of the entry of multinational corporates.

While all non-Congress parties vehemently opposed the Enron project, and while the Left parties hoped to mobilize public opinion on this issue, the BJP–SHS alliance was more successful in gaining political mileage out of the anti-Enron agitation. In the election campaign of 1995, BJP leader Gopinath Munde had declared that if voted to power, the opposition would 'drown the Enron project in the Arabian sea'. The BJP–SHS opposition to Enron however was less on grounds of economic policy and more on grounds of alleged kickbacks. Once elected to power, the SHS–BJP government sought to renegotiate the Enron deal and bring back the Enron company soon after assuming office in 1995.[2] While the 1995 election campaign did have a lot of focus on the 'Enron issue', it is noteworthy that as far as the main parties in the State were concerned, the debate was limited to the issues of modality and public propriety. As the decision of the new alliance government indicates, the BJP and SHS did not have any serious objection to the larger project of privatization and the public–private partnership model implicit in the Enron project. All that the new government did was to 'renegotiate' the deal. This episode indicated the unstated consensus among major parties over new economic policies.

In fact, while Sharad Pawar has been identified with initiating many new economic policies, actual changes in this regard were speeded up by the first non-Congress government of the SHS and BJP that came to power in 1995. This government pushed major decisions such as the construction of the Mumbai–Pune expressway by assigning the work to private players and by initiating the Slum Rehabilitation Scheme among others. The expressway model brought in the practice of road

---

[2] *India Today*, Why Gopinath Munde Will Be Missed as a Maharashtra Leader, 3 June 2014, https://www.indiatoday.in/india/west/story/why-gopinath-munde-will-be-missed-as-a-maharashtra-leader-195578-2014-06-03(accessed on 25 June 2020).

tolls as a long-term compensation to the investors in public infrastructure projects. The practice of adopting the 'Build–operate–transfer' (BOT) model or 'Public–private partnership' (PPP) model became a common strategy for augmenting infrastructure projects since the 1990s, and all governments since have followed the same path. Since the 1990s, an unstated consensus has always existed among the major parties of the State that active reorganization of the economic policies was needed. This new consensus was so pervasive that even the most famous field of sugar factories was opened up for private players. Thus, the privatization drive included the rise of private agro-industries including private sugar factories and milk dairies as also privatization of octroi collection (Nashik Municipal Corporation) and privatization of water supply in some cities (Sangli, Nagpur).

Consensus among major parties ensured that economic policies were never the key issue of contestations or political mobilization by the major parties. Successive governments were able to push specific steps in the direction of both privatization and restructuring of government-run services such as the State Electricity Board. The Left parties and other smaller parties did seek to mobilize the public against policies of liberalization and privatization. But such mobilizations lacked strength and also lacked political traction in electoral terms. They attracted public attention and support only when there were agitations against specific projects such as the special economic zone (SEZ) in Raigad district or the efforts to acquire agricultural land at Maan, near Pune, the Dow project (Mohanty, 2019; Sathe, 2017) in Pune district, etc., but such protests seldom transformed into movements for resistance to the overall policy.

Alongside sporadic agitations against specific projects, changes in the economic policy brought about three structural effects. One has been the slow but sure decline of cooperatives including sugar cooperatives. Another important factor has been the consolidation of the service sector as the main driver of the economy. We shall be discussing both these in greater detail in the chapter on political economy (Chapter 8). The third effect has been the unending spate of farmers' suicides representing the continuing crisis in the farm sector. Droughts, indebtedness and inability of successive governments to treat agriculture outside of the framework of liberalized economy have all contributed to the agrarian crisis in the State. We mention these factors here because all three have been present for a long time and have overshadowed politics in an indirect manner. These factors also help us understand the absence of large-scale mass movements and yet at the same time an unease about the economy and economic policies which get articulated through assertions of identities. Thus, at one level, the debate about economic liberalization took shape wherein the Left parties—PWP and the Republican faction led by Prakash Ambedkar, Bharatiya Republican Party (BRP)—could mobilize localized protests and gain some space in the politics of the State and at another level, issues of migration, rehabilitation and anxieties emerging out of economic uncertainties have dotted the political landscape of the State. As we shall discuss in Chapter 8, the uneven pace of urbanization accelerated during this period gave rise to routine struggles of poor workers—such as the domestic workers, street vendors and rag pickers—seeking legitimacy to their urban existence in various ways. These struggles often remained unarticulated or, worse still, led to conflicts among different sections of the poor (Deshpande, 2003). As a result, despite various diffuse contestations, questions of economic policy did not become central to electoral or party competition in the State during 1990–2014.

MANDAL AND THE CASTE CAULDRON

The late 1980s witnessed the northern parts of the country getting embroiled in a bitter controversy over the question of 'OBC reservations'. This conflict was occasioned by the decision of the V.P. Singh government to implement the recommendation of the Mandal Commission' to reserve 27 per cent seats in Central government establishments for both admissions to educational institutions and to employment. But it also represented the anxieties generated by caste relations, continued backwardness of supposedly 'lower' castes and competitive claims facilitated by democratic politics. These factors produced dramatic political outcomes in the late 1960s and again in the 1970s as far as the northern States are concerned. Comparatively, the caste factor remained limited in its salience in Maharashtra when 'politics of *pichchadas*' was shaping in the North. The Mandal controversy initially touched Maharashtra only peripherally. This muted response to the Mandal controversy in the State had many reasons. The demographic composition of the State made it difficult for 'OBC' communities to effectively organize politically.[3]

More importantly, unlike in the States of North India, perceptible political change had already come about in the State right from the time of the formation of a separate State in 1960 when political power was transferred to the intermediate Maratha community pushing the Brahmans on the margins of formal political power. This outcome of Brahmanetar movement meant that political aspirations of non-Brahman communities were partially fulfilled. As a result, there was limited excitement in Maharashtra on the issue of OBC reservations. Although the OBC Mahasangh was active in the late 1980s, Congress—being the vehicle of Maratha community—did not feel the need to take an initiative in this regard. While the BJP was initially at best ambivalent on this question at the all-India level, its State-level leadership had already become more diverse in caste terms by the late 1980s with the rise of non-Brahman leaders such as Farande, Dange and Phundkar. With the rise of Gopinath Munde in State BJP, the need for the party to vocally support Mandal became much less urgent because the party's State leadership included the major OBC and non-Brahman castes from Maharashtra. In any case, the ideological emphasis of the BJP at that time was on Hindu consolidation and hence less favourably inclined to caste as a basis for mobilization.

While core leadership of the SHS till the mid-1980s came from upper intermediate castes, the party had successfully mobilized the Marathi community of Mumbai and Thane across caste lines and a large section of its cadres there came from non-Brahman communities. By the mid-1980s, the SHS was about to make its mark in the Marathwada region where more than OBC platform, the communal platform paid dividends and as such, the SHS competed with the BJP

---

[3] As we saw in Chapter 1, Marathas constitute almost 30 per cent of State's population, but a section among them—Kunbis—was already included in the OBC category by Mandal commission. No other backward caste singly did have the capacity to mobilize all OBCs on the OBC platform.

for Hindu identity but in the process effectively amalgamated youth from non-Brahman communities. Both SHS and BJP were ideologically averse to taking up the Mandal issue and SHS chief Thackeray was openly against reservations and Mandal recommendations.[4] In fact, that was one of the reasons for Bhujbal's exit from the SHS in 1991. Subsequently also, like BJP, SHS too did not explicitly mobilize the OBCs on Mandal platform, although a large section of its followers in Vidarbh region was OBC during the mid-1990s. Nevertheless, many small Hindutva organizations emerged during this period which brought typically non-Brahman youth to the Hindutva fold. New organizations like Hindu Ekta and Patit Pawan Sanghatana brought the political energies of OBC youth to the forefront of Hindutva politics (Pawar, 2005). The 'neo-Hinduist' militant politics thus facilitated the entry of OBCs into Hindutva framework in a nascent manner (Vora and Palshikar, 1990) and SHS, in particular, appropriated much of this energy both in Mumbai and in the hinterland of the State during the late 1980s and 1990s—something that has been described as 'vernacularization of Hindutva' (Hansen, 1996).

Thus, two factors seem to have partially neutralized the 'politics of OBCs' in the State. First, as mentioned above, was the political transition that happened in two stages—first around the 1930s when the Congress facilitated entry of Maratha leadership alongside the Brahman leaders in the State and the second around the 1950s when around the formation of the State, the Marathas took full control of the Congress and State politics producing Maratha hegemony. While the OBCs were not necessarily part of that transition, it ideologically represented non-Brahman forces and Marathas represented the claims of OBCs. The other factor is the absorption of the OBCs into Hindutva politics by neo-Hinduist organizations—BJP and SHS. This provided the OBCs an opportunity that the then prevailing congress system would not give them. The platform of the Shetkari Sanghatana also performed a similar role. In Sharad Joshi's Shetkari Sanghatana, besides farmers from the Maratha community, the Mali and Vanjari farmers could easily rise to prominent positions. The emergence of

[4] *Times of India,* Sena Confused in Rural Maharashtra, Mumbai ed., 19 December 1990, p. 7.

platforms for effective participation both allowed OBCs a political space and reduced the need for a separate politics of OBCs. Because of these factors, main political parties had somewhat limited incentive to adopt the Mandal platform.

In effect, this meant that the politics of OBC mobilization was confined to less influential political parties and organizations in the State, like the JD in the late 1980s. In the early 1990s, Prakash Ambedkar, a leader of an RPI faction, also floated the BBM and aligned it with his BRP (1994), thus experimenting Dalit–Bahujan coalition. Much later, smaller parties like Jan Surajya Shakti (active since 2004) founded by Vinay Kore and Rashtriya Samaj Paksh (active since 2003) founded by Mahadev Jankar have sought to represent Lingayat and Dhangar communities respectively, mainly from the southern parts of the State.

But much before these smaller parties came on to the political scene, in post-1991 period, Chhagan Bhujbal sought to mobilize the OBCs and projected himself as the OBC leader—first within the SHS and subsequently through the Congress and then the NCP. In 1994, on the eve of the Assembly elections, Pawar government decided to implement OBC quota with further subcategorization of the OBCs in view of the State-specific internal divisions and expectations. One of the contentious issues was about the distinction between Banjara and Vanjari communities. The government, after considerable public debate, decided to treat them as separate and not as one community.[5]

In 1994, a demand by the Gowari community from Vidarbh that they be included in the list of STs suddenly acquired importance because of the mishandling of a demonstration by the community at Nagpur[6] and the Pawar government agreed to include the community

---

[5] This led to the decision of the State government to give sub-quotas to different categories such as Denotified Tribes (DNTs) and NTs. While named as 'tribes', these groups have been assigned separate share from the 27 per cent OBC quota. Among the NTs, the Dhangar community, which is an important caste in parts of South Maharashtra, is given a separate share of 3.5 per cent while the Vanjaris, who mainly inhabit central districts of Beed, Ahmednagar and Nashik, are accorded a share of 2 per cent. Other NTs are given a share of 2.5 per cent and DNTs are given a separate share of 3 per cent.

[6] The demonstration ended in a stampede resulting in the death of 114 demonstrators (November 1994) and subsequent resignation of Madhukar Pichad, Tribal

in the category of 'Special Backward Class', giving this group a separate share of 2 per cent. For some time now, the Dhangars have been agitating for their inclusion in the ST category instead of the Nomadic Tribe (NT) status, and this demand has been assiduously opposed by the other STs fearing that Dhangars may capture a larger share of the reserved seats available for the State's ST category. This issue has a potential of becoming a flash point in the State, though the decade of the 2010s has been more embroiled in the controversy surrounding the demand of the Marathas for OBC status.

These complications show that despite the apparent calm over the OBC issue, within different castes, the question of internal sharing of OBC quota involved serious contestation and bargaining. Instead of strengthening 'OBC politics', these claims and counterclaims actually ensured that there would not be any consolidated politics of the OBC community as such. While this is not fundamentally different from the experience of UP or Bihar, there were two key differences. One is the absence of a State-level OBC leader. Although Bhujbal tried hard, his role as OBC leader always remained circumscribed by his association with the Congress–NCP and with the Maratha leadership. Second, and more importantly, in North India, one comes across one large OBC community that anchored the politics of OBCs at the State level—the Yadavs in particular. In Maharashtra, as we have been arguing, the strength and spread of each of the major OBC castes have been quite limited. Most of the OBC castes (except Kunbis)[7] do not account for more than 3–4 per cent of the State population, and most of them are concentrated in some districts rather than being present across the State. The Kunbis, though more numerous than most OBC castes, have traditionally been closely linked to the Marathas and, in fact, many of them often claimed Maratha status too (Deshpande, 2007). This

Development Minister. State government appointed a commission of enquiry which exonerated both the political leadership as also the police in its report (1998; Guru, 1995).

[7] As stated earlier in Note 3, the Mandal Commission report had made a distinction between Marathas (high-caste Marathas) and Kunbis (low-caste Marathas) and included the latter in the OBC category. However, the Kunbis do not have a separate politics distinct from that of the Marathas either in terms of political aspirations or in terms of social claims.

association with the ruling and hegemonic community from the State meant that they would not be able to lead the politics of OBCs—neither would Kunbis be willing nor would they be accepted by other OBCs as leader of the larger OBC project.

Although no party became the political representative of the OBCs in the State, all parties accommodated leaders from various OBC communities. Almost from each major OBC community, its own leadership emerged effectively bringing about 'OBCization' of State's politics and posing a threat to the dominance of the Maratha community.[8] The growing number of OBC leaders active within parties including the four major parties suggests that in spite of the 'Maratha dominance' for which the State is famous, a 'silent revolution' of some sort has occurred in the State during the post-1990 period. While this may not be on the scale of and in the exact sense of the silent revolution that Jaffrelot speaks about (Jaffrelot, 2003), this development has definitely nuanced the dominance of the Maratha community and brought about at least a limited transformation in the composition of political elite in the State. It is another matter that it has not necessarily transformed the agenda and core power equations. Nor did it endanger numerical preponderance of Maratha elite until at least 2004 (Vora, 2009).

Unlike in the North, then, the OBC issue did not occupy political centre stage in Maharashtra. Also, as we saw above, no single caste like the Yadavs could lead OBC politics in the State. No major party operated as the political vehicle of the OBCs in the State and

---

[8] For instance, Bhujbal and Farande from the Mali community (respectively from Congress–NCP and BJP), Makharam Pawar from the Banjara community, who was the key leader of Bahujan Mahasangh in early years (but who later joined the BJP in 2009), Anna Dange from the Dhangar community, who was in the BJP for a long time but left the party in 2002 to briefly form his LokRajya Party and then joined the NCP (2006) at the fag-end of his career, Mahadev Jankar (also from the Dhangar community), founder of the Rashtriya Samaj Paksh, and Eknath Khadse of the BJP from the Leva community. Above all, besides Bhujbal, who had ambitions of becoming a State-level leader and leading the OBCs beyond his Mali community, Gopinath Munde emerged as the OBC leader of the BJP before his sudden death in 2014. His daughter Pankaja Munde has been in the limelight since 2014 and claiming to lead the OBCs in the State.

finally, the sections identified as OBC got politically dispersed in the State. As a result, rather than broader claims of OBCs for administrative and political power and mobilization of OBCs as a political constituency, Maharashtra's politics has seen caste-based mobilization of different OBC castes and their continuous reconfiguration and fragmentation. As such, the role of 'OBC politics' has remained limited in the State. Yet, the constant pressure of a possible OBC takeover did haunt the Maratha political elite as we shall discuss in Chapter 7 on Marathas.

HINDUTVA POLITICS

Like elsewhere in the country, the language of Hindutva began to occupy political space in the State by the late 1980s. Although the birthplace of both Savarkar and RSS and the home of the Brahman Peshwa rulers, Maharashtra was not much enamoured of Hindutva politics prior to the late 1980s. Except the Brahman community, political Hindutva did not have much attraction for the masses in the State. But from the late 1970s, the process of amalgamation of the many non-Brahman castes into Hindutva fold began slowly. As mentioned earlier, small local organizations mushroomed in parts of Maharashtra which attracted the non-Brahman youth to a militant Hindutva argument. In a sense, this was facilitated by the fact that aspiring youth from these castes did not have a political vehicle to locally engage with public affairs. During the late 1980s, this process of entry of 'OBC' youth from small towns into the Hindutva fold gathered momentum. In part, this was due to the new, pro-Hindutva narrative articulated by the SHS in its effort to enter the hinterland of Maharashtra. But besides the SHS, the RSS and BJP also contributed to this process. They not only accommodated the youth from non-Brahman castes into the Hindutva fold but also began to increasingly depend on the numeric strength of the non-Brahman entrants in order to penetrate both public discourse and the arena of competitive politics. Soon, the Ram Janmabhoomi agitation gave the BJP a platform to further attract cross-section of the Hindu society. Although response to that agitation remained somewhat lukewarm in the State compared to states like Gujarat or Madhya Pradesh, the Ram Janmabhoomi agitation did provide critical impetus to the process of associating many sections to political Hindutva.

The SHS was the main vehicle initially to exploit the communal cleavage and also to benefit from it; though later, the BJP also benefited from the expansion of Hindutva politics. Already, during the 1980s, communal sensibilities had become a key factor in shaping new social cleavages in many towns and also in rural areas of the State (Vora and Palshikar, 1990). Besides many small-scale clashes between Hindus and Muslims in different parts of the State where there was no prior history of communal clashes, the State witnessed a major riot in Bhivandi in 1984—a city with large Muslim population and a history of communal tension (Khopade, 1992). Around the mid-1980s, the SHS made deep inroads in the Marathwada region which was previously under the Nizam rule and had a history of deep resentment among Hindus over the atrocities perpetrated by the agents of Nizam—a Muslim ruler—and therefore against the Muslim community, more generally. Tactically exploiting the demographic composition of Aurangabad city where Muslim presence is quite high, the SHS demonstrated how Hindu consolidation can work effectively in local electoral politics by winning the city municipal corporation in 1987.[9]

The early 1990s saw a further and more vicious expansion of Hindutva politics. This was occasioned both by the increasingly ferocious rhetoric of the SHS through its Marathi publication (daily) *Saamana* and also by the events unfolding at the national level—the Rath Yatra by L. K. Advani and the subsequent destruction of the Babri Mosque in December 1992. Following the destruction of the mosque, communal clashes broke out in Mumbai, mainly resulting from the anger among Muslims and retaliated by Hindus. While the December riot was brought under control pretty quickly, much more severe violence against the Muslims ensued in January 1993. The January violence caused a collapse of the collective life of Mumbai

---

[9] This was the first time that the SHS stepped out of Mumbai–Thane belt and, tactically exploiting the local Hindu–Muslim divisions, managed to win 27 seats in the corporation out of 60. Since then, Aurangabad city continued to be an SHS bastion until, dramatically, in 2014 Assembly election, a candidate of the All India Majlis-e-Ittehad-ul-Muslimeen (AIMIM), Imtiaz Jaleel, won from Aurangabad central constituency.

amid allegations of police partisanship and direct involvement of many leaders of the SHS. The Congress government led by Sudhakar Naik was seen as ineffective in handling the situation competently and the one-sided violence against Muslims had an even more violent and subversive reaction in the form of a series of bomb blasts in different parts of Mumbai in March 1993.[10] Thus, between December 1992 and March 1993, the city of Mumbai had become the main theatre of worst-ever communal violence the State had witnessed so far. Besides the doubtful role of the police, this communalization altered the patterns of communal politics, taking communal orientation to almost all sections of the society.

Post-1993, the State did not experience any major communal clash but the following few years did see continued communal rhetoric as the mainstay of public discourse in the State. The Assembly elections of 1995 were the next major occasion for communal campaigning. Almost 10 years of communalization thus changed the overall pattern of political allegiances. While the OBCs could see in communal politics an opportunity to assert themselves, the Marathas, who traditionally constituted the bulwark of political support for Congress factions, also began to be attracted to communal propaganda. Maratha factionalism thus began to be played out beyond the confines of the Congress party. Some Maratha leaders joined the SHS or BJP around 1995, while many contested the 1995 elections as independents and after the elections joined the coalition government of the SHS and BJP. This development had a far-reaching impact in the sense that the rise of the SHS and BJP initially owed a great deal to communalization and, later, communalization constituted new political alignments in terms of changed voting behaviour.

Most importantly, what the events of the decade between 1985 and 1995 did was to alter the image of Hindutva politics in the State. What was supposed to be only a Brahmanical political cult now became truly pan-Hindu in its appeal and spread. What was thought to be an urban

[10] The State government appointed an enquiry commission consisting of Justice (Retd) Srikrishna in January 1993. The report of the commission is available online at https://sabrang.com/srikrish/sri%20main.html (accessed on 24 June 2020).

phenomenon also penetrated the rural areas of the State. A politics that was identified only with the middle class now became cross-class with substantial appeal among the lower-middle and lower-income groups. Subsequent elections bear this out. This changed social base of Hindutva in Maharashtra is comparable to what Jaffrelot has shown in the case of Madhya Pradesh and UP (Jaffrelot, 2003). At the same time, it is noteworthy that except the 1995–1996 elections, the SHS also did not rely much on direct Hindutva rhetoric. This was partly because it was by then identified with the Hindu cause and did not need further advertisement of that fact. But this also happened because other State-level issues and political configurations rendered the continued use of Hindutva as less relevant to State politics.

CONCLUSIONS

In sum, the three themes that dominated Indian politics during the 1990s and later too did play an important part in shaping politics in Maharashtra also. Nevertheless, they brought State-specific outcomes.

In the case of issue space, neither of the three themes emerged as the key element in electoral politics or in politics of mobilization. The simultaneous journeys of these themes have meant that the critical issue of agrarian crisis consistently remained out of focus. For long, farmers' suicides have failed to become a political issue just as overall farm crisis has remained only in the background. More importantly, no election—not even that of 1995—was based on any of these three themes exclusively. Instead, these themes seem to have neutralized each other from time to time, allowing many contingent, temporary and/or emotive issues to emerge as crucial.

But in the case of social space, economic liberalization and 'Mandalization' of politics combined to produce the most critical issue—the Maratha demand for reservations. It took a while for this issue to become central, but over the years, it has become most critical. We shall discuss this issue at greater length later in Chapter 7, but suffice it to mention here that this issue goes much beyond the scope of mere reservations. On the one hand, it touches upon the question of jobs while simultaneously bringing in sharp focus the issue of agrarian crisis. On the other hand, the contemporary mobilizations among the Maratha community have also created new fault lines such as between the Dalits and Marathas and Marathas and OBCs.

Finally, in the arena of party-political space, the intertwined politics of these three themes has not produced any single political force representing any of these themes. The politics of the post-1990 period has also not thrown up any single party as the central force. Instead, the quarter of the century, since the decline of the Congress began, has been marked by coalitions. In this competition among political players for political space, the inability of the four major parties to stabilize party competition has produced many small parties, which have proved to be critical to the success of coalitions from time to time. Although the smaller parties have yet not carved out a firm space for themselves as their counterparts in Tamil Nadu have already done, in each election since 1995, the role of either a third front or of smaller parties who join the two main coalitions has been quite important. And yet, despite interventions from smaller parties, the multi-party competition in the State was shaped within a bipolar framework without ceding much space to small parties. Only in 2014 did this framework seem to collapse, in terms of both bipolarity and role of small parties. That development was more due to the rise of Modi's leadership rather than the politics of the previous quarter of a century.

Maharashtra's First Critical Election

4

1995

As we saw in the second chapter, the 1980s came close to displacement of the Congress from power, but the party was to be removed from power only in 1995. Of course, the displacement of the Congress was culmination of a long-drawn process. As explained in Chapter 2, the crisis of the congress system dates back to the late 1970s. Nevertheless, the congress system manifested considerable resilience whereby many of its features continued to be present in State politics even after the initial weakening began. Moreover, the Congress party managed to outlive the congress system—as it did at the Centre and indeed in some States too. Thus, the party retained power for more than a decade after the initial crisis of the congress system became visible. Of course, in the 1980s, the rule of the Congress party was a pale ghost of its earlier dominance. Elections of 1989–1990 almost rehearsed the ultimate that happened in 1995. Thus, the 1990s mark the major departure from previous patterns of State's politics. While the Congress party was in power for much of nearly 25 years since that change began to occur (1989), three things have changed: the nature of politics and political discourse, the nature of party competition and political configurations and, more pertinently, the traditionally understood picture of social alignments behind parties. While the last chapter dealt with the first of these three shifts, this chapter aims to discuss the other two shifts that mark politics of Maharashtra during the 1990s.

This was also the time when the Congress had begun losing State after State. A weak Central government and emergence of coalition system since 1989 had meant that the importance of the State was beginning to increase. CMs were becoming increasingly important not only within their respective States but in national politics too. States began demanding a better deal and CMs began claiming a greater role in national configurations. This was perhaps most dramatically manifested when a State-level heavy weight became prime minister (PM) in 1996 or also by the fact that another very long-term CM was offered leadership of the Central government. Sensing this significance of the moment, early in the decade of the 1990s, Pawar sought to claim his party's leadership, albeit unsuccessfully. What is ironical is that Pawar, who was aiming to become the PM in 1991, should have lost the State election and the Congress would be losing many States precisely at the time when States were becoming important players, Maharashtra being one such State the party lost in 1995.

In Maharashtra, the Congress party lost power for the first time in the wake of Emergency (1978) when a united opposition party in the form of the JP confronted two Congress parties following the Congress's debacle of 1977—Congress (I) and Congress. However, that loss was limited by the fact that the JP also did not get clear majority. Although the PDF was a non-Congress government, it still had one Congress faction as its main anchor. The next time the Congress lost power was in 1995. This time, the Congress lost squarely and the alliance of the SHS and BJP managed to come very close to the majority mark. In this sense, the Assembly election of 1995 was not only 'historic', but it was also one of the few critical elections in the State because it changed the pre-existing political as also the social alignments.

A critical election is recognized as 'critical' only retrospectively through the effects it brings to bear on the political process, though some of these features may be noticed contemporarily too. In the contemporary assessment of 1995, some such features were identified (Vora and Palshikar, 1996). These elections were seen as realignment (Palshikar, 1996) because of the disgruntlement among the Marathas—both among Maratha elite and Maratha voters, as far as their association with the Congress was concerned. Vora (1996) argued that Congress's defeat in 1995 was suggestive of a broader churning caused by the 'shift' towards urban interests. 'Critical' elections implylarge-scale voter involvement expressed through turnout, changes in power relations and rise of new groups that have a long-term impact (Key, 1955). In this chapter, we discuss the process that led to the defeat of the Congress party in the Assembly election of 1995 and argue that the 1995 election qualified for being described as critical election in the political history of Maharashtra, since it fulfilled most of these features. Thus, not merely the actual outcome of the election, the politics preceding the election and the way politics in the State has shaped subsequently also require careful attention.

CONGRESS IN 'DECLINE MODE'

Around 1990, the Congress in the State seemed relatively healthy compared to its situation in many other States and particularly at the Centre. Yet, the build-up towards the 1995 debacle of the Congress began much earlier. We have seen earlier (in Chapter 2) that in the 1990 Assembly elections, the Congress barely won and the alliance of the SHS and BJP posed a major challenge to it. Subsequent to that, it might not be an exaggeration to say that serious decline of the Congress began as early as in 1992 itself. As discussed in Chapter 3, the communal violence that erupted in Mumbai in December 1992 and January 1993 followed by the bomb blasts in Mumbai, though localized in the physical sense, had State-wide implications. A new rhetoric of communalism was then attracting large sections of the Marathi society. Communalization of the electorate was further augmented by the hugely popular campaign by SHS chief Bal Thackeray. The period between 1993 and 1995 was also marked by a spate of allegations against Pawar for his association with the infamous Dawood Ibrahim, the mastermind behind the bomb blasts in Mumbai in 1993. Pawar was also alleged to have close links with Mumbai's real estate industry (Vora and Palshikar, 1996; 44–45, 54–57). While these remained only allegations, the public image of the Congress government as corrupt and having links with the underworld dented the party's ability to attract the voters. Besides the BJP and SHS, Pawar also had to confront bitter and biting criticism and charges by a maverick officer of the Mumbai municipal corporation, Khairnar, who claimed that Pawar was protecting the real estate mafia in Mumbai and was also shielding illegal constructions (which the latter was zealously demolishing).[1] Around the same time, Anna Hazare, who had not yet become an all-India figure but nevertheless enjoyed respect as a constructive rural worker and an anti-corruption crusader, waged his first State-wide anti-corruption agitation (Jenkins, 2004a). This agitation directly attacked Pawar along with many other politicians from the State.

MULTI-PARTY COMPETITION

The framework of political competition was also adversely stacked against the Congress. While the SHS and BJP were successful in forging an alliance, the Congress could only win over the RPI(A) to its side. Those were the times of 'third front' and despite the failure of the National Front government of 1989, many small political players were sensing an opportunity to situate themselves tactically away from both the Congress and the BJP. There were two such non-Congress and non-BJP groups contesting the elections in 1995—one was under the leadership of the JD. This was called 'Purogami Lokshahi Aghadi' (Progressive Democratic Alliance—PDA—different from Pawar's 1978 PDF). This alliance consisted of the JD, PWP, RPK and Kawade faction of RPI, Samata Party, Samajwadi Janata Party and Dalit Panther (Gade faction). The other front was more or less a 'Left front' comprising of the two communist parties, Kamgar Aghadi (led by trade union leader Datta Samant), Satyashodhak Communist Party, Lal Nishan Party and Prakash Ambedkar's BRP along with the Bahujan Mahasangh (which had also been floated by him). This front was called Bahujan Shramik Samiti (BSS) and had seat adjustments with the SP and Bahujan Samaj Party(BSP). Some smaller parties such as the Swatantra Bharat, Nag Vidarbh Andolan and Maharashtra Vikas Congress did not join any of the fronts. This mapping suggests the impending fragmentation of the political spectrum. As Table 4.1 shows, both the PDA and BSS had limited success (they together won 23 seats), but they took away at least 15 per cent votes. While such proliferation of smaller parties

[1] *The Hindu*, He Is Back with His Crowbar, 21 May 2000, https://web.archive.org/web/20080309150949/ http://www.hinduonnet.com/2000/05/21/stories/05211342.htm (accessed on 25 June 2020).

Table 4.1 *Region-wise Results: Assembly Elections, 1995*

Region	Seats	Turnout	Congress		BJP		SHS		JD		IND[a]		Others[b]	
			Won	Vote	Won	Vote	Won	Vote	Won	Vote	Won	Vote	Won	Vote
Mumbai–Thane	47	57.3	02	28.2	15	17.3	23	29.8	01	04.7	02	08.8	04	11.2
Konkan	18	76.3	02	30.3	03	09.0	10	33.2	00	04.1	00	09.0	03	14.4
North Maharashtra	36	71.3	10	31.5	10	16.1	05	12.6	03	06.2	07	26.3	01	07.3
Vidarbh	66	77.4	17	24.6	22	17.8	11	08.0	02	06.5	13	29.2	01	13.9
Marathwada	46	74.9	12	26.8	09	09.9	15	18.4	02	08.5	05	24.7	03	11.7
Western Maharashtra	75	76.8	37	41.1	06	06.5	09	12.0	03	04.7	18	29.7	02	06.0
Total	**288**	**71.7**	**80**	**31.0**	**65**	**12.8**	**73**	**16.4**	**11**	**05.9**	**45**	**23.6**	**14**	**10.3**

Notes: Turnout: 71.7 per cent.

[a]IND includes 35 Congress rebels and one rebel each from the BJP and SHS.
[b]Others include CPM (03), SP (03) and Swatantra Bharat Paksh (02; of Sharad Joshi).

during Assembly elections is not uncommon, their presence along with a major coalition challenging the Congress made a crucial difference to the dispersal of votes. Not surprisingly, therefore, the competitiveness index went up considerably in the 1995 Assembly elections—in terms of both seat dispersal and vote dispersal. For the first time, the 'effective number of parties' (ENP) in terms of seats went up to 5.14 and in terms of votes it reached almost 7 (6.96).[2]

More than the dispersal of votes, the sudden rise of multi-party competition during 1995 elections had another indirect consequence. All the three fronts targeted the Congress government in their campaigns. This was also the time when the Congress party had become rudderless, faction-ridden and weak at the all-India level. While the national government was led by the Congress, the party was seen as a declining force, devoid of capacity to reorganize itself. Two slightly different political strategies were in operation nationally. One was the rejuvenated non-Congressism and the other was a muted awareness of the rising power of the BJP. Those who found the BJP's Hindutva unacceptable often argued for a 'third alternative', that is, the alternative to both the Congress and BJP. Thus, the Congress found itself in the line of fire first because it was the ruling party both in the State and at Delhi; second, because it was seen as incompetent to take on communalism of the BJP; and third, the Congress party was also seen as responsible for the rise of the BJP. Besides these handicaps, as the previous chapter has detailed that in the 1990s, the new economic policies were projected by some non-Congress parties as a major deviation of the Congress. All these factors meant that the campaign was singularly anti-Congress and the larger and stronger alliance (the SHS–BJP alliance) was in a position to take advantage of the anti-Congress tone of the entire campaign. Thus, while the third and fourth fronts did not themselves gain much, they were indirectly instrumental in mobilizing voters against the Congress.

---

[2] Political competition is often better understood in terms of number of relevant or really effective parties in a system. Rein Taagepera and Mathew Shugart develop a measure of 'effective parties'. In their calculation, the ENP is calculated separately for their relevance in terms of votes—ENP/v—and seats—ENP/s (Taagepera and Shugart, 1989; 77–91).

ANTI-CONGRESS CAMPAIGN

The election campaign thus highlighted a sharp anti-Congress tone besides being focused on Sharad Pawar. Pawar was a once popular CM, seen as a competent administrator but also perceived as the faction leader within the Congress. He handled the Congress's campaign practically single-handed because not many Central leaders campaigned in the State, and within the State party unit, not many had the capacity to attract the voters. The anti-Pawar tone of the campaign also meant that other Congress leaders were disinterested in rebutting the charges. The opposition campaign had two main themes. One was the issue of corruption and the other was Hindutva. Thackeray on behalf of the *yuti* (alliance of the SHS and BJP) was the star campaigner and crowd-puller across the State. While till then he had confined himself mostly to Mumbai (and only partially campaigned in Marathwada in the previous election), Thackeray proved to be the most popular campaigner across the State and even in the rural areas. He presented himself as a renouncer who did not want power for himself. In fact, this was the time when he shifted to a saffron costume that was to become his hallmark in public life in the remainder of his political career. His earlier campaign in 1991 had brought the party into difficulty on the question of appeal to religious sentiments. In 1995, he refrained from direct mention of religion or Hindutva but all the same symbolized strident Hindutva and combined it with attack on corruption.

Pramod Mahajan and Gopinath Munde were the two BJP leaders who rose to prominence around this time. Mahajan was the key link between the party and its ally, the SHS, and he ensured smooth distribution of seats between the two partners. Munde matched Thackeray's oratorical skills with his strong appeal among young rural voters. Both Munde and his party avoided direct campaign on Hindutva platform. Instead, they took recourse to allegations of corruption against Pawar and Congress leaders at local levels throughout the State. One of the most evocative issues in the campaign was the 'Enron controversy' (discussed in the third chapter). This issue was also raised by the 'third' and 'fourth' fronts since they wanted to drive home the point about privatization, but the SHS and BJP chose to highlight the allegations of corruption instead and benefitted from the attack. Such allegations also lent credence to many other accusations of land grabbing and nexus with underworld that were hurled at Sharad Pawar (Vora and Palshikar, 1996; 54–58). Thus, a changed discourse, alliance by two main opposition parties and an atmosphere of suspicion towards the State leadership of the Congress combined to produce the defeat of the Congress party in 1995.

And yet, the story of 1995 and the 'victory' of the SHS and BJP would remain an incomplete story if we do not supplement it with the other critical aspect—factionalism in the Congress party. As in most other States, and perhaps even nationally, the Congress has always been its most efficient opponent. This is primarily because of the loose organizational structure and the umbrella coalition that the party has always been. This means that the party would have multiple groups and in times of crisis, these groups would not mind fighting with each other at the peril of the party's political interests (as we saw in the case of 1977, in Chapter 2). In fact, this is what we mean by the decline of the congress system—decline of its ability to hold different groups together. Maharashtra is an instance of such steady decline, resulting finally in the political fall of the party.

The 1990s were no exception to this larger trend. At the State level, the party was unable to function effectively and was also unable to have any fruitful mediation among the warring factions within. In 1995, this fragmentation of the party took the form of chaotic, individualized and mostly uncoordinated local revolts by local leaders who felt they need not depend on the party anymore. Thus, the non-Congress government that came to power in 1995 had a (not-so-hidden) Congress hand. A large number of Congress 'rebels' won as IND (as can be seen from Table 4.1) and then went on to support the SHS–BJP government and even participated in it as ministers. Of the 45 'IND' candidates who won the election, 35 were Congress rebels. The regional distribution of these rebels is also quite critical to understand the extent of organizational failure of the Congress. Vidarbh, which always supported the Congress and remained with it even in the post-Emergency elections, sent 9 Congress rebels while the other strong Congress bastion, western Maharashtra, elected as many as 18 Congress rebels. There were five Congress rebels elected from North Maharashtra and three from Marathwada. Moreover, Congress lost 24 more seats because of the presence of 'rebel' candidates who themselves could not win but nevertheless defeated the official candidates of the Congress party—this takes the total loss to a staggering 59 seats (Vora and Palshikar, 1996; 62–70). This suggests the extremely fragile organization the Congress had around this time. As we mentioned earlier, the weakness of the Congress was gradually building up since the late 1970s and the election of 1995 only highlighted it in a dramatic fashion. When a dominant party crumbles internally in this fashion, it creates a political space and an opportunity. The SHS–BJP coalition grabbed it with both hands in the 1990s.

They came very close to winning a majority in the Assembly but fell short by seven seats. Ordinarily, a party or alliance with such a close distance from majority would not find it difficult to form the government. Things became easier for the SHS and BJP when most Congress rebels chose to support the new government (expecting to benefit from the new dispensations). The SHS–BJP government could not have sailed smoothly without the crucial support coming from most of these ex-congress persons. At the time of the formation of the new government, 16 Congress rebels formed a group (Maharashtra Vikas Aghadi) and extended support to the SHS–BJP government, while many more extended support following the formation of the government.

MOMENT OF REALIGNMENT

The outcome of Assembly election of 1995 became historic for the removal of the Congress from power. However, as we have indicated before, more than being historic, this election deserves to be seen as a critical election. This critical nature manifests above all in the new alignments the election threw up. Not all the new alignments came to fruition immediately, but the outcome sufficiently indicates the footprints of new social configurations that were to shape later. In this sense, the characterization of the outcome as realignment (Palshikar, 1996) is relevant.

Three kinds of realignments began shaping around this election. One was the realignment among parties. We already noted the many 'fronts' that came into being before and after the elections, but the political realignment was most prominently manifested by the willingness of a large number of political actors steeped in politics of the Congress party to not only support the SHS–BJP government but also to join that government. The second realignment related to the spatial factor. Table 4.1 gives the election results by regions. Even in the times of Congress dominance, Mumbai was not exactly seen as its stronghold and, therefore, it is no wonder that the Congress lost so many seats in Mumbai—it could win only one seat in the metropolis. Even in 1977–1978 when the Congress was on the back foot, the party had faced severe decimation in Mumbai—it could not win a single seat in Mumbai either for 1977 LS or for the following Assembly election. Yet, what is remarkable about the outcome of 1995 is that out of 34 seats, the SHS–BJP won 30 seats between themselves, polling over 48 per cent votes. Taken together, in the Mumbai–Thane urban belt, the SHS and BJP won 38 out of 47 seats. Besides, the SHS and BJP both made deep inroads in traditional Congress bastion of Vidarbh. This region had steadfastly supported the Congress even during 1977–1978. But in 1995, the SHS and BJP took half of the seats from this region. In Marathwada, known for its volatility since the 1970s, the Congress was able to win only 12 seats. Thus, the political profile of each region was being redefined in one way or the other.

The third sense in which 1995 marked a moment or realignment was the social bases of parties. In the absence of reliable survey data on voter preference for the period prior to 1995, we can only conjecture the nature of realignment. But one study conducted after polling for the 1995 election indicates possibilities of change. Thus, almost one of every three who voted for SHS–BJP in 1995 had not voted for them in the previous election (Palshikar, 1996; 175). So, it is evident that many voters were attracted to the non-Congress coalition for the first time and looking at the votes polled by these two parties subsequently, it looks like those voters stayed with the SHS and/or BJP. The SHS/BJP voters, predictably, were below 40 years of age and more among urban educated sections. The differences between Congress and its opponents were stark in terms of the social composition of the two political camps. For instance, just about 3 to 4 of every 10 Congress voters were educated at the high-school level or above, while in the case of the BJP, more than 6 among every 10 voters were similarly educated. The SHS, even in 1995, looked more like the Congress in terms of its voter profile. In spite of its strong base in Mumbai, 65 per cent of its voters were from rural backgrounds (70% in the case of the Congress), whereas 63 per cent of the BJP voters were from urban locations. This is true of class too. In the case of both the SHS and Congress, two of every three of their voters came from low-income background, while almost half of the BJP voters came from middle-income sections (Palshikar, 1996).

Elections of 1995 threw up two other features of social bases of parties that were to crystallize later: the fragmentation of Maratha vote and the move of the OBC voters towards the BJP (and to some extent to the SHS too). In fact, Maratha voters voted for non-Congress candidates (including the rebels) and for Congress in equal proportion. While the Congress could attract barely one-third OBC voters, together the SHS and BJP polled 30 per cent votes among the OBC voters. As a result of this beginning of social churning, we find that both the Congress and SHS–BJP alliance had almost similar proportion of Maratha-Kunbi voters among their voters (33% and 31% respectively) and the SHS–BJP alliance had greater proportion of OBC voters among its voters (26%) than the Congress had (20%). Notably, the SHS–BJP alliance had a competitive share of Dalits among its supporters (8%) compared to Congress's 12 per cent (Palshikar, 1996; 176), though the bulk of Dalit vote went to parties other than the Congress and the coalition. In a sense, this too, was an early indication of the fragmentation of Dalit (and later Muslim) vote.

SHS–BJP GOVERNMENT

The leadership of the non-Congress government went to the SHS since it had larger number of MLAs. SHS chief Thackeray nominated his senior colleague and associate from the days of the SHS's formation, Manohar Joshi, to be the CM.

This choice raised eyebrows for three reasons. First, because of Joshi's caste. For the first time since the formation of the State and indeed for the first time since early post-independence times when Balasaheb Kher was the premier of the Bombay State, a Brahman became the CM. Although very influential in fields of culture, Brahmans had mostly been relegated to the background in the political arena because of their very small numbers in State population (barely 4%) and also because of the anti-Brahman sentiments in the State dating back to the Brahmanetar movement of the early 20th century. This sentiment was further strengthened due to the fact that Gandhi's assassin, Godse, happened to be a Brahman and following the assassination, anti-Brahman riots had taken place in some parts of the Marathi-speaking areas. All these factors would often weigh not only in distribution of cabinet portfolios but also in distribution of tickets. So there used to be very small number of prominent Brahman leaders in the State since the formation of the State.

Second, Joshi was a leader based in Mumbai and, again, Mumbai-based leaders often stood a thin chance of leading the government. This marginalization of Mumbai leadership also had a historical context. Most leaders from the city came from non-Marathi backgrounds and as we saw in Chapter 2, a Marathi leader from Mumbai, S.K. Patil, had opposed the formation of Marathi-speaking State and, in fact, actively supported the separation of Mumbai from Maharashtra. Thus, there was an atmosphere of suspicion about Mumbai-based leadership, and this leadership seldom had much organic linkages with rest of the State. Only Babasaheb Bhosale, who was based in Mumbai, had ever become the CM so far, and he too had close community connections outside of Mumbai, thanks to his caste. Third, Joshi was not a mass leader. A government that had come to power by defeating the Congress and particularly Sharad Pawar would have been expected to ensure that it would be led by a leader with mass following and connections across the regions of the State. Joshi's entire political career was shaped in the politics of the Mumbai city, and he had been the city Mayor too. In the previous Assembly, he was the leader of opposition. But he never rose to be a leader with a mass base, particularly outside of Mumbai.

SHS's choice of Joshi, despite the political tradition of the State, was an instance of the difference in the political strategy devised by SHS chief Thackeray. It also indicated the changes this new dispensation was set to bring about in State politics. The SHS would often argue that it did not take into account the traditional caste equations. Joshi's nomination as the CM exemplified this ability to neutralize caste considerations. Of course, it is also true that the SHS did not have any leader of experience belonging to the Maratha or OBC communities. All its key leaders were either Brahmans or Chandraseniya Kayastha Prabhus (a non-Brahman caste with a long literary background). The only non-Brahman leader with mass following that the SHS had was Chhagan Bhujbal, who had already left the party in 1991 when Joshi was made leader of the opposition in the Assembly bypassing Bhujbal. That Joshi was a product of SHS's pro-Marathi politics was reason enough to make him the CM because for the first time a Mumbai-based leader with a strong pro-Marathi background would be leading the government and this showcased the regional roots of the SHS. Also, the fact that the SHS won 33 of its 73 seats from the Mumbai and Konkan regions made it quite natural for the party to have a CM from Mumbai. That Joshi did not have much following was not seen as a handicap because Thackeray clearly intended to call the shots in the new government and did not want a CM who could independently cultivate a power base for himself. But above all, both Joshi's nomination and the composition of the new ministry indicated to change the 'transfer of power' brought about in political considerations and social equations.

THE URBAN TURN?

The election of 1995 deserves to be characterized as 'critical' for one more reason. It indicated the possibility of a change in political equations in terms of location of power and the shaping of public policy in a new direction. Like many other States of India, Maharashtra also displayed two key features of power and public policy. One was the preponderance of political elite belonging to, and/or coming from, rural backgrounds with entrenched interests in rural–agrarian economies. The other was the consequential emphasis on agrarian interests in the realm of public policy. In the case of Maharashtra, both these features had to face considerable challenges from social structure and the political economy. Because of the presence of Mumbai and also the emergence of many other large urban centres such as Pune, Nagpur, Aurangabadand Nashik, the State's urban population was always higher than the national average. Second, the expansion of industry in the State and the rise of service sector through its cities meant that non-agrarian interests would often compete with agrarian interests for greater state attention.

The year 1995 marked a fundamental shift that slowly stabilized in the politics of the State as an important development. While the outward social composition of the political elite did not change much, the moment marked a change in the policy orientation of the government along with a mild change in the composition of the government itself. We can thus notice three changes inaugurated by the 'urban turn' of 1995: the theatre of politics, the social composition of political elite and the priorities and policy directions of the Government of Maharashtra (GoM).

As already noted, the developments in Mumbai had a deep impact on the psyche of the voters—the riots of 1992–1993 and the bomb blasts of 1993 created questions of not only safety but also identity and endangered the plurality of the city of Mumbai. Besides, the virulent campaign of competitive communalism did not remain confined to the city and its surroundings. The entire State, particularly the cities and urban centres, resonated with the sensibilities that the events in Mumbai generated. These sensibilities were adroitly exploited during the campaign. The rallies by SHS chief Thackeray in most urban centres were attended by huge crowds of excitable dispositions and he ensured that their anxieties would be converted into electoral backlash. Thus, for the first time since the Samyukta Maharashtra Movement, the theatre of politics shifted to Maharashtra's cities, and the undercurrents of public opinion began to flow from cities to rural hinterlands. Stories of Pawar's alleged corruption related to Mumbai's real estate and the anti-corruption agitation by Anna Hazare resonated mainly in cities and small towns. The urban electorate thus dominated the campaign, though the State at that juncture did not have more than 40 per cent urban population.

Since then, another factor that has always been crucial to Maharashtra's electorate is the influence of urban centres on urban peripheries and semi-urban localities. This has been mainly due to the occupational patterns. Large numbers of residents from semi-urban towns regularly commute to the urban centres nearby for their liveli-hood and bring back urban sensibilities and urban political undercur-rents. Therefore, in 1995, the urban and semi-urban centres together emerged as key movers of the political atmosphere in the State. This interlinkage between the urban and the semi-urban worked in the favour of the SHS and BJP, since these two parties emphasized large rallies addressed by Thackeray and Munde. Such rallies are often a convenient moment to generate hysterical response to emotional appeals and convert a campaign into a theatrical performance.

The other effect of the urban factor that could be identified from the election of 1995 was the largely urban face of the SHS and BJP MLAs. Although the SHS had penetrated both Marathwada and Vidarbh since 1990 elections, its—as also the BJP's—main success in 1995 came from urban centres. Out of 138 MLAs winning on their tickets, as many as 63 came from urban and semi-urban constituencies (Vora and Palshikar, 1996; 89). As we saw above, Mumbai alone accounted for 30 such victories. Therefore, an urban imprint was clearly stamped on the social composition of the SHS and BJP victory. The two parties could not ignore the claims of these urban representatives when con-stituting the cabinet or, later, while appointing chairpersons of various government corporations. In Manohar Joshi's first cabinet, out of 22 ministers, 11 were from urban constituencies and of them, 7 came from Mumbai itself. So much so that even the chairpersons of two statutory development boards (Marathwada and rest of Maharashtra) were also from Mumbai (belonging to the SHS) along with the chair-manship of State Planning Board which went to the BJP (Vora and Palshikar, 1996; 90). Partly, this was inevitable because the MLAs, leaders and important office-bearers of the SHS in particular had their base in Mumbai and Thane regions. In fact, the SHS–BJP government would have appeared far more urban if they had not obtained the support of rebel congress persons who mostly came from non-urban backgrounds and many of whom later became members of the State council of ministers.

The third urban shift that came about in 1995 related to State's policies and initiatives. Although the SHS–BJP government soon chose the strategy of course correction, it started with a clear urban agenda and many of its schemes and programmes were aimed at benefitting the urban voter. Moreover, they also sought to rein in the rural entrenched interests.

One of the most ambitious schemes of the new government was to provide decent housing to about four million slum dwellers from Mumbai. Slums of Mumbai have always been a contentious issue, but the SHS had realized that along with its tough talk about not allowing 'outsiders' to settle in Mumbai, it was necessary to also cultivate and consolidate the huge constituency of the urban poor of Mumbai who have been living in the city for a long time. So, it had announced in its manifesto the plan of resettlement of Mumbai's slums. Once in power, the party vigorously pursued that plan. Similarly, the new government encouraged and subsidized the scheme of providing lunch at a nominal price of ₹1. While the Zunka Bhakar scheme was a State-wide one, it had an appeal in large urban centres like Mumbai where thousands of workers have to regularly eat out during the day. Such a scheme can be economically viable only in densely populated urban areas. In this sense, this was a typical pro-urban scheme which also allowed large number of SHS workers to obtain stalls/permits to run the Zunka Bhakar kitchen centres. To cater to its Mumbai-based lower-middle-class urban constituency, the government also announced a scheme to renovate Mumbai's dilapidated lower-middle-class buildings (chawls; Anubhav, 1996; Vora and Palshikar; 1996; 119).

At the same time, the new government sought to discipline the cooperative lobby. For this purpose, many new regulations were brought such as not giving extension to boards of directors of sugar cooperatives and instead appointing a government administrator on such cooperatives. The government also initially decided to suspend the scheme of giving loans to sugar cooperatives if they had not paid earlier loans from the apex cooperative bank of the State. These tactics not only cut the sugar bosses to size but also encouraged many of them to buy peace with the State government by shifting political allegiances (Vora and Palshikar, 1996; 116–117). Soon, the new government realized that it would be suicidal to ignore rural electorate altogether, and therefore it began showering populist slogans and schemes for rural areas as well. These included sale of *jowar* in public distribution system shops at ₹2 per kg up to a maximum of 10 kg, power supply to agriculture at a subsidized rate, etc. Most of these schemes failed to take off or run smoothly (Palshikar and Birmal, 2003; 207–211).

GOVERNMENT IN THE MIDST OF ELECTIONS

Despite a slew of schemes and subsidies, the SHS–BJP government had an imprint of an amateur government. Most ministers in the new SHS–BJP government being ministers for the first time, there was a certain amount of shakiness to the new government at least initially. The shakiness was further aggravated by the fact that the government was proudly 'remote controlled' by the SHS chief, Bal Thackeray. Besides weak implementation of most populist schemes, the SHS–BJP government faced internal problems, particularly pertaining to the SHS. In spite of a tightly controlled party organization marked by undisputed leadership of Thackeray, the party did face many problems both at the top and among its MLAs. Within one year of the formation of the government, Narayan Rane, a rival of the CM, had already started planning to remove the incumbent.

While many Congress rebels extended support to the new government, the SHS and BJP failed to establish themselves as a major force in rural areas of the State. This was very starkly brought out by the elections to the local bodies held in 1997. In ZPs (comprising of rural electorate only), the Congress did receive a setback confirming that it had not revived yet from its 1995 debacle. It could win a total of 45 per cent seats across the State and managed to acquire the position of ZP president in 18 of 29 districts (Kulkarni, 1997a). However, many ZPs were controlled by IND, and the SHS or BJP were not able to expand their base much. More interestingly, the SHS–BJP failed to make a mark in urban local bodies too. Elections were held in 175 urban local bodies during 1996–1997, and the SHS won only 13 per cent seats with both the BJP and Congress winning 11 per cent seats each in these bodies. Municipal Council chairpersons were elected by members of the councils and here the Congress, with the help of IND, trumped the SHS and BJP by grabbing as many as 101 municipal bodies (Kulkarni, 1997b).

Besides the local elections, the SHS–BJP government found itself facing two intervening parliamentary elections in quick succession—first, the routine one in 1996 and a mid-term election in 1998. The SHS–BJP alliance won the 1996 LS elections with a handsome majority of 33 seats against Congress's 15 (Table 4.2). This was no surprise since the State government was in office barely for a year by then and the Congress, both in the State and nationally, was in a bad shape. But in the next parliamentary election, Sharad Pawar brought many opposition parties on board. By then, the goodwill enjoyed by the new government was also on the decline. So, the Congress was able to reduce the SHS–BJP to mere 10 seats (Table 4.3).

Table 4.2 *LS Results: 1996*

Party	Seats Contested	Seats Won	Votes
Congress	48	15	34.8
BJP	25	18	21.8
SHS	20	15	16.8
CPI	3	0	0.6
CPM)	3	0	1.1
JD	12	0	3.3
RPI	11	0	4.9
Others	137	0	7.0
IND	806	0	9.7
Total	**1,065**	**48**	

Note: Turnout: 52.4 per cent.

Table 4.3 *LS Results: 1998*

Party	Seats Contested	Seats Won	Votes
Congress	41	33	43.6
BJP	25	4	22.5
SHS	22	6	19.7
CPI	2	0	0.1
CPI(M)	3	0	0.6
BSP	27	0	0.8
JD	19	0	1.7
RPI	4	4	4.1
Others	62	1	4.5
IND	172	0	2.4
Total	**377**	**48**	

Note: Turnout: 57.1 per cent.

Despite that adverse outcome, when the LS was again dissolved mid-term, in 1999, the State government decided to dissolve the Assembly and opt for early elections. The last time the State had a simultaneous election to LS and the Assembly was in 1967. Since then, Assembly elections always took place separately. This time too, the term of the State government was to end in March 2000, but the BJP was insistent on holding State elections along with LS elections probably hoping to cash in on the sympathy and support to Vajpayee. Following the split in the Congress party, the SHS also agreed to that proposal and the State government recommended dissolution of the Assembly in preparation of simultaneous elections.

Before this development, internal squabbling within the SHS had forced the decision to change leadership. Manohar Joshi was asked to step down and SHS leader Narayan Rane became the new CM (February 1999). He did not get enough time to settle down in office and make an impact because of the decision to hold early election. Before the 1999 elections, the State Congress was also in a turmoil. When three leaders—Pawar, Sangma and Tariq Anwar—expressed their opposition to Sonia Gandhi for being foreign-born, they were

Table 4.4 LS Results: 1999

Party	Seats Contested	Seats Won	Votes
Congress	42	10	29.7
NCP	38	6	21.6
SHS	22	15	16.9
BJP	26	13	21.2
BSP	16	0	0.3
CPI	2	0	0.1
CPI(M)	3	0	0.5
Others	34	3	6.4
IND	78	1	3.3
Total	261	48	

Note: Turnout: 60.9 per cent.

thrown out of the Congress party and they in turn formed the NCP (June 1999). This meant a clear split in the State Congress. Although Sharad Pawar was opposed by many internal factions, he had the skill and ability to organize the party and ensure better electoral performance. Once he left the party, the Congress in Maharashtra became considerably crippled once again, as had happened earlier in 1978. The State went to elections in October 1999 with two Congress parties trying to defeat each other and occupy the 'Congress space' available in the State while the SHS–BJP alliance was relatively intact. The Congress party had seat-sharing arrangement with SP, BBM and RPI (Gavai faction). The NCP, on the other hand, had an alliance with RPI(A) and the Janata Dal (Secular)—JD(S). The PWP and the Communists did not join either the Congress or the NCP. The two Congress parties could win only a limited number of seats—content with defeating each other—and the ruling coalition won 28 LS seats (Table 4.4).

RETURN OF THE CONGRESS: 1999

The BJP's gamble of holding Assembly elections along with LS did not pay. The ruling SHS–BJP coalition failed to win a clear majority in State legislature. From their previous strength of 138 seats, SHS–BJP came down to 125, 16 short of majority. The two Congress parties ensured that the SHS–BJP would not get enough support from Others/IND. They also decided to form a post-election alliance called Democratic Front consisting of their pre-election partners plus the PWP, while the Left parties agreed to extend support without joining the Front and without joining the government. The two Congress parties had a joint strength of 133 (Table 4.5) and with their allies, they could easily claim majority in the Assembly. Thus, despite electoral setback in 1995 and though it did not fully recover from that, the Congress party, along with its breakaway faction, NCP, returned to power in 1999 once again.

Since the Congress emerged as the single largest party, NCP agreed to have a Congress CM. Congress leader from Marathwada, Vilasrao Deshmukh, became the CM in October 1999 with NCP's Chhagan Bhujbal as the deputy CM. In January 2003, there was a change of guard when internal factionalism led to resignation of Deshmukh. Senior leader Sushilkumar Shinde (belonging to the SC community) became the CM. This was the first time a Dalit leader became the CM and till the end of the Assembly's term in October 2004, State's Maratha leadership was sidelined since both the CM and deputy CM were non-Marathas.

How far did this return of the Congress neutralize the 'critical' effects brought out by 1995? It may be more accurate to say that the neat division that seemed to be emerging in 1995, wherein the SHS and BJP were to be the mascots of the 'urban shift', began to get diluted. In order to combat the SHS and BJP and also in response to the changing political economy, the Congress and NCP needed to look beyond the rural. Both in terms of social bases and in terms of policy orientations, the Congress parties had to adapt to the urban turn. In a sense, this only underscores the critical change brought about by 1995. At the same time, the compulsions of politics of electoral expansion meant that the BJP (and to an extent, the SHS too) had to cater to rural constituencies. Thus, while the neatness was messed up, the predominance of the urban remained. At the same time, it is necessary to remember that tensions arising from the political economy did not allow a complete transformation. The year 1995 was a political

Table 4.5 *Region-wise Results: Assembly Elections, 1999*

Region	Seats	Turnout	Congress		NCP		BJP		SHS		Others [a]	
			Won	Vote	Won	Vote	Won	Vote	Won	Vote	Won	Vote
Mumbai–Thane	47	42.9	13	28.9	03	11.1	10	17.3	16	24.7	05	18.0
Konkan	18	61.2	00	20.1	02	20.5	03	07.7	10	32.6	03	19.1
North Maharashtra	36	61.7	08	25.9	07	26.8	07	15.6	10	15.0	04	16.7
Vidarbh	66	65.2	26	29.0	05	14.6	21	21.3	08	12.0	06	23.1
Marathwada	46	69.4	10	25.5	05	20.1	10	13.2	16	20.2	05	21.0
Western Maharashtra	75	67.6	18	27.4	36	36.0	05	08.8	09	14.0	07	13.8
Total	**288**	**60.9**	**75**	**27.2**	**58**	**22.6**	**56**	**14.5**	**69**	**17.3**	**30**	**18.4**

Notes: Turnout: 61.0 per cent.

[a]Others include IND (12), PWP (05), Bahujan Mahasangh (03), 2 each from CPM, JD(S) and SP, 1 each from RPI, Gondwana Gantantra Party, Native People's Party (NVPP) and Samajwadi Janata Party (Maharashtra)—SJP(M)].

moment that allowed the urban configuration to have an upper hand, but the State's politics was yet to accept the straightforward pre-eminence of the urban interests. Once the Congress and NCP came to power, they began readjusting the balance between urban and rural although not always successfully. We have discussed this earlier and argued that the coming back to power of the Congress parties led to a new 'disjunction' (Palshikar and Deshpande, 2003). From 1999 onwards, for the next 15 years, the Congress parties awkwardly presided over this disjunction. The rural political elite did control formal power in the State, but at the same time, they increasingly lost control over the shape of the economy.

The other critical factor that emerged in 1995 was about the 'realignment' of social forces across party lines. The elections of 1999 made only a marginal difference to that. In fact, like 1995, this round of elections consolidated the two trends—of fragmentation of social forces and of an uncertain and fluctuating voting behaviour by many social sections. This is borne out by a series of voter surveys between 1996 and 1999. Below we summarize some of the main trends emerging from voter surveys:

- During the three elections in quick succession, in spite of its limitations, the Congress continued to have a slight advantage among women compared to men, while the BJP drew more votes among men. This 'gender gap' must have imposed severe constraints on the BJP—Congress had a gender advantage of about 6 per cent, while the corresponding disadvantage for the BJP was an average of 7 per cent. The NCP and SHS did not have any specific gender profile during this period (Table 4.6).

- We have discussed the question of new urban assertion earlier in this chapter. This is not necessarily reflected in party choices of the voters in urban or rural localities. The Congress does draw greater support among rural voters but in 1999, the party lost out on this, probably as the NCP took away more rural votes. The BJP had a consistent advantage among urban voters, while the SHS did not have any particular profile. In fact, in 1998, the SHS got more support among rural voters than among urban voters (Table 4.7).

Table 4.6 *Gender and Vote: 1996–1999*

	Congress			NCP	BJP			SHS		
	1996	1998	1999	1999	1996	1998	1999	1996	1998	1999
Men	27	36	24	19	23	26	24	14	18	16
Women	32	42	31	21	15	15	15	15	17	15
Total	30	39	27	20	19	20	20	14	18	16

Source: For Tables 4.6–4.15: These Tables are derived from the Maharashtra data files from the National Election Studies (NES) datasets for 1996, 1998 and 1999 made available by CSDS Data Unit.

Notes: For Tables 4.6–4.15: This was a panel data, that is, same respondents were interviewed for the three waves. This led to considerable attrition. N for 1996 was 858, N for 1998 was 907 and N for 1999 was 1,028 after adding a booster sample.

Tables do not show the share of Others.

Except for urban/rural, for comparison of voting patterns across other social variables, we have used only 1996 and 1999 data files.

Table 4.7 *Vote by Urban/Rural Location: 1996–1999*

	Congress			NCP			BJP			SHS		
	1996	1998	1999	1996	1998	1999	1996	1998	1999	1996	1998	1999
Rural	33	41	27	18	15	15	18	15	15	14	22	16
Urban	23	37	28	21	28	28	21	28	28	15	12	15
Total	30	39	27	19	20	20	19	20	20	14	18	16

Table 4.8 *Vote by Age Group: 1996*

	Congress	BJP	SHS
Upto 25 years	27	22	14
26–35 years	30	18	16
36–45 years	33	22	12
46–55 years	28	13	16
Above 55 years	31	16	14
Total	**30**	**19**	**14**

- During the 1990s, age did not seem to be very relevant in explaining voters' party preferences. Of course, the Congress and NCP had greater support among the middle aged and the elderly, but correspondingly, the BJP and SHS did not draw extra support from the young voters at this point (Tables 4.8 and 4.9).
- Education was only mildly relevant during this period in deciding voter choices. For the Congress, it was the less-educated voters who constituted an important social base, though the relevance of that factor was quite limited as is seen from Tables 4.10 and 4.11. On the other hand, the BJP certainly drew more support from the better educated, particularly those with college education and above but its ally, the SHS, did not have any strong educational profile attached to its voters.

Table 4.9 *Vote by Age Group: 1999*

	Congress	NCP	BJP	SHS
Up to 25 years	25	17	22	18
26–35 years	27	16	23	14
36–45 years	29	20	16	15
46–55 years	30	18	19	19
Above 55 years	25	30	16	14
Total	**27**	**20**	**19**	**16**

Table 4.10 *Vote by Education: 1996*

	Congress	BJP	SHS
Non-literate	31	16	12
Up to primary	29	12	16
Up to matric	32	20	16
College and above	26	31	13
Total	30	19	14

Table 4.11 *Vote by Education: 1999*

	Congress	NCP	BJP	SHS
Non-literate	30	26	11	15
Up to primary	31	19	19	15
Up to matric	23	13	28	17
College and above	19	14	30	18
Total	27	20	20	16

- In 1996, the Congress was again back into business. But it could muster support among most communities almost in proportion to its overall vote share, meaning that its supposed advantage among the SCs (or OBCs) as also among Marathas was almost neutralized. Survey data for 1996 shows that the Congress could get 35 per cent votes among both these sections, same as its overall share. Only among the Muslims, the Congress polled a handsome 53 per cent vote share. In contrast, the SHS, with its overall vote share of 23 per cent, was far ahead among both Marathas (34%) and OBCs (30%; Table 4.12). This advantage for the SHS weakened but stayed in 1999 also. In 1999, the emergence of the NCP led to a three-way split among Maratha vote—Congress getting the least (23%) and NCP cornering the highest (29%; Table 4.13). While OBC vote was also split, the BJP along with the SHS emerged as the main recipient of OBC vote (Table 4.16). In nutshell, the process of Maratha fragmentation clearly continued during this period, and the Congress lost any particular social character.

Table 4.12 *Vote by Caste/Community: 1996*

Caste/Community	Congress	BJP	SHS
Maratha-Kunbis	35	09	34
OBCs	35	16	30
SCs	31	12	07
STs	37	26	00
Muslims	53	02	02
Others (including upper castes)	30	19	24
Overall vote share	35	13	23

Table 4.13 *Vote by Caste/Community: 1999*

Caste/Community	Congress	NCP	BJP	SHS
Maratha-Kunbis	23	29	18	24
OBCs	23	15	27	23
SCs	54	24	05	05
STs	33	13	16	03
Muslims	52	31	03	01
Others (including upper castes)	27	13	41	14
Overall vote share	27	20	20	15

- Data on class throws up complicated patterns. In 1996, the Congress already had lost any sharp class profile. If anything, it drew slightly greater support among the upper-class voters (Table 4.14). This was primarily because of the dispersal of the votes of lower-income groups who voted for 'Others'. At this point, the BJP did have an advantage among middle-class voters with the SHS also attracting middle- and upper-class votes more. By 1999 (Table 4.15), a clear polarization emerged between NCP (with greater share of poor voters) and BJP (with greater share of rich voters). As we shall see later, this pattern does not necessarily continue.

Table 4.14 *Vote by Class: 1996*

	Congress	BJP	SHS	Others
Very poor	28	15	11	34
Poor	31	19	13	22
Middle	29	24	19	16
Rich	32	10	19	13
Total	30	19	14	23

Table 4.15 *Vote by Class: 1999*

	Congress	NCP	BJP	SHS	Others
Very poor	27	29	17	13	9
Poor	31	20	10	17	15
Middle	25	11	29	17	7
Rich	26	19	25	15	7
Total	27	20	20	16	10

Of course, this was the time when, ostensibly, voter choices were either shifting or were in a flux. Therefore, the survey findings for 1996–1999 are unlikely to throw up stable patterns of voter loyalty. This is not typical of Maharashtra alone; in other States too, the 1990s witnessed the rise of new parties and new party loyalties. But unlike in Bihar in this period or Andhra Pradesh a little earlier, no new political force was able to establish long-term alignments with specific social forces. Survey data suggests that the first task before the SHS and BJP was to capitalize upon the disenchantment with the Congress by presenting an alternative and collecting votes from disparate groups. Thus, in the first half of the 1990s, the SHS kept vacillating between Marathas and OBC while the BJP also worked hard among the OBCs expecting that Marathas, who were perceived as traditional Congress-voters, could be countered by building an OBC constituency. As discussed in the previous chapter, the BJP had an advantage that it had a popular leader coming from the OBC background in the person of Gopinath Munde. However, once the 1995 elections manifested deep cracks within the Maratha elite, the SHS and BJP began trying to win over strong Maratha leaders on the one hand and expecting a division among Maratha voters on the lines of economic and political power on the other hand. This development was further complicated by the split in the Congress party and the emergence of the NCP—a development that presented an option to the Marathas between the two Congress parties.

All these complications come to the fore if one looks at the composition of the voters of the major parties during this period.

For example, the Congress seems to be losing a sharp social profile during this period in terms of caste or class. Like elsewhere in the country, it was losing support among most social sections and its voter profile can at best be described as residual. The non-literate and the less educated still dominated among its voters; and at least in 1996, more than half of its voters were from less-privileged economic background (Table 4.16). But the share of Marathas among Congress voters seems considerably limited during this period. This profile of the Congress party correspondingly allowed the BJP and SHS to try and evolve their respective social identities. The BJP was particularly interested during this period in attracting OBC votes besides the upper castes. Yet, by the late 1990s, the BJP had 30 per cent of its voters coming from the Maratha-Kunbi community (Table 4.17). At the same time, SHS voters also increasingly came from the same

Table 4.16 *Social Composition of Congress Voters: 1996–1999*

	1996	1998	1999
Non-literate or up to primary	53	55	72
Rural	77	62	65
Poor and very poor	63	NA	60
Maratha-Kunbis	24	33	27

Source: See note to Table 4.6.

Note: For Tables 4.16–4.19, figures indicate the 'percentage of voters among the party's voters' from the particular social group.

Table 4.17 *Social Composition of BJP Voters: 1996–1999*

	1996	1998	1999
Non-literate or up to primary	40	34	47
Rural	66	43	52
Poor and very poor	57	NA	38
Maratha-Kunbis	9	27	30

social section—48 per cent of SHS voters in 1999 were Maratha-Kunbi. Thus, all parties were competing with each other for Maratha votes (Table 4.18). The formation of the NCP further complicated this competition when in its first election itself, the NCP also had 46 per cent voters from the Maratha community (Table 4.19). This dependence of the Maratha community meant two things. One was the quick eclipse of the OBC constituency that attracted ideological attention in the early 1990s. The two Congress parties never even attempted to attract OBC votes, but the BJP and SHS began to challenge the Congress ostensibly on the platform of non-Maratha votes

Table 4.18 *Social Composition of SHS Voters: 1996–1999*

	1996	1998	1999
Non-literate and up to primary	50	61	61
Rural	68	72	68
Poor and very poor	52	NA	55
Maratha-Kunbis	37	28	48

Table 4.19 *Social Composition of NCP Voters: 1999*

	1999
Non-literate and up to primary	76
Rural	77
Poor and very poor	70
Maratha-Kunbis	46

and then abandoned that project. So the political clout of the OBCs did not shape further. At the same time, and as a consequence of this political setback, the OBC constituency itself failed to shape much. Although Munde in the BJP and Bhujbal in the NCP sought to appeal to all OBCs, their respective parties not being interested in this, the OBCs began to fragment caste-wise. Since the 1990s, the politics of OBCs never arose as an important factor in the politics of the State.

The other long-term effect of the dependence of all major parties on Maratha vote was that Maratha vote got fragmented. As already noted, the Maratha political elite had already begun to get divided and dispersed across parties. Now in the 1990s, the vote of the community also became fragmented, but since all parties depended on Maratha vote, politics in the State remained centred around the expectations, identity concerns and political claims of the Maratha community. No party was in a position to satisfy the expectations of the community and, therefore, every party chose to cater to identity demands and political claims of the community. So the 'critical' change brought about by the election of 1995—namely the relative setback for Maratha leadership—became weak and yet remained a crucial factor in competitive politics of the State.

SUMMING UP

The 1995 elections opened up new possibilities in terms of political power and new social equations. Within five years, both these possibilities were tamed. This is not surprising, given the resilience of the old order. Moreover, the criticality of the elections was circumscribed by limitations of the congress system—it was equally an outcome of those limitations as it was an outcome of the emerging social configurations. These emerging social configurations were represented by the SHS–BJP alliance, while the limitations of the congress system were represented by the rebels from the Congress party. The combination of these two produced the first non-Congress government in the State but could produce only half-hearted realignment of social forces. The next decade was to further overshadow this criticality and give a semblance of continuation of Congress's power—albeit without real hold over society or politics. In spite of the electoral successes of the Congress and the NCP, the critical tendencies that the mid-1990s produced were to continue to characterize State politics. We turn to this in the next chapter.

Return of the Congress

2004 and 2009

Once the coalition government of the Congress and NCP came to power in 1999, both parties managed to keep their competition under control in order to retain power. As mentioned in the last chapter, Vilasrao Deshmukh, a self-made leader from Latur district of Marathwada, became the CM in 1999 with NCP's Chhagan Bhujbal as the deputy CM. Despite the formation of the BJP-led National Democratic Alliance (NDA) government under Vajpayee in Delhi, the BJP in the State remained somewhat inactive during the period immediately following the election of 1999. The Congress–NCP government, which was also known as the 'Democratic Front' government, was to not only complete its term but also to get re-elected twice—in 2004 and then in 2009. Ordinarily, 15 years of governmental power would give any party an opportunity to consolidate itself. Therefore, the central question that we address in this chapter is: Did the electoral successes in 2004 and later in 2009 result into the strengthening of the Congress and NCP in the State? Given the backdrop of Congress's well-entrenched power structures in the State historically, this was the time when the party could strengthen itself in spite of the national-level challenges that it was facing and even bring about a new version of the congress system. However, the split in the party meant that the Congress party was constantly engaged in a two-level competition. At one level, it confronted the SHS and BJP alliance and, at another, it confronted the NCP. The competition between two Congress parties meant that neither could expand itself and neither could re-establish the older networks of political patronage. As we shall see in this chapter, therefore, the decade from 1999 witnessed the extension of Congress's life but not the strengthening of the party. In a sense, this was the wasted decade for the Congress and NCP, while at the same time, this fitted well into the all-India pattern of paving the way for a new party system to emerge. The SHS and BJP were also unable to take advantage of their position as the strong opposition to the Congress–NCP governments.

ELECTIONS 2004

When the Vajpayee government chose to advance parliamentary elections and hold the elections in the first half of 2004, the State government did not choose to go for simultaneous elections to Assembly. Thus, Maharashtra had two elections in quick succession—April and October—in 2004 and this has been the case since then for 2009, 2014 and 2019 also. The context of parliamentary election of 2004 was shaped by the rise of Pramod Mahajan as the key figure within the BJP, as its national general secretary and chief strategist. The BJP went into the election with a confident slogan of 'Shining India', whereas the Congress was still smarting under the stress of leadership crisis. Although Sonia Gandhi had assumed leadership of the party, many still saw her both as a 'foreigner' and as incapable of rejuvenating the Congress party. In fact, the BJP campaign harped on a foreigner becoming a PM. Besides that, Sonia Gandhi's skills to attract the masses were also limited. This was seen as a major advantage for the BJP that was led by Vajpayee, who had goodwill and an image to his advantage. There was a shadow of Gujarat violence of 2002 on these elections, but 'Shining India' slogan sought to deflect the issue of communalism and shift the focus to Vajpayee government's efforts to improve infrastructure and speed up development through aggressive liberalization.

While these national-level issues and concerns had their shadow on the campaign in the State, politics in the State also had the influence of State-level dynamics. It was, on the one hand, embroiled in local equations within the Congress party and, on the other hand, an emotive issue that suddenly cropped up early in 2004. Typical of the intra-party jockeying for power, in 2003, Vilasrao Deshmukh had to resign in favour of a new leader to take over as the CM: Sushilkumar

Shinde. Shinde was the first CM of the State belonging to the SC. He was also seen as being close to the Central leadership of the party. While he did cultivate a following within the State, he was seen as having less grassroots support than the outgoing CM. Following this change, the NCP also decided to change its deputy CM. Bhujbal was replaced by Vijaysinh Mohite-Patil from Solapur district.

Around the same time when these changes were taking effect, a controversy was gaining ground in the State's politico-cultural field. This was caused by a book published by an American historian, James Laine, on Chhatrapati Shivaji. The book had a controversial reference to Shivaji Maharaj, and while intellectuals and historians had already begun debating the book in 2003 following its publication, the controversy spilled over into the political domain when one scholar was manhandled by SHS activists accusing him of being of help to Laine.[1] In early 2004, a research institute located in Pune was attacked and ransacked by activists claiming to belong to the Sambhaji Brigade, an organization active in mobilizing the Maratha community. Another organization, the Maratha Sewa Sangh, also entered the controversy. The State government banned the book. But in the months to follow, the Laine controversy kept recurring in the political arena, and parties and leaders went on seeking to competitively support the ban and action against the author. While the controversy was about alleged insult to Shivaji Maharaj, its subtext included echoes of the century-old anti-Brahmanism (discussed in Chapter 1), and the controversy also became a rallying point for those groups which were trying to mobilize the Maratha community on the issue of 'reservations' (discussed in Chapter 7). These local developments were to overshadow many other issues in the parliamentary elections for Maharashtra.

The LS elections from Maharashtra produced a split result with the Congress–NCP alliance winning 23 seats and BJP–SHS alliance getting 25. Even in terms of votes, there was little difference between the two alliances (44.8% for the Congress alliance and 42.7% for the

---

[1] For details, see *Frontline*, Politics of a Ban, 24 February 2006, https://frontline.thehindu.com/the-nation/article30208459.ece (accessed on 7 June 2020). Also see Novetzke (2004).

Table 5.1 *LS Results from Maharashtra: 2004*

Party	Seats Contested	Seats Won	Votes
Congress	26	13	23.8
NCP	18	9	18.3
BJP	26	13	22.6
SHS	22	12	20.1
BSP	46	0	3.1
CPI	1	0	0.1
CPI(M)	3	0	0.7
RPI	1	1	1.0
Others	118	0	6.4
IND	151	0	3.9
Total	**412**	**48**	

Note: Turnout: 54.4 per cent.

SHS–BJP alliance). Even this difference of 2 percentage points was the contribution of the RPI factions and the JD(S). On their own, the two Congress parties polled 42.1 per cent votes (23.8% for the Congress and 18.3% for the NCP) in the LS election (Table 5.1). If we take into account the vote share for LS elections held in 1999, the SHS and BJP gained by 4 per cent votes and the NCP and Congress, together, lost 9 per cent votes (mainly because they had contested separately in 1999, whereas in 2004, they contested as allies).

After entering into a post-election understanding, the Congress and NCP had also included 'third force' parties like the JD(S), PWP, Samajwadi Party (SP), BBM and the Left parties in the 'Democratic Front' (formed in October 1999). On the eve of the 2004 LS elections, all these partners did not necessarily remain with the two Congress parties. The Congress and NCP reached an understanding between themselves and the JD(S) and RPI (Athavale, Kawade and Gavai factions). One seat each was conceded to these partners, while the Congress contested 26 seats and the NCP contested 18 seats. The Congress alliance could not reach a compromise with the BBM of Prakash Ambedkar, nor with the Left parties, PWP and SP.

Six months after the LS elections, the State went to polls again with almost the same coalitions pitted against each other. For the Assembly elections, the JD(S) was not part of the Congress alliance, while the RPI(A) and Gawai factions remained with the Democratic Front and they contested two and one seats respectively. The Congress alliance supported two IND and did not contest at three places in favour of the CPI(M). For Assembly elections, the BJP–SHS alliance had seat adjustments with Nag Vidarbh Andolan Samiti for one seat and with the Swatantra Bharat Party for seven seats, apart from supporting six IND seats. In contrast to the LS election, the Assembly election gave a lead to the Congress–NCP alliance in terms of both seats and vote share (Table 5.2). The Congress alliance lost 3.5 per cent votes between April and October, while the BJP–SHS alliance lost 7.5 per cent votes—these votes going mostly to smaller parties and IND, as is typical in Assembly elections. This led to the 'victory' of the Congress and NCP.

REGIONAL VARIATION

A prominent feature of the result was its regional variation. In the LS election, the two Congress parties were virtually wiped out in the Vidarbh region. However, the BJP and SHS gained only a minuscule percentage of votes in this region (0.6%) and yet managed to add four more seats to their tally there. This was mainly due to the dispersal of Congress votes to IND and the BSP. (The entry of BSP complicated the political calculations of all other parties not just in the Vidarbh region but all over the State. While in the LS election the BSP contested 46 seats, in the Assembly election it fielded candidates for 272 seats.) The SHS–BJP gained as much as 6 per cent votes in the North Maharashtra region, compared to the LS election of 1999, but actually lost one seat. In the Assembly election, the Congress–NCP alliance lost 9 per cent votes and yet gained five seats in North Maharashtra, while BJP–SHS lost four seats in spite of gaining 5 per cent votes. On the other hand, the SHS and BJP did badly in their traditional bastion of Mumbai and Konkan, albeit without losing their vote share in any significant manner.

Table 5.2 *Assembly Results from Maharashtra: 2004*

Party	Seats Contested	Seats Won	Vote
Congress	157	69	21.1
NCP	124	71	18.8
RPI	4	—	0.2
RPI(A)	20	1	0.5
CPI(M)	16	3	0.6
Cong IND	2	2	0.6
BJP	111	54	13.7
SHS	163	62	20.0
BJP allies	8	1	0.5
BJP IND	6	2	1.0
CPI	15	—	0.1
PWP	43	2	1.3
SP	94	—	1.1
JD(S)	34	—	0.6
BSP	272	—	4.0
BBM	83	1	1.2
ABHS	20	1	0.2
JSS	19	4	0.9
Others	411	—	1.3
IND	1,075	15	12.4

Note: Turnout: 63.4 per cent.

The Congress and NCP faced a less supportive electorate in Marathwada and western Maharashtra. In the Marathwada, the SHS–BJP gained 6 per cent votes, though there was no change in the number of seats won by the two coalitions in the LS election. In the Assembly election, Congress and NCP lost 9 per cent votes in this region but gained three seats, while the SHS–BJP gained 3 per cent votes but lost one seat. In western Maharashtra, the SHS and BJP added 12 per cent vote share to their previous votes and in the Assembly election too, they gained 8 per cent votes. In the Assembly election, they also managed to convert this advantage into seat gain by adding six more seats from the region (Tables 5.3 and 5.4).

The LS result for 2004 shows a combined effect of two factors: alliance of the Congress and NCP and lack of sting in the campaign by the SHS–BJP. In the case of the Assembly election, the two Congress parties benefited from a combination of factors: the goodwill enjoyed by the newly elected Central government, an opposition that was demoralized by defeat in the LS election and an absence of any clarity about the issues the opposition wanted to raise, etc. But more importantly, both elections indicated two things: one, the instability of the social bases of parties and, two, the emergence of a new structure of competition. It may be said that coalition politics, which produced bipolar competition, changed the structure of competition in the State after 1999. The picture that we witness through the competition between the two coalitions is somewhat unreal: In the post-election survey in the aftermath of 2004 parliamentary election (NES 2004), when asked whom one would vote for if there were no alliances, only Congress fared satisfactorily. Over 71 per cent of Congress voters said that they would still vote for the party. On the other hand, only one-third of NCP voters would stay with the party, another one-third would turn to the Congress in the absence of an alliance, while 7 per cent of NCP voters were likely to turn to the SHS–BJP. The SHS was also likely to retain only 45 per cent of its present voters, while the BJP could retain 51 per cent if there were no alliances. A survey of the voters conducted after the Assembly election shows that two-thirds of those who voted for the Congress alliance in April remained with this alliance in October as well, while 70 per cent of the SHS–BJP voters also continued to favour the same combine.[2] Political competition was further complicated by the entry of large numbers of rebel candidates from the NCP and Congress. This adversely affected the ability of

---

[2] Source: NES 2004, CSDS Data Unit and Assembly election post-poll survey jointly conducted by Lokniti (CSDS) and Department of Politics and Public Administration, Savitribai Phule Pune University (SPPU). The sample size from Maharashtra for the NES 2004 was 1,498 and for the Assembly survey it was 1,448. The two surveys were administered to the same sample.

Table 5.3 *Region-wise Results: LS Elections, 2004*

Region	Seats	Turnout	Congress		NCP		BJP		SHS		Others	
			Seats	Votes	Seats	Votes	Seats	Votes	Seats	Votes	Seats	Votes
Mumbai–Thane	09	47.5	05	31.3	01	17.9	00	16.1	03	28.7	00	06.0
Konkan	04	56.1	02	21.7	00	17.5	00	08.1	02	31.1	00	21.6
North Maharashtra	06	46.7	02	23.6	01	16.5	03	35.1	00	08.2	00	16.6
Vidarbh	10	59.1	01	27.3	00	03.8	06	29.7	03	11.8	00	27.4
Marathwada	08	60.1	00	22.1	02	21.4	03	24.3	03	23.0	00	09.2
Western Maharashtra	11	56.3	03	16.7	05	30.3	01	19.7	01	20.0	01[a]	13.3
Total	48	54.4	13	23.8	09	18.3	13	22.6	12	20.1	01	15.2

Note: [a]RPI(A).

Table 5.4 *Region-wise Results: Assembly Elections, 2004*

Region	Seats	Turnout	Congress		NCP		BJP		SHS		Others	
			Seats	Votes	Seats	Votes	Seats	Votes	Seats	Votes	Seats	Votes
Mumbai–Thane	47	49.2	15	25.9	09	14.4	07	14.9	12	27.3	04	17.5
Konkan	18	69.2	02	18.0	04	19.9	02	08.3	09	28.2	01	25.6
North Maharashtra	36	64.0	09	18.5	10	23.8	06	14.8	07	20.4	04	22.5
Vidarbh	66	67.6	19	25.5	11	08.5	20	18.7	10	13.4	06	33.9
Marathwada	46	69.9	07	20.2	11	16.3	11	15.5	14	19.9	03	28.1
Western Maharashtra	75	66.5	17	16.7	26	29.1	08	08.1	10	19.2	14	26.9
Total	**288**	**63.4**	**69**	**21.1**	**71**	**18.8**	**54**	**13.7**	**62**	**20.0**	**32[a]**	**26.4**

Note: [a]Others include IND (10), Jan Surajya Shakti (04), CPM (03), PWP (02) and 1 each from BBM, RPI, Swatantra Bharat Party and Akhil Bharatiya Sena and 19 IND.

these parties to retain the votes they had got in April, during the LS elections. The Congress alliance lost as many as 24 per cent of the votes it had received in April to 'Others'—mostly rebels. At the same time, 28 per cent votes of the 'Other' parties (non-BJP–SHS) shifted towards the Congress and NCP.

Data from NES 2004 suggests that the Congress was able to get more votes among women voters (both compared to its vote share among men and compared to women's vote to other parties), and this put it in a position of apparent advantage. However, less support among male voters was the party's key weakness; as against 24 per cent women, only 17 per cent men voted for the Congress. Both the NCP and SHS had a more balanced share of votes from both genders. The BJP, on the other hand, received greater support from men (22%) than from women (16%). Contrary to its reputation, the Congress did not get a larger share of the rural vote (it could get only 16% votes among the rural voters). The SHS and NCP were the main recipients of rural votes (27% and 26% respectively). The Congress alliance had a slightly upper hand among the poor and very poor voters, though the SHS and BJP were behind the Congress alliance just by 4 and 3 per cent respectively in these categories. The Congress and NCP were ahead of the SHS–BJP among the lower-middle-income group. In the middle-income group, the SHS and BJP clearly had a lead of 13 percentage points (Palshikar and Birmal, 2009; 120–121).

In spite of getting an edge in both parliamentary and State elections, the Congress and NCP were not able to consolidate their social base through these elections. As we shall discuss further, the fragmentation of the Maratha vote could not be stalled by these parties and, in fact, the Marathas tended more towards the BJP–SHS alliance. Along with this development, the inability of the two Congress parties to gain among the OBCs also imposed a severe limitation on their success. In this sense, the electoral outcome may have been favourable, but the social configuration was not favourable to the Congress parties. Data for 2004 studies indicates that the social base of the NCP and SHS was identical except for the support to the former by the Dalit and Muslim communities. This is a continuation of the trend from the 1999 election (Palshikar and Birmal, 2003). The social base of different parties in 2004 did seem to have a regional pattern: In Mumbai, the Congress got the support of the Dalit, Muslim and non-Maharashtrian voters. In Vidarbh, Maratha-Kunbi and OBCs voted for the SHS–BJP alliance, while in Marathwada, this alliance got over 64 per cent of the votes from the Maratha-Kunbi community. The churning among Marathas was most visible in western Maharashtra. The Congress and NCP together got support from 43 per cent of Maratha voters in this region, but another 42 per cent votes from that community went to the SHS and BJP.

ELECTIONS 2009: THE CONTEXT

Following the success of the Congress and NCP in winning majority in Assembly elections of 2004, there was initially some tussle between the two partners of the Democratic Front. The NCP had managed to emerge as the single largest party—two seats more than the Congress—and hence it staked its claim over the post of CM. By this time, the United Progressive Alliance (UPA) government was settled in office at the Centre for a second term and being part of that alliance, NCP leader Pawar decided not to insist on the demand for the CM's post. This cleared the way for the Congress to lead the ministry. Vilasrao Deshmukh was able to wrest the position from his intra-party competitors. Although this time too, he was not to complete his full term. He had to resign in the aftermath of the Mumbai terror attack of November 2008,[3] making way for another Congress leader from Marathwada region, Ashok Chavan. The deputy CM, who held the home portfolio, R.R. Patil, too had to resign in the wake of the terror attack, and he was replaced by Chhagan Bhujbal. While these were relatively minor tremors in the parties in power, the SHS underwent a major crisis during this period.

SHS leader and CM for a brief period in 1999, Narayan Rane left the party (July 2005) in the backdrop of increasing clout of Uddhav

---

[3] *The Indian Express,* Deshmukh Resigns, Ends the 2nd Longest Term in Maha, 4 December 2008, http://archive.indianexpress.com/news/deshmukh-resigns-ends-the-2nd-longest-term-in-maha/394192/0 (accessed on 4 May 2019).

Thackeray, son of Bal Thackeray. On joining the Congress party, he was promptly inducted in the State cabinet but had a somewhat uneasy relationship with the State party and also with the national leadership of Congress. Probably expecting his elevation to CM's position once Deshmukh resigned, he left the cabinet in December 2008 when Ashok Chavan became the new CM. He later agreed to return to the cabinet (February 2009).[4] But SHS's troubles were not confined to only Narayan Rane. The long-time competition between the cousin brothers from Thackeray family, Uddhav and Raj (nephew of Bal Thackeray), came out in the open following Rane's departure from the SHS. Raj Thackeray quit the party in 2006 and founded a separate party, Maharashtra Navnirman Sena (MNS; March 2006).[5]

When LS elections approached in 2009, the Congress and NCP faced double 'anti-incumbency' in the sense that they were now in power for two terms at the State level and also holding power at the Centre for one full term—that too, under a PM who did not have mass following—though, of course, Sonia Gandhi did enjoy considerable goodwill among the masses and enough control over the party. In Maharashtra, the UPA included RPI(A). The NDA was nationally relatively rudderless and smarting under the loss of Pramod Mahajan. In Maharashtra, besides the factionalism between Gopinath Munde and Nitin Gadkari,[6] the NDA also had a disadvantage due to

[4] Ever since he left the SHS, Rane's political career has been bumpy. He was always uncomfortable in the Congress and finally left the Congress to form his own party, Maharashtra Swambhiman Paksha in 2017; was elected to Rajya Sabha with BJP support in 2018 and finally merged his party with the BJP in October 2019. *The Hindu*, Finally Konkan Strongman Narayan Rane Joins BJP, 15 October 2019, https://www.thehindu.com/news/national/other-states/finally-konkan-strong-man-narayan-rane-joins-bjp/article29690503.ece (accessed on 13 June 2020).

[5] Raj Thackeray initially indicated that his party would interest itself in the well-being and rejuvenation of the State of Maharashtra. But soon, this turned out to be the same pro-Marathi agenda that the SHS was known for. After its initial success in denting the SHS bastion (see below), MNS came to be known for the strong-arm street action that the SHS was known for (Palshikar, 2010).

[6] Munde even resigned briefly from the party only to withdraw the resignation. See *Frontline*, Brief Revolt, 23 May 2008, https://frontline.thehindu.com/other/article30196018.ece (accessed on 13 June 2020).

semi-retirement of SHS chief Bal Thackeray on account of old age. The latter factor was further underscored by the departure of Raj Thackeray, who had been a crowd puller like his uncle. Both these factors put the NDA in a somewhat defensive and weak position in spite of the double anti-incumbency that the Congress and NCP were facing. These factors ensured the continuation of bipolar competition because none of the four major parties had been in the position to face the electorate on its own and with any new agenda.

The configuration arising from the artificial bipolarity also meant that the deep-seated resentments flowing from demand for OBC status to Marathas and also the competition between Marathas and OBCs simply remained muted in the election season. No party explicitly supported the demand of the Maratha groups for reservations under OBC category, but no party opposed it either; no party attempted any experiment in forming its political constituency by giving prominence to either Marathas or OBCs. This meant that the tentative and fragmented nature of social support to various parties was to continue in the elections of 2009.

ELECTORAL OUTCOMES

A relatively disheartened opposition, a somewhat improved economy of the State and goodwill earned by the UPA government at Delhi combined in shaping the two outcomes in the State in 2009. For LS, the Congress (and UPA) nationally improved its situation, and similarly in Maharashtra, a slight improvement in Congress's performance marked the outcome of parliamentary election. A much better performance in the Assembly elections a few months later ensured a third term for the State government.

As Table 5.5 shows, the Congress won 17 seats from the 25 it contested for LS. If one looks at Congress's performance for the two decades starting from 1999, when there was a split in the party, there seems to be some recovery of lost ground: In 1999, immediately after the split in the party, the Congress could win barely a quarter of the seats it contested for in the LS. Following an alliance with the NCP, the party contested fewer seats in both 2004 and 2009 LS

Table 5.5 *LS Election Results: 2009*

	Seats Contested	Seats Won	Vote
Congress	25	17	19.6
NCP	21	08	19.3
BJP	25	09	18.2
SHS	22	11	17.0
BSP	47	00	4.8
MNS	11	00	4.1
BBM	39	00	1.3
RPI(A)	01	00	0.6
SWP	01	01	1.3
BVA	01	01	0.6
RPI	01	00	0.6
SP	10	00	1.0
JD(S)	04	00	0.2
CPI	03	00	0.1
CPI(M)	02	00	0.5
Others	196	00	2.7
IND	410	01	8.1
Total	819	48	100

Note: Turnout: 50.7 per cent.

elections. Of the seats it contested, the party won half the seats in 2004 and more than two-thirds of the seats in 2009. In a sense, this improvement appears to be a function of its alliance with the NCP. As Table 5.6 shows, there is a regional pattern. The SHS and BJP swept the election in the contiguous belt of North Maharashtra and western Vidarbh while the Congress–NCP captured a large number of seats from the Mumbai–Thane belt, which happens to be more urban. Another remarkable feature of 2009 parliamentary outcome was the inability of the Congress and NCP to retain their stronghold in western Maharashtra. Yet, six months after the parliamentary election, the Congress and NCP retained power in State elections also. With this,

Table 5.6 *Region-wise Results: LS, 2009*

Region	Seats	Turnout	Congress		NCP		BJP		SHS		Others	
			Seats	Votes	Seats	Votes	Seats	Votes	Seats	Votes	Seats	Votes
Mumbai–Thane	10	41.2	06	25.9	02	10.7	00	14.6	01	15.3	01	33.5
Konkan	03	52.3	01	28.2	00	12.9	00	00	02	49.3	00	09.6
North Maharashtra	06	46.8	01	12.5	01	24.8	04	34.0	00	03.8	00	24.9
Vidarbh	10	55.7	04	25.3	01	09.9	02	19.3	03	16.4	00	29.1
Marathwada	08	56.7	02	18.8	01	20.7	02	22.6	03	20.3	00	17.6
Western Maharashtra	11	52.8	03	11.6	03	32.0	01	13.5	02	14.5	02	28.4
Total	**48**	**50.7**	**17**	**19.6**	**08**	**19.3**	**09**	**18.2**	**11**	**17.0**	**03[a]**	**25.9**

Note: [a]Others include 1 each from Swabhiman Paksha and Vanchit Bahujan Aghadi (VBA) and 1IND.

Maharashtra joined Delhi, Odisha and Gujarat where the same party/ alliance had remained in power for three consecutive terms.[7]

In Assembly elections, the Congress–NCP improved their condition (Table 5.7). Region-wise disaggregation of Assembly results shows that the success rate of the Congress party (proportion of seats won to seats contested) varied from region to region (Table 5.8): Compared to 2004, it declined in the regions of Mumbai, North Maharashtra and western Maharashtra, while the party improved its success rate in Konkan (only marginally and mainly due to the entry of Narayan Rane from the SHS into the Congress), Vidarbh and Marathwada. Gains in the Marathwada region were most impressive.

In both 2004 and 2009, Maharashtra witnessed a bipolar competition between two coalitions, and the outcomes did not indicate much difference between the two. There were many smaller players in the field, and they tried to intervene by forging third alternatives. But these made only a limited impact on the outcome. More than the 'third' players, the MNS emerged as a major factor in 2009—particularly in the Assembly election—since it dented the SHS vote in a sizable manner. Its overall vote shares of 4 per cent in LS elections and under 6 per cent in Assembly elections do not tell the full story. In the Mumbai–Thane region, the MNS polled more than 18 per cent votes in LS elections and almost 20 per cent in Assembly elections. While the party surely must have drawn voters from across the political spectrum, it is reasonable to believe that a larger chunk of its voters in Mumbai and Thane would have come from the SHS (and in part the BJP too). In other

---

[7] This was also the time when anti-incumbency of the 1990s had become less troublesome as a trend in many States and a number of State governments across parties were getting re-elected; for instance, while in Gujarat the BJP got re-elected despite internal factionalism, the Congress, which almost consensually was not in a strong position organizationally, did manage to get re-elected in Delhi, Haryana and Assam. Similarly, Navin Patnaik's Biju Janata Dal also successfully retained power in the State. Thus, the re-election of the Congress–NCP government in the State was not an extraordinary happening; it fitted into the new pattern of pro-incumbency—probably supported indirectly by the quiet buoyancy of the economy nationally and in turn also allowed these States under stable governments to also post better growth on economic indicators, thus leaving at the disposal of the governments greater resources to manage popular expectations. That of course does not mean that any of these States actually embarked on any radically different path of managing the economy.

Table 5.7 *Assembly Election Results: 2009*

	Seats Contested	Won	Vote
Congress	170	82	21.0
NCP	113	62	16.4
SHS	160	44	16.3
BJP	119	46	14.0
BSP	281	00	2.4
MNS	143	13	5.7
RLDS[a]	286	12	5.4
BVA	2	02	0.3
JSS	37	02	1.3
BBM	103	01	0.9
LSG	1	01	0.2
Other Parties	321	—	0.9
IND	1822	23	15.3
Total	**3,558**	**288**	**100**

Note: Turnout: 62.1 per cent.

[a]Republican Left Democratic Samiti was forged by Ramdas Athavale of RPI(A) as a third front of parties in 2009 Assembly elections. The front consisted of a large number of smaller parties, mainly the communist parties, the PWP, JD(S), SP and some RPI factions (for details, see Palshikar et al., 2009; 43).

words, the MNS certainly made it easier for the Congress and NCP to return to power in 2009.

ROUTE TO CONGRESS'S SUCCESS

After its defeat in 1995 and the split in 1999, it was not easy for the Congress to make a comeback. The return to power in 1999 was only providential—there was no real victory, but the BJP and SHS were unable to gain majority in the State legislature. Since 2004, however, the Congress (and NCP) began gaining some lost ground. Getting the third term was particularly difficult; power generation was not sufficient—leading to only limited industrial growth; in the

Table 5.8 *Region-wise Results: Assembly Elections, 2009*

Region	Seats	Turnout	Congress		NCP		BJP		SHS		Others	
			Seats	Votes	Seats	Votes	Seats	Votes	Seats	Votes	Seats	Votes
Mumbai–Thane	60	47.6	18	20.0	08	10.4	09	11.0	09	20.1	16	38.5
Konkan[a]	15	67.0	02	20.9	05	19.0	01	05.5	04	23.2	03	31.4
North Maharashtra	35	59.9	06	15.1	09	22.3	04	13.4	07	20.6	09	28.6
Vidarbh	62	62.0	24	28.0	04	07.3	19	23.0	08	11.0	07	30.7
Marathwada	46	65.7	18	22.5	12	19.1	02	14.8	07	17.3	07	26.3
Western Maharashtra	70	63.1	14	17.7	24	22.7	11	10.0	09	14.2	12	35.4
Total	288	59.7	82	21.0	62	16.4	46	14.0	44	16.3	54[b]	32.3

Notes: [a]This was the first election after delimitation of 2007–2008. Accordingly, some regions lost the seats and some gained.

[b]Others include: IND (24), MNS (13), SP and PWP—4 each, Jan Surajya Shakti and BVA—2 each and one each of BBM, Swabhimani Paksha, CPM, Loksangram and Rashtriya Samaj Paksha.

agricultural sector, the government was not able to stop the steady incidence of farmers' suicides; the Mumbai terror attack had brought disrepute to the government; and, so, the overall image and performance of the government were only lacklustre. However, there was no explicit resentment against the State government either in 2004 or in 2009 (Palshikar and Birmal, 2009; see also, Deshpande and Birmal, 2009; 137–138). In our earlier work in collaboration with Nitin Birmal, we have shown that the popular image of the State government was not very negative and the UPA government at the Centre was seen as quite satisfactory during this period. This helped the Congress and NCP to neutralize the effect of anti-incumbency. Overall satisfaction about the Congress-led governments at the Centre or State was not very high, but the Congress was able to contain dissatisfaction. Besides, there seems to be marginal improvement in satisfaction levels both between parliamentary and State election and between 2004 and 2009. After its first term, in 2004, at the time of parliamentary election, the State government had slightly negative 'net' satisfaction, meaning more people were dissatisfied than those satisfied with it, and this negative trend, in fact, somewhat strengthened at the time of Assembly elections; that is, the gap between dissatisfaction and satisfaction widened a little. However, what is significant is that at both points in time, the proportion of those satisfied with the Central government was greater than those dissatisfied (for details, see Palshikar et al., 2014; 438).

But beyond the ability of the Congress and NCP to retain power, the larger question was whether the two parties were able to retain a consistent social base during this period, after its debacle in 1995. We attempt to answer this question by looking at the survey data for 2004 and 2009.[8] As Tables 5.9 and 5.10 show, no particular social group

[8] Note on 2004 surveys and 2009 surveys: Data for 2004 parliamentary election is part of Lokniti's NES, NES 2004 and for the 2004 Assembly election, data is from a study jointly done by Lokniti and Deptartment of Politics & Public Administration, SPPU. For both these, the same sample was canvassed, that is, the data is for a panel study. In the year 2009, two voters' surveys were conducted in Maharashtra, after LS and Assembly elections (May 2009 and October 2009). Both surveys were conducted by the Department of Politics and Public Administration, SPPU, in collaboration with Lokniti (CSDS) and were supported by the UGC under two separate major research projects granted to the authors during 2009–2011. The total achieved sample of the

Table 5.9 *Volatile Social Bases of Congress and NCP: 2004 and 2009*

	LS 2004	N	VS 2004	N	LS 2009	N	VS 2009	N
Upper castes	26	52	25	108	39	132	42	158
Maratha-Kunbis	30	411	35	404	34	603	35	456
OBCs[a]	34	181	39	243	39	500	31	490
SCs	61	182	38	165	46	295	48	220
STs	59	108	58	139	46	225	35	237
Muslims	72	130	66	109	59	143	66	117
Others	35	190	49	48	35	108	35	130
Upper class	34	211	39	103	35	304	40	227
Middle class	39	218	40	319	36	711	38	538
Lower class	46	431	35	185	39	200	39	393
Poor	43	396	44	553	43	792	34	551
Rural	41	846	37	816	35	984	34	1,034
Urban	45	410	46	400	43	1,023	43	674
All	42	1,255	40	1,216	39	2,007	37	1,708

Source: Adapted from Palshikar et al. (2014; 440).

Note: [a]Other than Kunbis.

Table 5.10 *Social Bases of SHS and BJP: 2004–2009*

	LS 2004	N	VS 2004	N	LS2009	N	VS 2009	N
Upper castes	67	52	54	108	41	132	35	158
Maratha-Kunbis	57	411	38	404	49	603	30	456
OBCs	47	181	47	243	47	500	42	490
SCs	16	182	25	165	26	295	22	220
STs	27	108	16	139	15	225	24	237
Muslims	10	130	10	109	09	143	19	117
Others	42	190	30	48	10	108	23	130
Upper class	50	211	42	103	41	304	25	227
Middle class	48	218	38	319	39	711	28	538
Lower class	36	431	32	185	38	200	32	393
Poor	43	396	28	553	28	792	34	551
Rural	46	846	32	816	38	984	30	1,034
Urban	37	410	38	400	33	1,023	30	674
All	43	1,255	34	1,216	35	2,007	30	1,708

Source: Adapted from Palshikar et al. (2014; 441).

can be identified as the stronger and consistent supporter of either the Congress–NCP or the SHS–BJP for this period. In fact, the two alliances are pretty closely engaged in a competition with each other in order to win over various social groups. The Congress and NCP, in particular, are weak in retaining a consistent base among their voters compared to the BJP and SHS.

Tables 5.9 and 5.10 make it clear that every social group—in caste terms or otherwise—was somewhat volatile in its political choices. Upper castes are often supposed to be supportive of the BJP (and SHS). But in 2009, the Congress and NCP managed to get the support of 38 per cent from upper castes compared to SHS–BJP's 40 per cent among this group. As seen from 1995, the Maratha-Kunbi vote has been quite volatile. During 2004–2009 too, this volatility continued. By 2009 (LS election), almost half of the Maratha-Kunbi voters supported the SHS–BJP (this support declined during Assembly election in the same year). The same is the case with OBCs. As stated earlier, there has been a gradual consolidation of the OBC constituency in favour of the BJP–SHS since 1995. And yet, in 2009 Assembly elections, they moved away from these parties. As a rule, the Dalits supported the Congress–NCP more than the BJP–SHS. However, their support for the Congress alliance dipped suddenly in the 2004 Assembly elections as political competition opened up and became multi-polar. The Adivasis, on the other hand, showed a consistent shift away from the Congress fold.

The earlier pattern of the Congress as a party of the poor and marginalized sections changed in these elections when the poor voted for both rival alliances in equal degrees. And between 2004 and 2009, there was a clear shift of poor classes from the two Congress parties to the BJP and SHS. Despite the 'urban' turn of the late 1990s, urban voters preferred the Congress and the NCP in these elections rather than the BJP–SHS. Thus, the return of the Congress and NCP into electoral reckoning meant that no set pattern could emerge as far as the social support for parties was concerned, except a clear gender advantage for the Congress–NCP in comparison to the SHS–BJP. The

first survey was 2,459 and the second survey used a sub-sample of the first consisting of 1,966 respondents.

latter continued to receive greater support among men than among women.

Three things emerged from this overview of voter choices during 2004–2009. In the first place, every social section faced political fragmentation. This refuted the role of vote banks based on caste as key drivers in electoral outcomes. Second, it is clear that political competition based on coalitions concealed social instability or volatility because alliance partners brought votes from diverse groups. Third, it seems that the Congress did not have any firm social base that it could rely upon.

DID THE CONGRESS 'REVIVE'?

When the Congress retained power in the State for the third time in 2009, coupled with its success nationally, it was natural to imagine whether the party was recovering from its continuous decline since the mid-1990s. In hindsight, we know that this was not the case. Even in 2009–2010 itself, it was not easy to imagine the recovery of the party and, therefore, we described the electoral outcomes of 2009 as survival of the Congress (Palshikar et al., 2014). The party did have momentary goodwill nationally, but it still lacked strong leadership and was ridden with factionalism. Soon, it was to get embroiled in crisis situations resulting from alleged corruption and chaotic decision-making. But this was more about the national-level party and its government. At the State level, the party singularly lacked leadership that could connect to all regions of the State. Vilasrao Deshmukh, who was slowly shaping as the State-level leader, found himself in the midst of a controversy following the Mumbai terror attacks. This cut short his tenure and also reduced his stature, though he was inducted in the Union cabinet later. As mentioned earlier, the apparent atmosphere of Congress recovery in the State was triggered mainly because of the relative disarray in the opposition camp. The Congress retained power partly because of the happenings at the national level and partly because of a somewhat weak opposition within the State.

To these extraneous factors, one must add a somewhat improved economic condition of the State as a background factor. We have noted above how there was mild satisfaction about the performance of State government in 2009. Besides that, in the survey after the 2009 Assembly elections, 42 per cent respondents felt that their economic condition had improved over the last few years compared to only 13 per cent who felt that it had deteriorated (Palshikar et al., 2009; 46). This factor of voter satisfaction is also related to the fact that compared to the 1990s, State's economy did show signs of some improvement in the next decade. Except the bad performance of the year preceding the 2009 elections, the Congress–NCP government could actually claim a decent growth of the economy of the State throughout its second term and consolidation during the first term as far as the increase in the net state domestic product and the per capita income are concerned (GoM, 2013; 2–4). Thus, election outcome in 2009 was partly shaped by the better performance of the economy. It also connects with our earlier observation on the basis of the survey data (Palshikar et al., 2014) that between class and caste, the significance of class was a more pertinent factor in determining vote choice. While this needs to be examined further in the light of subsequent elections, at least for 2009, the 'revival' of the Congress depended on the performance of the economy.

Of course, this revival had an in-built contradiction. As Table 5.9 shows, the Congress drew more votes from the better-off classes than the poor. Better performance of the economy may have driven the economically better-off sections to support the Congress. Thus, the momentary survival of the Congress hinged on a combination of improved economic condition, support by the better-off sections and fragmentation of the vote of the poor. This obviously could not be a long-term solution to the decline of the Congress as was seen in the next election itself.

Second, in this discussion of the revival of the Congress, the question about its base among the Marathas is crucial. Since the mid-1990s, politics of Maharashtra began undergoing dramatic changes not only because of the all-India trends but also because of the glaring failure of the Congress to retain its base among Marathas. As data presented in this chapter shows, more than a decade after the 1995 elections, the Congress was still unable to win back the Maratha voters. On the other hand, the Congress also did not seem to inspire confidence among the members of the OBC sections. OBCs went on to become supporters of the SHS and BJP rather than the Congress. This left the Congress with a narrow social coalition of only Dalits, Adivasis and Muslims, not sufficient to regain its power in the State. The main battlefield between the Congress and NCP, of course, has been the Maratha community. The NCP quickly managed to win a sizeable section of the Maratha community towards itself so much so that it came to be identified as a party of the Marathas in the State (Birmal, 1999), and political interests of the Maratha community facilitated the post-election coalition between the two Congress parties in 1999 (Palshikar and Birmal, 2003). However, the support among Marathas became a battle of dual battlefields. Once the unease among Maratha voters shaped, they soon also began exploring other political alternatives and as such, while the Congress and NCP were vying with each other for Maratha vote, the two coalitions between themselves also kept competing for Maratha vote. As Table 5.10 shows, the SHS and BJP together were able to muster support from a large section of the Maratha community. This meant that the coalition between the two Congress parties would not necessarily ensure Maratha support.

Therefore, election results from 2004 and 2009 suggest only a limited point: that the decline of the Congress in the State was momentarily arrested. In the arena of electoral competition, the Congress—along with the NCP—could claim some space despite the inability to strengthen itself organizationally, ideologically or socially. In a sense, this matches the developments at the all-India level where Congress's decline appeared to be arrested by developments since 2004. The outcome that appeared in 2009 as the party's recovery soon evaporated under the pressures of inefficient governance and absence of organizational effort to revive. By 2011, the same Congress was beleaguered by multiple challenges.

In Maharashtra too, the post-election developments between 2009 and 2012 indicated the hollowness of the survival of 2009. The somewhat unexpected survival of the Congress neutralized the ambition of the BJP to emerge as the main party in the State. This also had an implication for opening of the party competition. Sensing that the collapse of the Congress would facilitate entry of new players, in the post-JD period, attempts were consistently made to float new, non-Congress and non-BJP parties. Earliest of this was the formation of the BBM by Prakash Ambedkar. Throughout the 1990s, Ambedkar tried to keep his distance from the Congress and imagine a third front. The 1990s also witnessed the entry of the BSP and SP in the politics of the State. Subsequently, in the period 2000–2010, besides the MNS, many other experiments took place. These included the Jan Surajya Shakti (JSS), a party founded by Vinay Kore just before the 2004 Assembly elections, mainly trying to gain a foothold in southern parts of the State. Another similar effort was the Rashtriya Samaj Paksha (founded in 2003) also in the same region of the State. The third player, also expecting to intervene in the region traditionally dominated by the Congress, was the Swabhiman Paksha formed by Shetkari Sanghatana followers in 2004. While it is interesting that all these three parties aimed at occupying the space vacated by the Congress, it is also noteworthy that they were not able to create enough space for themselves and while they did survive beyond 2009, their ability to bring about a new party system that would go beyond the bipolarity of two coalitions did not succeed during the period 2004–2009.

As the next elections approached and as Modi arose as the central mobilizer around late 2013, the 15-year-old edifice of Congress rule crumbled rapidly and, as we shall see in the next chapter, reopened the possibilities of new political configurations—the possibilities that were left incomplete in 1995.

Towards BJP's Shaky Dominance

The Congress that survived in the State after 2004 was obviously not the 'older' Congress that enjoyed deep roots and a kind of hegemony. It was a much battered and maligned Congress that was also torn asunder by its ongoing war with its breakaway faction, NCP, and its own many factions. Yet, once it made the decision in 1999 to ally with the NCP, the two Congress parties managed to remain allies until 2014. Much of this was of course done under double duress: In the first place, they both feared marginalization if they operated separately in the wake of continuing alliance of BJP and SHS and the other reason was that the compulsions of all-India politics forced the State Congress to accept an alliance with the NCP.

In fact, all-India developments influenced the course of events in the State to a great extent in the post-1999 context. Thus, in 2004 and 2009, the fact that Assembly election followed close on the heels of parliamentary elections proved to be an asset for the Congress and NCP in that they benefited from the electoral victory at the Centre and rode on the goodwill created by that victory. Both of those elections also demoralized the BJP even at State-level elections. This was also the time when all was not well with the SHS (as discussed in the previous chapter). Thus, more than the performance of the coalition government of the Congress and NCP, other political circumstances were more influential in the survival of both Congress parties in post-2004 period. Similarly, when the 2014 election approached, the larger, all-India scenario mattered more than the issue of the performance of the State government.

By the time the elections for LS commenced in 2014, the issues of coalition and State government's performance had become less important in the backdrop of the rising popularity of Narendra Modi and once the LS election assumed critical importance, the Assembly election of 2014 also became part of that critical moment. Thus, the two elections of 2014 became completely dominated by the change of political atmosphere prevailing at the all-India level and contributed to the complete decimation of the two Congress parties. So much so that even after five years from that defeat, the two Congress parties did not show signs of recovery and the party system came to be artificially dominated by a new player—the BJP.

In this chapter, we shall take a closer look at the State-level electoral process in 2014 that produced the dramatic transformation in Maharashtra's political landscape, and which continued in the next round of elections in 2019. Like 1995, this was more than dramatic; it constituted the second critical moment in the electoral history of Maharashtra. As we show in this chapter, after 1995, 2014 was another critical election and it was so mostly because it strengthened most of the critical features that characterized the 1995 election: first, it hastened the collapse of the Congress; second, it facilitated further reconfiguration of social bases of parties; third, 2014 aggravated the crisis of Maratha politics; fourth, it underscored the rising importance of the urban factor in State politics; and finally, it ruptured the bipolarity that was sustained by coalition politics, leading to the rise of the BJP as the main political force in the State and at the same time its isolation—with the formation of one of the more awkward coalitions in the history of the State, the MVA (2019).

CONGRESS'S CONTINUED DECLINE

In the parliamentary elections of 2014, the Congress witnessed its steepest fall when it dipped to its lowest ever seat share in the State winning only two LS seats on its own, while its partner, NCP, won four seats. While the emergence of Modi's leadership hastened the complete decline of the Congress party, the party was more or less in a vulnerable position for over a decade before this happened. Besides the organizational weakness from which the party suffered for long, the third term of the Congress-led State government unfolded in the backdrop of leadership changes in the State and the overall negative publicity the UPA received at the national level from 2011 onwards. As elaborated elsewhere, we have described the return of the Congress and NCP to power in 2009—for the third term in a row—as 'survival in the midst decline' (Palshikar et al., 2014). As mentioned in the last chapter, the economy of the State showed improvement between 2000 and 2009 and, as a result, on the eve of the 2009 elections, popular perceptions about the State government were not at all negative. But after its third consecutive victory, the fate of the Congress party in Maharashtra, instead of becoming stronger, began to rapidly slide down along with its national-level weakening. It needs to be reiterated that the developments in 2014 and 2019 were the product of a combination of all-India trends and the State-specific factors.

Ashok Chavan, who had succeeded Vilasrao Deshmukh in December 2008 as the State CM, continued to lead the State government after the Assembly elections of 2009. But things did not go smoothly for him and the Congress party. He had to resign within a year from the Assembly elections under the pressure of allegations due to the Adarsh scam.[1] He was succeeded by Prithviraj Chavan (November 2010), who was seen as inexperienced in the politics of the State since much of his political career had shaped in Delhi. Ever since he became the CM, partly due to his clean image and arduous efforts to retain that image (but also due to intra-party factionalism), Prithviraj Chavan ran into trouble with his party MLAs for his alleged indecision. He also did not have a very good equation with his coalition partner, the NCP. Yet, the Congress

---

[1] The 'Adarsh scam' refers to Adarsh Housing Society at a prime location in Mumbai where alleged misappropriation took place through bureaucratic and political connivance. The land belonging to military was supposed to be used for war widows and other military personnel, but flats were allotted to relatives of politicians and bureaucrats. The scandal erupted in 2010 followed by appointment of an enquiry committee that indicted a number of political leaders including the then CM Ashok Chavan and many civil servants. See *Hindustan Times*, First Case in Adarsh Scam Registered, 15 November 2010, https://www.hindustantimes.com/mumbai/first-case-in-adarsh-scam-registered/story-gfxsmVLpXbay1odXOn-B1AL.html (accessed on 26 June 2020); see also report on the enquiry commission, *The Indian Express*, Adarsh Panel Indicts Former CMs, Maharashtra Cabinet Rejects Report, 22 December 2013, http://archive.indianexpress.com/news/adarsh-panel-indicts-former-cms-maharashtra-cabinet-rejects-report/1209897/ (accessed on 26 June 2020).

party (and NCP) fared well in the 2012 elections to local bodies in the State. In the district-level ZP elections, the Congress and NCP together won almost 60 per cent seats across the State (NCP—31% and Congress—27.5%). BJP won 14 per cent seats, while the SHS won a little under 14 per cent seats. The SHS and BJP were able to get a majority only in 5 of the 27 ZPs—Ratnagiri, Jalgaon, Jalna, Hingoli and Nagpur (SECM, 2015; 379–381). Out of the 26 municipal corporations, the Congress and NCP managed to gain combined majority in 11 corporations during the period 2009–2013 (SECM, 2015; 29) and in municipal councils, the Congress polled 27 per cent votes, followed by the NCP (26%) while both the parties won 27 per cent seats each in the municipal bodies as against 9 per cent seats each won by the BJP and SHS (SECM, 2015; 365–366).

But around the same time, the political atmosphere in the country had begun to shift away from—and against—the Congress on the issue of corruption. While this was caused by the anti-corruption movement that was centred in Delhi, the Congress–NCP government in Maharashtra also began facing corruption charges at the State level. While the CM ensured that his image remained clean, the party and the government got embroiled in many corruption charges. After the exit of Ashok Chavan, Congress MP from Pune Suresh Kalmadi was charged in corruption cases involving the Commonwealth Games.[2] Subsequently, the deputy CM, Ajit Pawar, belonging to the NCP became the target of charges involving the irrigation department under his charge.[3] At the same time, Prithviraj Chavan came under

---

[2] *The Hindu*, CWG Scam: Kalmadi Named 'Main Accused;'in First CBI Charge Sheet, 20 May 2011, https://www.thehindu.com/news/national/cwg-scam-kalmadi-named-main-accused-in-first-cbi-charge-sheet/article2035048.ece (accessed on 25 June 2020).

[3] *Business Standard*, What Is Maharashtra Irrigation Scam, 25 September 2012, http://www.business-standard.com/article/economy-policy/what-is-maharashtra-irrigation-scam-112092503026_1.html (accessed on 4 March 2019). The State government appointed a committee to enquire into the allegations under the chairmanship of a retired expert and civil servant, Madhav Chitale. The report of this committee was tabled in the Assembly in June 2014. It exonerated the minister for direct involvement and irrigation projects initiated without proper permissions: *Times of India*, Chitale Committee Report, 4 June 2014, http://timesofindia.indiatimes.com/city/mumbai/

criticism both from his party men and from the NCP for his inaction and overcautious approach.

Throughout this period, the economy of the State was stable but marked by agricultural stagnation. While many infrastructure projects were begun, the image of the State government remained somewhat negative. This was in part due to the negative image of the UPA government at the Centre and also because of the lack of coordination between the two parties ruling the State. The State government, and NCP in particular, also received very negative press coverage, leading to a public impression that the State was on the verge of ruin.

Ironically, during this period, the main opposition parties, the SHS and BJP, were not very active in mobilizing protests. Popular protests, however, occurred at Jaitapur in the Konkan region over its nuclear plant.[4] This project, like the Enron project of the 1990s, deeply divided the Konkan region over matters of development and destabilization of local livelihood patterns. The SHS took a strong stand against the project, though the BJP did not join its partner in these protests. Even after its victory as an alliance partner with the BJP in the 2014 parliamentary elections, the SHS announced that it would continue its protest.[5] Besides this agitation, local unrest in western Maharashtra kept recurring during the five-year period mainly on the issue of sugar cane prices payable from the cooperative factories in the region.[6] These factories being mostly under the control of the Congress and NCP leaders, such agitations created an atmosphere against the local elite from ruling parties. So the failure of the ruling parties in maintaining

Irrigation-projects-initiated-without-proper-permissions-Chitale-committee-report/articleshow/36505180.cms (accessed on 4 March 2019).

[4] Rediff.com, Jaitapur Protests: Sena Goes on Rampage, 19 April 2011, https://www.rediff.com/news/report/ramesh-slams-shiv-sena-over-jaitapur-protests/20110419.htm (accessed on 4 March 2019).

[5] *DNA*, SHS Opposition to Jaitapur Project a Big Test for New Government, 9 June 2014, https://www.dnaindia.com/india/report-shiv-sena-opposition-to-jaitapur-project-a-big-test-for-new-government-1994278 (accessed on 4 March 2019).

[6] *The Indian Express*, Sugar Cane Farmers Begin 48 Hour Bandh in Maharashtra, 28 November 2013, http://archive.indianexpress.com/news/sugarcane-farmers-begin-48hour-bandh-in-maharashtra/1200615/ (accessed on 4 March 2019).

a close connect with the rural population helped in creating a negative impression.

All these negatives combined into a sentiment against the ruling coalition since mid-2013, once the popularity chart of Modi began rising up. Like the North, the western region was also witness to the effect of Modi's appeal on the electorate. In addition to the effective role played by Gopinath Munde, Nitin Gadkari and Devendra Fadnavis, the ability of Modi to turn the election into a plebiscite over his personal leadership became the single most crucial factor that had the potential of swaying the voters.[7] We shall discuss in greater detail the nature of this decline of the Congress later in this chapter. But before that, let us simply look at the electoral magnitude of the 2014 defeat that the party faced.

RESULTS: LS, 2014

Table 6.1 summarizes the results of the 16th LS election from Maharashtra. It was clearly a one-sided affair on an unprecedented scale for the State. Of the 48 seats, the BJP-led NDA won 42 seats, leaving only 6 for the Congress-led UPA. Just as the seat tally tells a one-sided story, the vote shares also intimate the one-sided nature of the outcome.

For the Congress, this was probably one of its most humiliating defeats in the State. Maharashtra is traditionally seen as a Congress stronghold, but the party dipped to its lowest-ever seat tally in 2014. Even the two seats that the Congress won did not give it much comfort. The victory at Nanded was narrow, though a stronghold of ex-CM Ashok Chavan. The other seat won by the Congress, also from the Marathwada region—Hingoli—was wrested by the party from its partner NCP, after much haggling, for a candidate close to Rahul Gandhi—Rajeev Satav. While he did win the seat, the victory margin was a paltry 1,632, whereas elsewhere the SHS and BJP won with huge margins.

---

[7] In the following analysis of 2014 parliamentary elections, we draw on two of our previous writings: Palshikar and Birmal (2015) and Deshpande and Birmal (2017).

Table 6.1 *LS Election Results: 2014*

	Seats Contested	Changeover from 2009	Won	Changeover from 2009	Votes	Changeover from 2009
BJP	24	–1	23	14	27.3	9.2
SHS	20	–2	18	7	20.6	3.6
NDA allies	4	3	1	1	3.4	3.4
Congress	26	1	2	–15	18.1	–1.5
NCP	21	—	4	–4	15.9	–3.3
UPA allies	1	–1	—	—	0.6	–0.7
MNS	10	–1	—	—	1.5	–3.4
BSP	48	1	—	—	2.6	–2.8
Others and IND	743	79	—	–3	10.0	–3.9
Total	**897**		**48**			

Note: IND: 446; turnout: 60.5 per cent; change over from 2009: 9.8 per cent.

In comparison to Congress's two victories, NCP's victory on four seats may create a wrong impression that the party fared better. In reality, all four seats that the NCP won represent its inability to go beyond family networks and personalized style of organization. Its candidate from Satara in western Maharashtra has been known for his personal stranglehold over the constituency and the party had practically no control over him (he joined the BJP ahead of the 2019 Assembly elections). The Satara victory, thus, was his personal victory, rather than the party's victory. The second seat, Kolhapur, was also not much to the credit of the party. Like Satara, this was the victory of its candidate who has a stronghold over the city, independent of any party. In 2004, he contested on an SHS ticket and lost. In 2009, though he had joined the NCP briefly, he contested against the party as an IND and lost but also ensured the loss of the NCP candidate. So the Kolhapur victory was also a personal victory, rather than the party's victory. Another 'personal' victory came from Baramati, the home constituency of Sharad Pawar, where his daughter Supriya Sule was contesting as a sitting Member of Parliament (MP). Finally, NCP won Madha, the fourth seat, also in western Maharashtra, which Sharad Pawar had won in the previous election. This time, another senior party leader Vijaysinh Mohite-Patil contested it but won only by 25,000 votes. In other words, the four seats won by the NCP in no way suggest its organizational strength over the western region despite having a network of institutions over which the party leaders have had a long history of control.

The NCP and the Congress did have some weak partners. These included the Bahujan Vikas Aghadi (BVA; influential only in Vasai–Virar constituencies near Mumbai), and RPI (Kawade faction) having support among Dalits of Marathwada. In contrast to the Congress and NCP, the BJP entered the contest with an advantage: Modi was already gaining in popularity and the Congress was reeling under the burden of anti-incumbency and the shock of the anti-corruption movement. The BJP successfully retained its alliance with the SHS and further expanded the NDA in the State by bringing in not only the RPI(A) but also Raju Shetti's Swabhimani Paksha (SWP). The latter had a following in parts of western and southern Maharashtra, particularly among farmers. The NDA also included the Rashtriya Samaj Party (RSP) of Mahadev Jankar with his following among the Dhangar community in the same region. This strategy ensured that the NDA could take on the Congress and NCP in their bastion of western Maharashtra.

As Table 6.2 shows, the outcome of 2014 was devoid of any regional variation. For the first time in the electoral history of the State, we witnessed such a 'flat' outcome. Traditionally, Vidarbh and western Maharashtra have been strongholds of the Congress and NCP respectively. But the outcome of 2014 LS wiped out any traces of this traditional influence. Victory of BJP and SHS this time was also characterized by large margins in all regions. Not only did the NDA win seats in all regions, but the coalition also registered a high vote share in each of the regions of the State. Given the overwhelming advantage for the BJP and SHS, the urban–rural distinction also did not matter. The traditional wisdom about the Congress being stronger in rural and the opposition being somewhat influential in urban areas has always been less applicable in the post-1990 electoral politics of the State (although, as we discuss below, this election underscored the importance of the urban factor). This domination of the NDA was also reflected in the huge victory margins enjoyed by its candidates. All 23 victories of the BJP came with a victory margin of above one lakh votes, and 16 out of SHS's 18 victories also belonged to the same category. These victory margins indicate a fundamental shift in the structure of competition. With these margins, it is difficult to ascribe the NDA victory to only the structural aspects of the 'first past the post' system. It is quite clear that in 2014, the BJP (and SHS) simply emerged as a potentially new dominant force rather than fledgling challengers to the Congress and NCP.

RESULTS: ASSEMBLY, 2014

In the backdrop of such a massive victory of the BJP (and NDA) both in the State and at national level, it was unlikely that the trend would suddenly alter within the intervening five months at the time of State Assembly elections. The Congress was completely demoralized and, in contrast, the BJP was upbeat. However, what made the Assembly

Table 6.2 *Region-wise Result: LS Elections, 2014*

Region	Seats	Turnout	Congress		NCP		BJP		SHS		Others	
			Won	*Vote*	*Won*	*Vote*	*Won*	*Vote*	*Won*	*Vote*	*Won*	*Vote*
Mumbai–Thane	10	51.6	00	17.9	00	08.1	05	29.5	05	25.5	00	19.0
Konkan	03	63.0	00	11.2	00	18.9	00	00	03	45.8	00	24.1
North Maharashtra	06	61.5	00	14.5	00	19.2	05	48.4	01	8.2	00	09.7
Vidarbh	10	62.9	00	20.8	00	10.8	06	30.9	04	18.8	00	18.7
Marathwada	08	64.3	02	23.8	00	15.3	03	26.0	03	25.0	00	09.9
Western Maharashtra	11	61.9	00	15.4	04	24.7	04	19.8	02	15.0	01	25.1
Total	**48**	**60.3**	**02**	**18.1**	**04**	**16.0**	**23**	**27.3**	**18**	**20.6**	**01**[a]	**10.3**

Note: [a]SWP.

election complicated was the decision of all major parties to contest the elections on their own. Although the SHS decided to participate in the Modi-led national government, its leadership was not comfortable with a newly buoyant BJP at the State level. It also must have sensed an opportunity to fill the vacuum created by the complete decimation of the Congress. In any case, neither the BJP nor the SHS genuinely wanted their alliance to continue and, therefore, the two parties chose to part ways for the State election. The BJP was successful in retaining the support of the smaller partners such as the SWP, Jankar's RSP and RPI(A).

Following this development, the two Congress parties also decided to disband their coalition and contest independently. Thus, the State was plunged into a four-cornered competition. Besides complicating the electoral competition for the October 2014 Assembly elections, this development indicated the crumbling structure of party competition in the State. Ever since the BJP and SHS had entered into a coalition, they were not able to displace the Congress either on their own or through their combined power (except once in 1995). However, their coalition gave an artificial appearance of bipolarity to State politics which was actually undergoing the process of fragmentation. This fragmentation was not only represented by the limited strength of the BJP and SHS, but it was also represented by the internal factionalism within the Congress and the split that occurred in 1999. Third, the ensuing fragmentation was also represented by the continuous emergence of smaller parties and their attempts to enter the electoral arena. The so-called main parties or larger parties such as the BJP, SHS and Congress had to perforce make adjustments for the smaller parties because of the fragmented nature of party competition. The SHS–BJP alliance, however, gave a superficial sense of bipolarity because in order to ward off their challenge, the Congress, and NCP too, had to agree to a coalition. Since 1995, all State governments were coalition governments. These forced coalitions meant that no party could systematically attempt to develop and expand. Parties had to make room for each other and give up their 'seats' to their alliance partners.

Once the BJP managed to situate itself as the main party in the State, a fundamental transformation quickly shaped in the form of

Table 6.3 *Assembly Election Result: 2014*

Party	Seats Contested	Votes	Seats Won
BJP	260	27.8	122
BJP allies	22	1.3	1
SHS	282	19.4	63
Congress	287	18.0	42
NCP	278	17.3	41
IND and Others	2,990	15.3	19
NOTA		0.90	-
Total	**4,119**		

Note: Turnout: 63.3 per cent.

breakdown of the coalitions that were existing for almost 25 years (in the case of SHS and BJP). As we shall see below, the coalitions did come back again in the aftermath of the Assembly election, but by then the process of reconfiguration of party system had already been under way (and continues as the coalition broke once again after the Assembly elections in 2019, although the BJP–SHS contested the 2019 LS elections as alliance partners).

As a result of the collapse of the SHS–BJP coalition, the Assembly election of 2014 took a multiparty shape. This allowed the BJP to post its best performance so far in State Assembly—it won 122 seats, pushing the Congress and NCP to third and fourth positions respectively (Table 6.3). Except Konkan, the BJP posted a reasonably good performance across other regions of the State. Whereas its success in Vidarbh was most handsome, the noteworthy fact about BJP's success was that it managed to win a significant number of seats (25) in western Maharashtra. The SHS emerged as the second largest party. Its comparatively better performance in Marathwada besides Mumbai and Konkan helped the party become the second largest party in the legislature (Table 6.4). Ever since the BJP and SHS forged their alliance in 1989, this was the first election when they were contesting separately, and the two Congress parties were also contesting separately. Therefore, in a sense, this election was a test of each party's strength.

Table 6.4 *Region-wise Result Assembly Elections: 2014*

Region	Seats	Turnout	Congress		NCP		BJP		SHS		Others	
			Won	Vote	Won	Vote	Won	Vote	Won	Vote	Won	Vote
Mumbai–Thane	60	52.0	05	13.6	04	09.8	24	29.7	21	26.2	06	20.7
Konkan	15	68.2	01	16.9	04	14.5	01	15.6	07	32.4	02	20.6
North Maharashtra	35	64.8	07	16.7	05	22.9	14	29.2	07	18.7	02	12.5
Vidarbh	62	64.8	10	22.3	01	09.7	44	35.3	04	12.3	03	20.4
Marathwada	46	68.3	09	18.6	08	19.9	15	27.4	11	16.9	03	17.2
Western Maharashtra	70	67.6	10	17.7	19	24.4	24	22.6	13	19.9	04	15.4
Total	**288**	**63.5**	**42**	**18.0**	**41**	**17.2**	**122**	**27.8**	**63**	**19.4**	**20[a]**	**17.6**

Note: [a]Others include IND (07), 3 each for PWP and BVA, AIMIM (2) and 1 each for MNS, BBM, CPI(M), SP and RSP.

Table 6.3 gives their respective seat and vote shares. But if one looks at the votes polled by them in the constituencies where they contested, we find that the BJP managed to poll 31 per cent votes in seats it contested, whereas for other parties this share was much less (under 20 for the SHS and 18 for the Congress and NCP). This suggests that the BJP did emerge as a party with more independent support in 2014 Assembly. It also appeared to be less dependent on alliance if one looks at respective vote shares for previous two elections (Deshpande and Birmal, 2017; 141).

Since the BJP did not get clear majority, there was some amount of uncertainty on the political horizon but after initial hesitation, the SHS decided to enter into a post-election arrangement with the BJP. This was the second government to be formed by the BJP and SHS in the State. The difference from the first was not only about their mutual relationship but also the internal composition of the ministry; being the larger party, the BJP got the post of CM and most important ministries in the BJP–SHS coalition of 2014. Devendra Fadnavis, BJP's leader from Vidarbh and a trusted Modi supporter, became the CM. Fadnavis could overcome the factional difficulties in his party with relative ease. In the first place, the most popular mass leader of the State BJP, Gopinath Munde, had unfortunately died in an accident much before the Assembly elections, leaving behind a political vacuum in the party. Eknath Khadse, BJP's powerful OBC leader from Jalgaon, and Pankaja Munde, Munde's daughter who looked upon herself as his political heir, both claimed to be mass leaders during the campaign and even afterwards sought to compete for leadership position, but Fadnavis, having successfully campaigned both during LS and more particularly the Assembly election, managed to win the confidence of Central leadership of the party and became BJP's choice despite murmurs of his being from Vidarbh region and also about his Brahman background.

EXPLAINING 2014

In order to understand what factors contributed to the outcomes in 2014, it is necessary to take into account anti-incumbency, the Modi factor and the changed social configuration of party support.

To what extent did anti-incumbency cause this outcome? Since the Congress and NCP were in power both at the Centre and the State, this 'double-incumbency' became a burden for them. In the pre-election surveys conducted by Lokniti, we found that the popular dissatisfaction with both the governments kept increasing from July 2013 onwards. In July 2013, 29 per cent respondents said that they were dissatisfied with the UPA government in Delhi, and 17 per cent were dissatisfied with the State government. As against this, in February 2014, 37 per cent were dissatisfied with the Central government and 39 per cent with the State government.[8] This, however, also alerts us to the fact that dissatisfaction soared only in the run up to the election. In other words, the perceived dissatisfaction was only an external indication of the change in the public mood that did not necessarily originate in anti-incumbency alone. If we take into account the fact that compared to 2009, the BJP and SHS added 21 more seats to their tally while NCP and Congress lost 19 seats (in LS election), the extent of NDA victory becomes evident. The two Congress parties together lost almost 5 per cent votes compared to last time, whereas the gains of the BJP and SHS amount to almost 13 per cent—more than double the loss of the ruling parties.

Besides anti-incumbency, the all-India context also mattered heavily in shaping the outcome. State-level incipient processes often require an external push. The Congress and NCP were already sitting on a weak throne with declining legitimacy. Their earlier victories were products of contingent factors and as such, when the push came, they crumbled rather dramatically. That push came in the form of the 'national mood' or the overall drift away from the Congress everywhere (Deshpande and Birmal, 2017). Since the middle of 2013, the popular opinion started shifting away from the UPA, and later that shift became very pronounced. The 'tracker' polls (done by Lokniti) measuring the public opinion consistently indicated that Modi was ahead of all other leaders in terms of popularity for becoming the PM. In July 2013, 21 per cent respondents from Maharashtra favoured Modi as the future PM, while in February 2014, this proportion rose to 31 per cent. Not surprisingly,

[8] Source: CSDS Data Unit.

therefore, 16 per cent BJP voters in the State said that they voted for BJP because Modi was its prime ministerial candidate.[9] This ability of Modi to decisively impact the electorate was also borne out by the response he received across the State during the campaign both during the LS elections and then in the Assembly elections.

Thus, both anti-incumbency and the 'Modi factor' contributed to the outcomes in 2014. Of course, three things combined against the Congress leading to most social sections deserting it in the 2014 elections. One is the long-term slow decline that the party was facing. This meant that the social base of the party was eroding and getting dispersed among different players from time to time over past two decades. The last chapter has shown this in the case of elections between 1999 and 2009. Two, quite a few locally powerful leaders from the Congress and NCP shifted their loyalties to the BJP, either in the wake of the LS election or afterwards. This facilitated the entry of the BJP in many Congress bastions in the State. Third, as a matter of routine political alternation that is bound to happen in electoral politics, the Congress was up against a long-term incumbency in 2014. Having been in power in the State since 1999, it was completing three terms in the State. Therefore, even in the absence of the so-called Modi wave, the BJP and SHS had a good chance of ousting the Congress–NCP government in the State.

But to explain the outcome, it is necessary to also look at the social configuration which made it possible for the BJP to emerge as the most preferred party in the State that has had a long tradition of deep-rooted Congress networks. Survey data helps us map the social bases of the four major players in the two elections that happened in quick succession in 2014. Tables 6.5–6.7 report the findings of the two surveys conducted after the LS and VS elections, respectively. As Table 6.5 shows, there is a flatness to the social profile of Congress and NCP voters. This means that no group is a stronghold of these parties; they tended to receive votes more or less equally from voters

[9] Source: CSDS Data Unit. Data for July 2013 and February 2014 was collected through the surveys conducted as part of the Lokniti Tracker Polls and data for post-poll survey was collected through NES 2014.

Table 6.5 *Party Choice by Gender, Age and Education: 2014*

	Congress		NCP		BJP+[a]		SHS	
	LS	VS	LS	VS	LS	VS	LS	VS
Gender								
Men	18	18	17	19	32	29	20	19
Women	19	18	15	16	30	29	22	20
Age								
18–25	18	18	13	19	31	27	28	22
26–35	20	18	16	18	32	29	20	21
36–45	19	18	11	18	36	31	20	18
46–55	17	14	18	18	29	28	19	18
56+	17	19	21	14	25	31	20	18
Education								
College	16	14	13	17	32	31	20	22
Matric	14	17	14	15	34	31	23	20
Primary	21	23	22	18	28	25	21	19
Non-literate	23	16	18	17	27	32	18	21

Source: NES 2014, N=1,790; State Assembly Study 2014, N=1,542.

Both the studies were conducted by the authors with Nitin Birmal and in collaboration with Lokniti—CSDS and Department of Politics and Public Administration, SPPU.

Note: [a]For LS, BJP includes its allies except SHS and for VS too, figures include BJP+.

Table 6.6 *Class and Vote: 2014*

	Congress		NCP		BJP+		SHS	
	LS	VS	LS	VS	LS	VS	LS	VS
Upper	16	16	21	12	33	36	19	20
Middle	16	17	15	20	29	29	26	20
Lower	20	19	17	17	34	28	19	20
Poor	19	19	15	14	28	28	17	19

Source: As per Table 6.5.

Table 6.7 *Caste–Community and Vote: 2014*

	Congress		NCP		BJP+		SHS	
	LS	VS	LS	VS	LS	VS	LS	VS
Upper Caste	8	16	7	10	51	52	19	9
Maratha-Kunbi	14	11	24	18	33	24	20	30
Peasant OBC	9	13	15	24	22	42	32	14
Other OBC	14	12	8	15	37	34	30	23
SC	25	28	17	17	20	19	16	13
ST	31	14	9	16	35	33	14	9
Muslims	71	53	13	16	6	13	—	11
Others	12	18	16	15	28	32	20	17

Source: As per Table 6.5.

of different age groups and educational attainments. Gender-wise too, they do not have much advantage among either men or women. Such flatness emerges either when a party's popularity skyrockets or when it dips—across social sections. Another feature of voters' social profile that emerges from Table 6.5 is the relative fragmentation of voters from most social groups. As a result, even while BJP does have an advantage among the less elderly and more educated voters, that advantage remains limited. The party did not perform extraordinarily well in any one social section. Like in the case of regions and rural–urban divisions, the appeal of Modi's leadership influenced many social sections and attracted them to vote for the BJP.

A somewhat sharper division emerges when we look at the class and caste–community base of the voters of different parties. While the profile of the Congress party remains somewhat flat, more voters from lower income groups voted for the party while in the case of the BJP, the rich and middle class constituted its main supporters. In the case of caste and community, the Congress was reduced to only receiving votes from STs, SCs and Muslims, and there too, it can be seen losing its grip on these communities as they got divided and a section voted for the BJP. The most striking feature of the social basis of BJP voters, however, was the extraordinary polarization of upper castes in favour of the BJP. As we discuss later, the story of Maratha vote is more complex: For quite some time, there has been a consistent fragmentation of Maratha vote and that is evident in the data for 2014 also. However, for the first time, more Maratha voters voted for the BJP and SHS than those who voted for the Congress and NCP together. In the LS election, the BJP gained from this surge among the Maratha voters to vote for it; in the Assembly elections, more Marathas voted for the SHS than for the BJP. The data for Assembly survey indicates that the success of the BJP hinged on the upper-caste and OBC alliance more than anything else.

EROSION OF THE CONGRESS'S SOCIAL BASE

Although the Congress and NCP were not very strong during the entire period following 1995, they could still manage limited electoral victories and even retain their power in 2004 and 2009. The massive victory of the BJP–SHS combine in 2014 brought to the forefront the inability of the Congress to now regain its erstwhile position in the State. This inevitably changed the rules of the game as far as State politics is concerned and hence political processes during 2014 brought the State onto the threshold of a new party system.

The more serious aspect of the defeat of the two Congress parties in the State in 2014 is about the rapid erosion of their support base among major social groups. As already discussed above, the BJP victory in Maharashtra was hugely supported by a drift of voters towards the BJP, which happened across different social sections. The BJP–SHS voter was still more likely to come more from the young, more educated, middle and higher-middle classes and also, most importantly, from those who are highly exposed to media. However, even the lower classes and those with lower level of education seem to have voted for the BJP–SHS in large numbers in both parliamentary and Assembly elections. Around a quarter of Dalit voters had supported the saffron alliance in the previous LS elections in 2009, whereas more than half of the Dalit voters (56%) preferred them in 2014. The BJP–SHS's support among the rural voters jumped up from 38 to 53 per cent in 2014. Strictly speaking, in terms of social support, the Congress and the NCP could compete with the saffron alliance only among the non-literates and among those who are not at all exposed to media. Otherwise, even among the elderly and the poor, the BJP–SHS alliance enjoyed a much-enhanced support in 2014.

The voting patterns among different communities during the Assembly elections also bring forward similar trends. Besides continued fragmentation of Maratha-Kunbi vote, and fragmentation among SC voters, there was a mild pro-BJP trend among Adivasis in these elections, while the Congress continued to enjoy support by Muslims. The Assembly elections in the State showed a massive consolidation of upper-caste and OBC vote in favour of BJP. In particular, the BJP got more support among peasant OBCs than rest of the OBCs. But the larger point emerging from the discussion of voter choices is about the erosion of Congress's base. The vote that the Congress party polled during 2014 lacked any social profile or sharp trend. The BJP and SHS may still continue to compete for the votes of different communities, but the Congress and NCP lost the capacity to craft a social base for themselves. Thus, the elections of 2014 took forward the process of decline of the Congress.

MARATHA VOTE

We have already noted above the loss of Maratha support for the Congress party. Fragmentation of the Maratha vote has been a big story of Maharashtra elections throughout the post-1990 period. It constitutes another feature of the erosion of the Congress support base in 2014 elections. But over and above that, this development suggests a crisis of what is known as 'Maratha politics'. More than half of the Maratha-Kunbi voters supported the BJP–SHS rather than the Congress–NCP alliance in the 2014 LS elections. Earlier also, 49 per cent of the Maratha-Kunbis had preferred the BJP–SHS over the Congress–NCP in the 2009 parliamentary elections. The elections in 2014 saw a consolidation of the Maratha support for the saffron alliance, and there was also an interesting mix of caste and class factors

Table 6.8 *Internal Divisions among Maratha-Kunbis (LS 2014)*

	Congress + NCP	BJP +SHS
Agriculturist Maratha-Kunbis	40	52
Maratha-Kunbis in non-agricultural occupations	33	46
Rich Maratha-Kunbis	44	43
Poor Maratha-Kunbis	40	39
Rural Maratha-Kunbis	42	48
Urban Maratha-Kunbis	25	51

Source: Deshpande and Birmal (2017; 147).

in this trend suggesting that Marathas may not be able to consolidate their power as a community anymore (Deshpande and Birmal, 2017; 146). As shown in Table 6.8, while the emerging divisions among the community do not necessarily operate as between rich and poor Marathas, their occupations and location matter in shaping—and fragmenting—their politics. Marathas having access to urban and non-agricultural resources seem to have favoured the BJP–SHS alliance more than the rural, agriculturist Marathas. This pattern jells well with the overall nature of social support to the BJP and SHS from the privileged groups. In the parliamentary elections, the internal divisions among Maratha-Kunbis did not play much role since it was a one-sided election.

However, Assembly elections threw up more complicated patterns of fragmentation among the Maratha-Kunbis (Palshikar, 2014). The SHS rather than the BJP benefited more from the Maratha vote. In the Assembly elections, it was able get a larger share of Maratha-Kunbi vote (29%) than the BJP (24%).

Maratha politics in Maharashtra had been in trouble over the past two decades before this election. The Marathas had somehow managed to retain power in the electoral arena (Palshikar and Birmal, 2003). And yet, the long surviving, complex patterns of Maratha dominance were challenged in several ways as we discuss in the next chapter. BJP's victory in 2014 elections further aggravated the crisis of the Marathas as the BJP attempted new social equations consisting of urban, upper-caste and OBC voters.

LIMITED RELEVANCE OF CASTE

But it is inaccurate to look at the crisis of Maratha politics in isolation. The continued fragmentation of the Maratha community and the arrival of the BJP in Maharashtra in 2014 may also be seen as a gradually unfolding shift from caste to class, as hinted in the previous chapter. In our earlier work (Palshikar et al., 2014), we had indicated the changing nature of caste-based voting patterns in Maharashtra in post-1990 period. During this period, not only Marathas but also each social section in the State was internally divided rather than becoming the strong base of any one political party. On the other hand, class emerges as a statistically significant factor for all parties (Palshikar et al., 2014). These observations have important implications for the politics of Marathas. Caste remains an inadequate but inevitable survival strategy for the Marathas and also for the other smaller castes as they are pushed into using the empty rhetoric of caste. At the same time, they are also forced to import the class content in their community politics. The campaign and the outcome of the 2014 of Assembly elections clearly bring forth these processes surrounding caste. While the Congress and the NCP played up the issue of Maratha reservations as an important issue in their election campaign, the BJP strived hard to bring to its fold leaders and voters of peasant and service OBC castes. The rise of Pankaja Munde within the BJP[10] and the party's appeals to the Vanjari community may be seen as a case in point. Indeed, upper castes and OBCs increasingly polarized behind the BJP. However, the nature of the Maratha vote cannot be explained only in terms of caste. In other words, the pattern of social support to different political parties in 2014 points to a transitory, fluid nature of processes of social realignment in the State's politics.

---

[10] *The Hindu*, BJP Banks on Munde's Daughter Pankaja, 9 October 2014, https://www.thehindu.com/news/national/other-states/BJP-banks-on-Munde%E2%80%99s-daughter-Pankaja/article11062503.ece (accessed on 15 June 2020).

'URBAN' RETURNS AGAIN

The 2014 elections discerned yet another trend which can be identified as the continuation of the earlier 'critical' election. This was the rise of the 'urban' factor in the politics of the State. We have dwelt on this issue in the discussion of 1995 election and the rise of BJP–SHS alliance. The 2014 election outcomes reinforced this shift and unfolded an important narrative in the contemporary politics of the State (Deshpande and Birmal, 2017; 148). After the latest delimitation exercise, a total number of 100 out of 288 Assembly constituencies became fully urban constituencies (Birmal and Bhoiwar, 2020; 378). As we will discuss in Chapter 8, the changing nature of the State's political economy has shaped a new 'urban' constituency in Maharashtra. This constituency was easily attracted to the developmental agenda put forward by the BJP and contributed to its electoral success in 2014. The BJP contested from 92 urban and 49 semi-urban Assembly constituencies. It won from 81 of these 141 constituencies, thus claiming victory in nearly 60 per cent of the urban constituencies. As against this, the party contested from 119 rural constituencies and could win only around 35 per cent (41 seats) of them. Among the urban voters of the State, 34 per cent supported the BJP, 17 per cent preferred the Congress, and 10 per cent supported the NCP, while 20 per cent voted for the SHS (Deshpande and Birmal, 2017; 149).

PARTY SYSTEM CHANGE?

In the last instance, elections of 2014 would have to be assessed as critical in terms of the changes they brought to the party system in the State (despite the anti-climax following the 2019 Assembly election which we discuss below). As already discussed at the beginning of this chapter, the immediate effect of the BJP victory in parliamentary elections of 2014 was that the coalitional system of political competition suddenly came under pressure. Although the BJP rode to a massive majority from the State along with its long-term alliance partner, the SHS, the BJP understood the outcome as its own success. This was not surprising for three reasons. One was that since 2004, there were tensions between the two partners and the BJP particularly believed that it had the potential to compete on its own power and that the SHS was an unnecessary burden (Palshikar et al., 2014; 144–148). The tenacity of Pramod Mahajan in dealing with the SHS chief Bal Thackeray had ensured the continuance of the coalition. Second, increasingly, the BJP must have felt that the SHS under Uddhav was not able to sustain the momentum and, as such, there was no advantage in further continuing the alliance. Third, in the specific context of 2014, the BJP understood the outcome as solely due to the 'Modi wave' and saw that moment as an opportunity to expand itself across the State. So, the BJP took a calculated risk and severed the alliance in the run up to the Assembly election of October 2014.

Parallel to this, there were deep-rooted tensions between the Congress and NCP (Palshikar et al., 2014; 149–150). The NCP saw itself as a party with a larger base than the Congress in Maharashtra; it also saw itself as indispensable to the Congress both in the State and nationally. Congress leadership in the State, on the other hand, always saw Pawar and the NCP as usurpers of the Congress legacy and an obstacle to the party in Maharashtra. Their alliance was purely out of the compulsion to ensure that both would get share in formal power in the State. For reasons of the history of State politics, the NCP was not enthusiastic about aligning with the BJP, and the Congress could not think of aligning with the SHS—at least not at that point! Hence, the two Congress parties needed each other lest the SHS–BJP combine sweep them out of reckoning. Therefore, defeat in 2014 LS and subsequent break-up of the SHS and BJP facilitated the end of Congress–NCP alliance. With this, party competition in the State assumed a multipolar dimension for the first time. At the same time, BJP's success in not just becoming the largest party in State Assembly but in coming very close to majority also meant that this multipolarity simultaneously brought in a new dominant player.[11] The compulsions that forced the SHS to cement its ties with the BJP in the aftermath of Assembly elections indicated this new dominance very starkly. The SHS was left with the only option of becoming one of the 'opposition

---

[11] This is comparable to the 'second dominant party system' emerging at the all-India level as argued by Palshikar (2017b).

parties' if it did not join the BJP-led government. Over the next four years, the SHS continued to provoke the BJP by being a partner and an opponent at the same time but the manner in which the BJP sustained this tactic and finally ensured that the SHS would come around and accept a pre-election alliance for 2019 parliamentary election further indicates the stabilizing dominance of the BJP.

A direct outcome of this emergent dominance of the BJP was that the competition got confined to lesser number of players per constituency. This election witnessed a narrowing of the main players in political competition, in terms of both votes and seats if we adopt the Taagepera–Shugart measure of competitiveness (Taageepera and Shugart, 1989, 77–91). In the case of the LS elections, the effective number of parties (in terms of votes) dropped to 5.6 from 7.1 in 2009 and 2.6 from 4.1 in 2009 in terms of seats. Table 6.9 shows the fluctuations in these figures for Assembly elections from 1962 onwards. When the dominance of the Congress was at its height, the ENP

Table 6.9 *Effective Number of Parties in Maharashtra Assembly*

Year	ENP/By Votes	ENP/By Seats
1962	3.6	1.5
1967	4.1	1.7
1972	3.0	1.5
1978	5.5	4.4
1980	3.9	2.3
1985	4.4	2.8
1990	5.0	3.3
1995	7.0	5.1
1999	5.7	4.7
2004	7.1	5.0
2009	8.2	5.6
2014	5.6	3.7
2019	6.7	4.4

Source: CSDS Data Unit.

used to be much smaller than during the period of Congress decline during 1989–2009. In this sense, 2014 comes close to the one-party dominance system.

A caveat is in order here: This dominance of the BJP in the State was disproportionately dependent on the success and popularity of Modi. In this sense, the new dominant party system that began shaping in the State post 2014 was based on reflected or borrowed dominance. Being in power at the State level further helped the party in gathering more and more dominance in terms of locally powerful leaders. At the same time, the way the BJP and the CM handled the Maratha agitation and pacified the Maratha youth definitely suggested that the State BJP was also about to gain dominance in its own right. In this sense, 2014 was not only about the defeat of the Congress party, but it was also about a new party system being ushered in through the dominance of one player and inability of others to counter that dominance between 2014 and 2019.

As we shall see further, although the BJP could not expand on this, elections of 2019 witness a firm grip of the BJP in State's politics despite its loss of governmental power due to vagaries of coalition politics.

ONWARD MARCH OF BJP: 2019

This detailed discussion of Maharashtra's second critical election shows that it had the potential to change the nature of State politics quite fundamentally. Compared to 1995, when a sudden change happened and then political system in the State relapsed into Congress rule once again, 2014 had the capacity to deepen the change. As a result, most of these trends continued and stabilized during the parliamentary election of 2019. The outcome of these elections indicated that the change that 2014 had brought about was not momentary but much deeper and long term in nature. In this sense, the second critical election has proved to be far more critical to reshaping of politics in the State. This process was exacerbated by the re-emergence of the BJP at the all-India level.

The parliamentary elections of 2019 indicated continued dominance of the BJP and yet Assembly election of 2019 threw up complications that not only tested the political skills of contesting parties but also put a question mark on the emergent dominance of the BJP.

Despite the continuous bickering between the SHS and BJP during the period 2014–2018, the two parties had managed to run the State government after bitterly fighting against each other in the 2014 Assembly election. As the parliamentary elections of 2019 approached, the BJP made up its mind to ensure that the SHS would be a part of its electoral alliance. Having been part of the coalition government in the State, the SHS also did not have much of an option but to agree to be part of the NDA for parliamentary elections. This development encouraged the two Congress parties to also form an alliance with a view to avoiding division of non-BJP votes. Thus, politics in the State returned to bipolarity once again. This meant that other smaller parties would have a limited role and space. Accordingly, most of the smaller parties chose to align with either of the two large coalitions. The PWP and Left parties did not opt for this, but the most notable exception to this was the new front formed by Prakash Ambedkar, leader of the BBM. He chose to float a broader platform, the VBA—a front of the deprived majority—and also tied up with Owaisi's AIMIM. In plain terms, this emerged as a major threat to all established calculations of caste–community configurations since the VBA–AIMIM could attract votes from three key social segments—the Dalits, OBCs and Muslims. If that happened, the worst sufferer could be the Congress–NCP, since they depended heavily on the votes by SCs and Muslims. On the other hand, if the VBA polled well among OBCs, it could ensure that those votes would not go to the Congress–NCP. So, either way, this was seen as a major setback to the Congress parties.

Another interesting development witnessed during 2019 parliamentary election from Maharashtra was the turnaround made by the MNS. Its leader, Raj Thackeray, had earlier praised Modi but after 2014,[12]

---

[12] *Times of India*, Raj Thackeray praises Narendra Modi, Says His Govt India's Best, 4 August 2011, http://timesofindia.indiatimes.com/india/Raj-Thackeray-praises-Narendra-Modi-says-his-govt-Indias-best/articleshow/9468326.cms (accessed on 8 July 2019). Raj Thackeray then had a good equation with the Gadkari faction within

he turned into a critic of Modi and the BJP. On the eve of the 2019 parliamentary election, efforts were made by the NCP, in particular, to bring MNS into the UPA alliance. While that did not materialize, the MNS chose not to contest the election but nevertheless campaigned vigorously in some parts of the State against the BJP and SHS. While the MNS campaign gave an impression that it could hurt the ruling coalition, in the end, the outcome was on similar lines of the 2014 election. Tables 6.10 and 6.11 give the details of this outcome, which only underscored the emerging trend since 2014—the ascendance of the BJP and its ability to ensure good fortune for its partner, the SHS. While the BJP polled on an average over 52 per cent votes in seats it contested, the SHS was also not far behind with 49 per cent votes in seats it contested. This gives an idea of the advantage gained by both the parties vis-à-vis their rivals. Given the fact that the BJP was in power both at the Centre and also in the State, this victory clearly indicated a positive vote in its favour. In fact, 43 per cent voters had probably made up their minds much before the campaign began and a large majority among them (Birmal and Deshpande, 2019; 29)[13], 58 per cent, ended up voting for the BJP–SHS alliance.[14] More than half the respondents in the post-election survey from the State were willing to give Modi government another chance and over two-thirds were satisfied with the performance of the State government and the same proportion were satisfied with the performance of the Central government (Deshpande and Birmal, 2019; 31). Like in 2014, the victory of the BJP (and SHS) was driven largely by the popularity of Modi. More than one among every five NDA voters (22%) said that they would have voted differently if Modi did not happen to be the PM

the BJP and hoped to have some role to play in the expanded NDA. But the SHS ensured that the MNS did not become an NDA partner (for more details on the MNS, see Palshikar, 2010). Even then, the MNS declared its intention to not only contest but also to support Modi in case MNS candidates won the election: *India Today*, Raj Thackeray Says He Will Support Narendra Modi for LS Polls, 26 March 2014, https://www.indiatoday.in/elections/highlights/story/will-support-narendra-modi-for-pm-says-mns-chief-raj-thackeray-184268-2014-03-09 (accessed on 27 June 2020).

[13] Birmal, N., & Deshpande, R., Replicating 2014, But with a Higher Vote Share, *The Hindu*, 29 May 2019, https://www.thehindu.com/elections/lok-sabha-2019/replicating-2014-but-with-a-higher-vote-share/article27277460.ece (accessed on 7 July 2019).

[14] Source: CSDS Data Unit for NES 2019.

Table 6.10 *LS Election Results: 2019*

Party	Seats Contested	Seats Won	Votes
BJP	25	23	27.6
SHS	23	18	23.3
INC	25	01	16.3
NCP	19	04	15.5
VBA[a]	47	00	6.9
AIMIM	01	01	0.7
SWP[b]	02	00	1.5
BSP	43	00	0.9
CPI	02	00	0.1
CPM	01	00	0.2
BVA[c]	01	00	0.9
SP	04	00	0.02
MSWP[d]	02	00	0.5
Other parties	302	00	1.0
IND	418	01	3.7
NOTA	—	—	0.9
Total	**915**	**48**	

Notes: [a]VBA.
[b]Swabhimani Shetkari Paksha.
[c]BVA.
[d]Maharashtra Swabhimani Shetkari Paksha.

candidate of the BJP. This proportion was almost 3 in every 10 voters (28%) for BJP voters.[15] This gives an idea of not only the popularity of the BJP leader but also how the election was turned into a plebiscite on Modi and as a result, like 2014, State-level competition was sidelined in favour of an all-India political context.

In the backdrop of this overall favourable political atmosphere and 'nationalization' of political competition, it is no surprise that

[15] Source: CSDS Data Unit for NES 2019.

Table 6.11 *Region-wise Results: LS Election, 2019*

Region	Seats	Turnout	Congress.		NCP		BJP		SHS		Others	
			Won	*Vote*	*Won*	*Vote*	*Won*	*Vote*	*Won*	*Vote*	*Won*	*Vote*
Mumbai–Thane	10	54.1	00	19.5	00	08.7	04	23.2	06	34.3	00	14.3
Konkan	03	61.0	00	01.9	01	30.1	00	00	02	49.6	00	18.4
North Maharashtra	06	61.5	00	18.3	00	13.8	05	46.9	01	08.3	00	12.7
Vidarbh	10	62.8	01	25.7	00	07.3	05	30.0	03	18.4	01	18.6
Marathwada	08	64.5	00	16.4	00	15.2	04	26.1	03	21.8	01	20.5
Western Maharashtra	11	62.6	00	08.0	03	25.3	05	26.7	03	21.8	00	18.2
Total	**48**	**61.0**	**01**	**16.3**	**04**	**15.5**	**23**	**27.6**	**18**	**23.3**	**02[a]**	**17.3**

Note: [a]Others include IND (1) and AIMIM (1).

most social sections turned towards the BJP and SHS alliance in large numbers. As Table 6.12 shows, the BJP and SHS were able to bridge the gap in their support among rural and urban areas. Similarly, while they had an overwhelming support among the upper castes, the more noteworthy feature of the findings of the post-election survey (as part of NES 2019) is that the BJP–SHS mustered almost equally high level of support among the OBCs. Together they outdid the Congress and NCP as far as Maratha support was concerned. In other words, the BJP–SHS brought together the upper, intermediate and OBC communities in 2019. With large proportion of farmers and the poor voters supporting the BJP–SHS alliance, these two parties managed to establish themselves not just as challengers to the Congress (and

Table 6.12 *Vote Share among Different Social Sections: LS Elections, 2019*

Social Group	Congress+	BJP+
Rural	35	49
Urban	33	54
Men	33	52
Women	36	49
Upper Castes	10	86
Marathas	39	56
OBCs	19	75
SCs	32	3
STs	53	34
Muslims	87	12
Buddhists	12	07
Poor	40	45
Rich	26	59
Farmers	31	54
Non-farmers	36	48

Source: Adapted from Deshpande and Birmal (2019; 31).

NCP) but also as the new political forces replacing the two traditionally important parties of the State.

The growing control of the BJP over the urban local bodies and over the local financial institutions along with its national-level clout had attracted many leaders of the Congress to its fold immediately after the parliamentary elections. The pragmatic attraction resulted in a large-scale exodus of the big and small Congress leaders into the BJP camp effectively neutralizing political opposition to the BJP ahead of the VS elections. And yet, the party ran a high-voltage campaign in the State. Even before the announcement of the Assembly elections, it had organized the Mahajanadesh Yatra (literally, a mega march for people's verdict) in order to showcase the achievements of the State government over the past five years. The official election campaign saw multiple rallies of many national leaders including the PM and the party president in order to make sure that the party wins a majority of seats on its own. Such aggressive campaigning has generally remained a trademark of BJP politics at the national-level and in all State-level elections so far. But in this case, it also indicated recognition to a somewhat shaky, contingent nature of BJP's dominance despite its electoral successes in the LS elections, as the election outcome was to testify.[16]

The LS election outcomes indicated effective control of the BJP–SHS alliance in 230 out of the total 288 VS constituencies. The trends did not materialize in the actual elections though and the alliance could win 161 seats in the State assembly in October 2019. The Congress–NCP alliance that had control over merely 44 VS constituencies, if one goes by the victories in LS elections, could significantly improve its performance by winning 98 seats. The real success for the Congress–NCP alliance came from the region of western Maharashtra. In the previous State Assembly elections held in 2014, the NCP had won 19 seats in this region. The tally increased by eight seats in 2019. The Congress also added two seats from this region. The BJP faced

[16] Deshapnde, R., In Pursuit of Complete Dominance, *The Hindu*, 19 October 2019, https://www.thehindu.com/opinion/lead/in-pursuit-of-complete-dominance/article29738480.ece (accessed on 25 June 2020).

major losses in the region of Vidarbh where its tally came down to 28 as against 44 in 2014. The BJP–SHS alliance was able to keep intact its control over the urban constituencies. However, the NCP under Sharad Pawar's leadership could attract the rural voters to the Congress fold in the 2019 VS elections (Birmal and Bhoiwar, 2020).

As expected, the SHS tried to assert its independent identity and also faced the wrath of the disgruntled elements within its own ranks as the VS elections approached. Internal factionalism was already rampant within the BJP. As discussed earlier, this aspect has more to do with the overall structuring of the contemporary party system in Maharashtra which is marred by the weak nature of party organization and lack of effective leadership. The organizational weakness combined with social and material frustrations of different social groups has resulted in localization and fragmentation of the party system. Political resurrection of the Raj Thackrey-led MNS, rise of VBA as a new political platform and the possible outbursts of suppressed political ambitions of political aspirants in each party contributed to the weaknesses of the party system.

One result of the uncertainty which marked the party system was the inability of the BJP to improve its position from 2014 and another was its inability to retain its alliance with the SHS after the Assembly elections. The BJP did not exactly lose the Assembly election, but it also couldn't exactly win these elections since its seat tally got reduced from 2014. It is also important to bear in mind that the BJP polled over 44 per cent votes in seats it contested—highest among all the parties. The SHS and NCP both polled a little over 38 per cent in the seats that they contested tagged by the Congress which polled a little under 33 per cent votes. In other words, the overall performance of the BJP indicates its relatively firm grip on the electoral process. Like in the times of Congress's dominance, the BJP could not expand its dominance adequately across the State as can be seen from Table 6.13.

It is another matter that the inability of the BJP to actually win a majority on its own put it in a difficult position vis-à-vis its partner, the SHS. Sensing an opportunity, the SHS stuck to its demand for the

Table 6.13 *Region-wise Results: Assembly Elections, 2019*

Region	Seats	Turnout	Congress		NCP		BJP		SHS		Others	
			Won	Vote	Won	Vote	Won	Vote	Won	Vote	Won	Vote
Mumbai–Thane	60	50.5	04	13.8	04	07.5	24	24.3	20	23.7	08	30.7
Konkan	15	64.2	00	05.3	02	16.4	03	13.7	09	38.8	01	25.8
North Maharashtra	35	62.38	05	13.9	06	20.2	14	26.4	06	15.8	04	23.7
Vidarbh	62	62.6	15	25.7	07	7.6	28	32.1	04	07.2	08	27.5
Marathwada	46	66.4	08	16.2	08	18.3	16	23.8	12	17.0	02	24.7
Western Maharashtra	70	65.0	12	11.7	27	27.3	20	24.2	05	15.5	06	21.0
Total	**288**	**61.4**	**44**	**15.9**	**54**	**16.7**	**105**	**25.7**	**56**	**16.5**	**29**[a]	**25.2**

Note: [a]Others include IND (13), BVA (03), 2 each for AIMIM, SP and Prahar Janshakti Party and 1 each for MNS, JSS, Krantikari Shetkari Party, PWP, RSP, SWP and CPI(M).

position of the CM which the BJP did not agree to. This disagreement opened up the doors for political calculations for isolating the BJP. After a surreptitious attempt on its part to win over a faction of the NCP led by Ajit Pawar, in order to be able to form a government, the BJP had to accept defeat when the SHS, having severed its ties with the BJP, joined hands with the NCP and the Congress to rule the State. These developments not only underlined the volatility of the post-Congress, regional party system in Maharashtra but also highlighted the still shaky nature of dominance of the BJP in the politics of the State (Deshpande and Birmal, forthcoming). In isolating the BJP, the Congress and NCP certainly scored over the BJP and in ensuring that they would return to power, they also grabbed one more opportunity to control structures and resources of the State. However, setting aside this advantage, it is not easy to shake off the fact that the BJP did retain its overall hold over the electorate.

In both the parliamentary and State Assembly elections, BJP's support came from a range of social groups, and the overall support for the two Congress parties was seen to be shrinking. And yet, as Table 6.14 shows, the Congress in Maharashtra could retain, at least to some extent, its earlier identity as a party of the poor and marginalized. The Congress alliance kept intact its support among the Adivasis, although a sizeable section from among them favoured the BJP and its allies. Despite the entry of the AIMIM in the politics of the State, the Congress alliance remained a popular choice among the Muslims. The AIMIM support was concentrated only in one LS constituency where it probably benefited from the Dalit votes as well. Growing internal differentiation within the Dalit votes was evident in the LS as well as VS elections. The polarization of Dalit voters along caste and religious identities was witnessed in the past elections as well. With the entry of the VBA in the 2019 elections, the internal divisions among Dalit voters surfaced clearly. The Buddhist voters predominantly voted for non-Congress, non-BJP parties, whereas the other Dalit castes had moved away from the Congress and voted for the NDA. Along with the Dalits, the BJP–SHS alliance also received significant gains among the OBCs.

Table 6.14 *Vote Share among Different Social Sections: Assembly Elections, 2019*

Social Group	Congress+	BJP+	Others[a]
Rural	36	41	23
Urban	31	55	14
Men	35	42	23
Women	31	42	27
Upper Castes	16	53	31
Marathas	35	46	19
OBCs	28	48	24
Adivasis	27	46	27
Muslims	54	15	31
Dalits	28	35	37
Poor	31	39	30
Rich	40	39	21

Source: 'Citizen Assessment of Governance and Welfare', Centre for Public Policy and Democratic Governance (CPPDG), SPPU.[17]

Note: [a]This was a pre-election survey conducted 15 days before the date of polling. As a result, a large number of citizens were undecided regarding their voting preferences. Nevertheless, the trends are useful to estimate how different sections may have actually voted in the Assembly election; N = 1,669.

Maratha fragmentation continued even in these elections, as more Marathas voted for the BJP–SHS alliance than the Congress parties in parliamentary as well as Assembly elections of 2019. Between the two partners of the saffron alliance, the SHS benefited more among the Marathas and so did the NCP from the other alliance. The BJP, on the other hand, mobilized OBCs when it provided candidature to major caste communities from among the OBCs.

---

[17] The study 'Citizen Assessment of Governance and Welfare' was conducted by the CPPDG established at SPPU, Pune, under the RUSA (IInd phase) research grant. The study was coordinated by Rajeshwari Deshpande, Nitin Birmal and Vivek Ghotale.

The tentative nature of social coalitions and the element of competitiveness in the regional party system in Maharashtra kept in check BJP's aspirations to acquire a more dominant role in Maharashtra's politics than in 2014—and that too, on its own. The outcome of the LS elections set in motion a transition in Maharashtra that establishes the State firmly within the BJP fold. But as the VS election outcome showed, it still remains a challenge for the BJP to establish and retain its complete dominance in the politics of the State. As a result, the BJP's ambition of *shat pratishat Bhajapa*[18] (cent per cent BJP) in Maharashtra remained an incomplete project in the 2019 elections (Deshpande and Birmal, forthcoming).

CONCLUSIONS

This chapter suggests that the BJP came close to becoming the dominant party in 2019, albeit with three differences.

First, it was not able yet to post a victory on its own. It is possible that the BJP may have won handsomely even if it did not align with the SHS, but having entered into an alliance with the SHS, BJP had to curtail its ambition to become the dominant party in the State—at least the test of that dominance had to be postponed. Second, even in times of its rising power, the BJP was still away from becoming another Congress. It did accommodate a large number of important Maratha leaders from the Congress and NCP in both 2014 and 2019. In 2019, it managed important victory morally and, in optic terms, over the Congress and NCP. Son of the (then) leader of opposition in Assembly, Sujay Vikhe-Patil, joined the BJP on the eve of election and was given ticket too. His father, Radhakrishna Vikhe-Patil, subsequently joined the BJP postelection. Similarly, an important NCP family from Solapur district, Mohite-Patils, joined the BJP before the election, while

---

[18] Despite its alliance with the SHS, the State BJP for long aimed at doing it alone and capturing power on its own. This is often described as *shat pratishat Bhajapa,* that is, cent per cent BJP in power. See *The Indian Express,* BJP Reverts to '100%' Mantra Ahead of Local Polls, 9 January 2015, https://indianexpress.com/article/cities/mumbai/bjp-reverts-to-100-mantra-ahead-of-local-body-polls/ (accessed on 15 June 2020).

following the parliamentary election, a prominent Adivasi leader of the NCP Madhukar Pichad and his son Vaibhav also joined the BJP. Nevertheless, during the parliamentary election of 2019, the BJP was still not able to comfortably win support of the Maratha community despite having successfully assigned them the status of socially and economically backward class. Third, it was not sure by 2019 whether the BJP was going to enjoy a hegemony as it did in Gujarat or even MP (despite its defeat there in the Assembly election).

In a sense, developments of 2014–2019 draw our attention back to 1995 once again. In 1995, the Congress still had possibilities of regaining itself, but 2014 left very little space for rebuilding the party in the State—if being in power in the State helps the Congress in post-2019 scenario is a puzzle that only time will resolve. In 1995, the defeat of Congress was the main story; in 2014, the rise of the BJP was the central theme. In 1995, there was a power balance between the SHS and BJP; in 2014—and again in 2019, the SHS simply had to drag itself unwillingly along with the BJP (and later, with the two Congress parties). If we compare 2014 and 2019 with 1995, it becomes clear that since 2014, party competition begins to move closer to the all-India pattern of 'second dominant party system' (Palshikar, 2017b) and the outcome of both elections of 2019 also witnessed the continuation of that tendency. How far being away from State-level power will adversely affect the BJP's chances to retain this advantage is of course a riddle because the exercise of power is indeed a key factor in retaining and expanding dominance. To the extent its opponents have managed to keep it out of power, they might have arrested the dominance of the BJP.

Do these developments mean that the eclipse of bipolar competition was momentary or that rise of a new dominant party system was becoming a real possibility—in comparison to 1995? We shall turn to these issues in the last chapter.

The Crisis of Maratha Politics

Although politics had already assumed a more competitive turn since the 1990s, as we saw in the last chapter, it became much more complex and competitive from the 2014 elections onwards. As noted earlier, elections since 2004 saw fragmentation of Maratha vote across the four main political parties. During this period, the BJP employed an ambitious strategy to expand its social base in the State. It tried to manufacture an alternative to Maratha dominance on the basis of a possible social alliance of the upper castes and the OBCs. However, the party also could not afford to altogether neglect the numerically dominant Maratha community and had to resort to balancing mechanisms in order to keep at least some sections of the Marathas within its fold. The two Congress parties also faced a similar problem. As the political space available to them shrunk, neither the Congress nor the NCP was able to hold on to their traditional support bases. And yet, they relied heavily on the Maratha support instead of looking for new social allies. As a result, the social support base of the Congress and the NCP remained weak and contingent in post-2004 electoral politics.

This is also the period when politics of Maratha community also entered a more critical phase. While some dimensions of that crisis have been discussed in the preceding chapters, this chapter will attempt to bring together the overall narrative of crisis of Maratha politics not only in terms of party politics but also in terms of its identity and the threat of loss of its long-held hegemony.

CONTEXT OF THE CRISIS

The political crisis of Marathas did not begin in 2014 or even in 2004. It goes back a long way to the decade of the 1970s and is rooted in the first shocks to the congress system in the State. As we saw earlier, the crisis became evident in the 1990s. Maratha politics has been in flux since then. At the formal level, the Marathas managed to retain power in the electoral arena (Palshikar and Birmal, 2003) and the Maratha leaders continued to occupy most of the key political positions in State politics (Datar and Ghotale, 2013; Ghotale and Kulkarni, 2019). However, at the more intricate levels of political competition, the long surviving, complex patterns of Maratha dominance stand challenged in several ways.

First, the internal power sharing mechanisms among the different Maratha factions are broken. There is a dispersal of Maratha elites and the voters resulting in an evident leadership crisis. Second, the Marathas have not been able to project a cohesive political identity of the community. A combination of factors is at work here. Internal economic stratification within the community, distancing between elite Marathas and the masses and their constant political splintering have all contributed to the identity crisis of the Marathas. As the community split internally, the need to showcase a unified caste identity became an urgent necessity for the Marathas. It has resulted in complex patterns of Maratha identity politics. The third dimension of the Maratha crisis is economic. Marathas have essentially been an agrarian community. Despite their diversification into other occupations over the years, a large number of Maratha families are still dependent on agriculture. Naturally, the agrarian crisis in India in general and in Maharashtra in particular had a huge impact on Maratha lives as sections of the community suffered economically. These sufferings, along with the growing internal economic stratification within the community, have resulted in a material crisis for the Marathas. Their growing material anxieties along with the cracks in communal solidarity and political splintering have led to a sense of loss of power and to a deeper indication of loss of the longstanding Maratha hegemony (Deshpande and Palshikar, 2017).

The State-specific context of Maratha politics that we discuss here spills over to the all-India context of patterns of caste–politics interaction in shaping the politics of 'dominant castes' over the years. The caste dominance, as it shaped along with the structuring of Indian democracy, had three noteworthy aspects to it. The first was the idea of internal homogeneity. This was linked to the claims of numerical strength of any caste. As the idea of representative democracy gradually unveiled, initially in the 1920s and later in the 1950s, numerical strength of castes became an important aspect of representative claims on behalf of castes. Internal homogeneity helped in making such claims. The bolstering of numerical strength became an important part of the transfer of power from upper castes to the middle peasant castes in the post-independence period in many states. The other aspect of caste dominance was about acceptance of a caste's leadership by other caste communities. This may be called as the criteria of external acceptability of the caste dominance. As a result, the caste rule gained legitimacy in the new democratic set-up. The third element of caste dominance—as it shaped in the democratic set up—was the extent of a community's control over material resources. In case of the Marathas we see an effective combination of the above three elements at work as their political role unfolded in the regional politics of Maharashtra.

As discussed in the first chapter, Maratha dominance in Maharashtra shaped initially when a well-knit Congress system evolved during the 1950s and the 1960s. This process of shaping of Maratha hegemony has been discussed in detail by the earlier studies of Maratha politics (Lele, 1982b, 1990a; Vora, 1994, 2009) These studies document how the Maratha hegemony was a combination of three main factors. The first was the numerical preponderance of the Marathas. Second, their control of material resources in the form of landownership also contributed to their dominance. Third, the Marathas could make use of a historically nurtured sense of identity in Maharashtra.

The Maratha-Kunbi caste cluster is estimated to constitute nearly 30 per cent of Maharashtra's population.[1] In none of the other Indian States does any single caste community enjoy numeric preponderance to such an extent.[2] The Marathas in Maharashtra are spread in all regions of the State, although they have a more significant presence in

[1] Caste or castegroup population shares are only estimates partly derived from the data of 1931 Census. Except in the case of SCs and STs, for no other caste or caste group is there official data available so far.

[2] Haryana comes close with Jats having around 25 per cent share in State population (Yadav, 2003; 146).

the regions of Marathwada and western Maharashtra. It is obviously a highly stratified caste cluster. Most members of this caste cluster are peasant cultivators. However, historically, it reached up to feudal aristocrats and rulers. Compared to other similar peasant–warrior caste clusters in other parts of the country, Marathas showed a greater degree of unification and a greater absorptive power (Deshpande, 2007).

As we discussed in the first chapter, along with the collective historical memory of Maharashtra, the idea of *Bahujan Samaj* popularized by Y. B. Chavan in the 1960s helped the Marathas as an important part of the legitimating ideology of their dominance. The idea of *Bahujan Samaj* had its origins in the discourse of the non-Brahman movement of the pre-independence period (Gore, 1989; Kulkarni, 1991). As is well known, the movement had put forward a case of discrimination against the non-Brahman castes at the hand of the Brahmans and the Brahmanical social frameworks and was active in Tamil Nadu and Karnataka along with Maharashtra. The politics of the non-Brahman movement and its claims of social backwardness of the non-Brahman castes subsequently acquired different tones in the politics of these States. The Lingayats in Karnataka, for example, used the legacies of the movement to demand official backward status to the community in the early post-independence period. Tamil Nadu witnessed mainstreaming of the backward caste politics initially under the leadership of the Justice Party and that of the Dravidian parties later on.

The Marathas in Maharashtra chose a different route. In order to ensure an almost hegemony like acceptance of their political domination, the Marathas used the legacies of the non-Brahman movement. The legacy helped them take over the political initiative from the Brahmans. It also contributed to the political construction of a numerically strong caste cluster of Marathas and Kunbis. More importantly, the non-Brahman legacy helped in establishing the Marathas as natural leaders of the Shudra masses. At this level, the appropriation of the non-Brahman legacy facilitated an ideological construct of Maratha leadership. Finally, it was also used to maintain non-antagonistic relations of Marathas with other sections of the society. These successful appropriations of legacy of non-Brahman movement helped the Marathas to establish their status as a natural ruling community.

And the politics of backwardness initially articulated by the non-Brahman movement subsided in the post-independence politics of the Marathas. In other words, the Marathas could manipulate the shared idea of backwardness to gain a more robust hold over the regional polity without obviously resorting to it (Deshpande, 2014a). Marathas were forced to abandon these strategies during the 1990s when their political and material desperations became unmanageable. That is when they openly resorted to claims of backwardness on behalf of the community. We will return to this discussion later in this chapter.

CHALLENGE SINCE THE 1970S

The helpful arrangements for Marathas in political as well as socio-economic arenas were unsettled for the first time in the early 1970s. Maratha leaders in Maharashtra felt the tremors of Indira Gandhi's politics at that time when she sought to destabilize the State-level leadership. As we discussed in the second chapter, Indira Gandhi's takeover of the Congress leadership at all-India level marked the beginning of the end of the congress system. In Maharashtra, this signalled the beginning of gradual decline of the dominance of Marathas. It was only the beginning though. Because, although the Congress as well as the Marathas were torn into factions, they could maintain their hold over the State politics. In subsequent years, internal factionalism produced further cracks in Maratha domination.

The results of 1977 elections in Maharashtra amply showcased the factionalism within the State Congress (Vora et al., 1983). Indira loyalists contested elections against the established Maratha lobby in the 1978 Assembly elections as well. A key reason why Marathas could still manage to control formal power at the State level was the absence of a non-Maratha alternative. While Sharad Pawar did break away from Indira Gandhi-led Congress, the core basis of his politics was not different from what the State Congress always enjoyed—the Maratha community. Karnataka (Manor, 1989) witnessed mobilization of backward castes as a counterpoint to dominant caste politics during this period. This was not the case in Maharashtra. In Maharashtra, political contestations mainly took the form of internal conflicts of

Maratha factions. In this sense, even during this first phase of the crisis, Maratha hegemony suffered cracks but was not challenged. While Indira Gandhi did try to bring in non-Maratha elements to the forefront of State politics after 1980, that did not succeed, and she had to settle for a Maratha faction that agreed to work under her leadership. On the other hand, Pawar also primarily focused on winning over the Maratha factions and shape his party's (ICS) politics in the mould of older congress politics. These developments postponed the crisis and breakdown of the system of Maratha dominance, but the hegemony of the Maratha community came under stress.[3]

Since the early 1980s, Marathas tried various political vehicles while responding to this stress and impending crisis. Initially, it was the Shetkari Sanghatana led by Sharad Joshi (Lenneberg, 1988; Omvedt, 1993). Marathas were obviously an important part of the farmers movement in the State (Deshpande, 2004). Later on, the SHS mobilized Maratha youths—especially from the more backward regions like Vidarbh, Marathwada and Konkan (Palshikar, 2004). These developments weakened both the Congress party and the dominance of the Marathas during the 1990s.

NUMERICAL PREPONDERANCE

In our discussion of electoral politics in the 1990s in Chapter 4, we have already pointed out the declining fortunes of the Congress, rise of the 'rebel' factor and finally the split in the party yet again, when the NCP emerged in 1999. All these developments dovetail with the fragmentation of Maratha politics. Table 7.1 shows that since 1999,

---

[3] In this context, it is noteworthy, as we shall discuss below, that the Maratha Mahasangh, a leading caste organization of the Marathas established in 1981, vehemently opposed the reservation policy till 1985 and took great pride in their anti-Dalit rhetoric (Pawar, 1996). The same organization was in the forefront in aggressively articulating the Maratha claims of backwardness in the more recent times. The altered tone of Maratha politics in the early 1990s indicated the initial troubles for this dominant caste. The troubles were both about their political anxieties and the material frustrations. These combined frustrations gave rise to complex narratives of deprivation and domination, leading to the politics of backwardness. As a part of this politics, Marathas tried to appropriate State resources for their political survival and also for re-assertions of their dominance in nuanced ways.

Table 7.1 *Maratha Vote by Party since 1999: LS and VS Elections*

	LS 1999	VS 1999	LS 2004	VS 2004	LS 2009	VS 2009	LS 2014	LS 2019	VS 2019
Congress + NCP	52	47	30	35	34	35	39	39	35
BJP + SHS	44	34	57	38	49	30	51	57	46

Source: Palshikar et al. (2014; 440–441) and Deshpande and Birmal (2019; 31).

Maratha vote has been rather badly divided between the Congress and NCP on the one hand and the SHS and BJP on the other.[4]

Despite their dispersal across parties and despite the changes in the nature of the party system, the formal political power still remained with the Marathas during the 1990s and beyond. In almost all State Assembly elections, Marathas were able to secure around 50 per cent of seats in the legislature. Datar and Ghotale (2013) studied the social and regional profile of the Maharashtra Cabinet. The study shows that Maratha leaders, and more prominently those from the region of western Maharashtra continue to retain key positions of power within the Cabinet. We studied the profile of candidates in LS and Assembly elections in Maharashtra during 1999–2019.[5] As shown in Table 7.2, on an average, 40 per cent of the candidates of main political parties contesting Assembly elections during this period belonged to the

[4] In 1999 and 2014 Assembly elections, the Congress and NCP were not in an alliance with each other; similarly, in 2014 Assembly elections, the BJP and SHS were not in an alliance. Their votes among Marathas are shown together in Table 7.1 to give a sense of continued division of Maratha vote.

[5] The candidate profile studies were conducted by the authors in association with Nitin Birmal and Vivek Ghotale. The studies in the year 1999, 2004, 2009 and 2014 were supported by Special Assistance Programme of the Centre of Advanced Study (SAP-CAS) of UGC at the Department of Politics and Public Administration, SPPU. The 2019 studies were supported by the Center fro Public Policy and Democratic Governance (CPPDG) at SPPU established under RUSA. We collected information of candidates of the main four political parties of the State, namely Congress, BJP, SHS and NCP in each VS constituency and also the other politically important IND candidates and candidates of smaller parties whenever relevant. The N for each study was as follows: 1999 (656), 2004 (555), 2009 (1,006), 2014 (1,276) and 2019 (1,028).

Table 7.2 *Caste Composition of Candidates of Major Parties: 1999–2014*

	1999	2004	2009	2014	2019
Brahmans + Upper Castes	04	07	04	05	06
Marathas	30	41	33	32	27
Kunbis	11	10	06	13	07
Dalits	13	09	18	12	23
Adivasis	09	08	09	10	09
Peasant OBC	20	11	14	23	11
Artisan OBC	01	02	02	02	01
Service OBC	06	04	03	03	07

Source: See Note 5; compiled by the authors.

Note: Column percentages do not add up to 100 as only select caste categories are reported in the table.

Maratha-Kunbi caste cluster.[6] Their share rose up to more than half of the candidates in the 2004 and 2014 elections. In all these elections, the OBCs got a share in candidatures roughly equal to their proportion in the State's population. However, even in the post-Mandal phase, there was no gradual increase in the number of OBC candidates in the State's elections. Among the OBCs, we see an overwhelming presence of the relatively dominant peasant OBC castes. There is a significant jump in the number of Kunbi candidates between 2009 and 2014. As we will discuss further, this was the period in which Maratha politics of reservations had gained momentum and the attempts to fuse Maratha and Kunbi identities were encouraged both by the Maratha organizations and by the State government (Deshpande, 2004). Although formally included in the list of OBCs, Kunbis always shared close affinities with the Marathas rather than the other OBC castes. In the light of both these factors, it is possible to suggest that the surge in number of Kunbi candidates in the 2014 elections could be attributed to the shifting official identities of the Marathas. Figures for 2019

[6] That is why in his studies of the social profile of elected representative from Maharashtra, Vora (2009) asks a question: Whether it is 'Maharashtra or a Maratha Rashtra?'

throw up a little different pattern, both pertaining to decline in the number of candidates from Maratha-Kunbi caste cluster and rise in the candidates belonging to SCs. However, this is mainly because the study included candidates of the VBA which fielded many candidates from OBC and SC background.

Anderson et al. (2016) conducted a large-scale household survey in three regions of Maharashtra to study patterns of political representation of Marathas in the local self-government institutions. They observed that if Marathas are present in a village, they almost always fill the gram pradhan (sarpanch; elected chief of village panchayat) position if the position is not mandatorily reserved for the lower castes. Maratha caste comprised roughly 38 per cent of the population in their sample. However, Marathas occupied 63 per cent of the unreserved gram pradhan positions (Anderson et al., 2016; 15). These gram pradhans were typically larger landowning cultivators.

Using these micro-level studies, Anderson et al. (2016) and Kotwal et al. (2015) argue how Maratha elites appropriate the democratic space locally even today. They use the framework of clientelism to explain the continued dominance of Marathas in local politics. In his analysis of the 2014 elections in Maharashtra in the context of sub-regional variations and local power structures, Bagchi (2019) also points to continued dominance of Marathas through import to other political parties. These studies provide important empirical data for understanding the contemporary Maratha situation. However, our main concern here is not about the strategies adopted for continuing local dominance, but rather the State-level response from the community and its leaders to the growing challenges to Maratha hegemony. Also, we suggest that in order to explain the growing scale of frustrations among Marathas since the 1990s, we need to move beyond the realm of elections. Instead, we locate the Maratha crisis in the changing nature of political economy of the State. Electoral politics tended to camouflage the Maratha sense of frustration and crisis, but developments outside the electoral arena unmistakably point to the multiple crises—of power, identity and community's well-being—that haunted the Maratha community, leading to their uneven responses resulting in continued share in formal power and yet hollowing of hegemony.

ANATOMY OF MARATHA CRISIS

The 1990s symbolized a moment for Indian democracy in which the formal realm of democratic politics was slowly delegitimized in the wake of new economic policies and the arrival of discourse of globalization (Harriss, 2001). This moment had several repercussions on patterns of State and local politics. Bureaucrats, social technocrats and corporate sector largely controlled the decision-making process, and the elected representatives were sidelined. Politics was reduced to management and appropriation of limited resources at the local level and thus forced politicians to become mere contractors. We discuss the impact of new economic policies of the 1990s on Maharashtra's regional political economy in the next chapter. The point here is that these changes seriously jeopardized the status of Marathas as a ruling community and injured their sense of pride.

The changing nature of the regional political economy of the 1990s also had a deep impact on the economic condition of the Marathas and led to anxieties of the community over material concerns. As mentioned in Chapter 3, the State of Maharashtra embraced policies of economic liberalization since the late 1980s. The policies advocated commercialization of agriculture that benefited only a few. This was also a phase of rapid industrial expansion in and outside of Mumbai. In the earlier phases of industrial expansion, the rulers had tried to maintain a balance between the agrarian and industrial sectors. The balance was lost in the new drive of industrialization and the subsequent expansion of the service sector. The capitalist development in Maharashtra became more skewed during this time. This was in terms of both neglect of agriculture and regional imbalances (we discuss the details of the skew in the next chapter).

How did this affect the Maratha community? Despite their strong political position, the nature of material domination of the Maratha community has always remained open to examination. Marathas dominated the agrarian resources and had also built an elaborate institutional mechanism to protect and further their material interests in the form of cooperatives (Damodaran, 2008; 216–223; Vora, 1994). Nevertheless, it always shaped within the context of industrial capitalism, and the latter had an upper hand over Maratha interests. In this sense, the Marathas could never effectively dominate the economy of the State fully; on the contrary, they had to take a secondary position vis-à-vis the industrial capitalists. Although sections of Maratha elite could enter the modern urban sectors—both industrial and the service sectors—majority of the Maratha community remained trapped in agriculture. Besides, with the advancement of liberalization, urban interests dominated political decision-making and added to the existing imbalances (Vora, 1996; 172). This process symbolized a decoupling of political power from material power where formal political positions did not have a substantive connect with the operation of dominant material interests (Deshpande and Palshikar, 2017; 88). As a result, the Maratha elite could no more claim that they could divert the flow of material resources to their followers in the rural areas.

Rapid expansion of the industrial, urban centres definitely encouraged migration of the young Marathas among others to the cities. However, they did not have access to urban resources for various reasons. There were only a few elite Maratha families who could invest in large industrial projects in urban as well as rural areas. The ordinary Maratha youth lacked skills and training required for the industrial sector. Maharashtra saw a disproportionate expansion of the service sector and the IT industry in the 1990s (Bhandari and Kale, 2007; 28–33). Brahmans monopolized high-profile jobs in these sectors. However, the young Marathas could not compete with them. They entered into lower-rung service sector jobs or were mostly accommodated in the sundry networks of the informal economy. With the privatization mantra, the public sector opportunities were already shrinking when young Marathas began to aspire for them through State Public Service Commission examinations. At all these levels, the Marathas could not claim adequate access to urban economic resources and thus developed a deep sense of relative deprivation.

A similar narrative shaped in other States too. Just like the Marathas, a large section of the Lingayats of Karnataka also remained trapped in the agricultural sector and did not have enough access to urban resources (Deshpande, 2014a; 178). Jaffrelot and Kalaiyarasan (2019; 29–36) discuss a similar predicament of Jats in Haryana. The Patidars of Gujarat also joined the chorus in 2015 when the Gujarat model of development did not prove to be inclusive enough to cater to their ambitions (Shah, 2015).[7] The expansion of capitalist market in the regional political economies in the post-1991 phase was essentially linked to educational attainments and acquisition of skills. It was also about a rapid delinking of the agricultural and non-agricultural sectors resulting in a disproportionate dependence on the service sector of the economy. Primarily, agrarian castes such as Marathas, Jats or Patidars could not gain entry into these expanding economic sectors due to their lack of skills and education.

Jaffrelot and Kalaiyarasan (2017)[8] have used the Indian Human Development Survey (IHDS) data[9] to gauge the current socio-economic status of Marathas and other similarly placed caste communities. The 2011–2012 round of this data clearly reflects the rural character of the Marathas. As per this survey, 43 per cent of the Marathas had reported cultivation to be their main source of income as against 32 per cent of the OBCs and 10 per cent of the SCs. No doubt that the Marathas are better off compared to OBCs and SCs in terms of per capita income; they are second only to the Brahmans (₹36,548 against ₹47,427 for Brahmans). However, as stated earlier, Marathas are highly differentiated in socio-economic terms. As per the IHDS data, the top 20 per cent of the Marathas get 48 per cent of the total income of the caste group with a mean per capita income of ₹86,750. On the other hand, the lowest strata among them earn 10 times less. In other words, the lowest 40 per cent of the Marathas get less than 13 per cent of the total income of the caste and lag behind the SC elite in Maharashtra.

As per the NES data of 2004 for the State of Maharashtra, more than 70 per cent Maratha-Kunbis lived in villages. After more than a decade,

[7] Shah, G., The Shrinking, the Rage, *The Indian Express,* 28 August 2015, https://indianexpress.com/article/opinion/columns/the-shrinking-the-rage/ (accessed on 25 May 2020).

[8] Jaffrelot, C., & Kalaiyarasan, A., Quota Is the Wrong Answer, *The Indian Express*, 3 May 2017, https://indianexpress.com/article/opinion/columns/quota-is-the-wrong-answer-4637872/ (accessed on 25 May 2020).

[9] The IHDS was conducted by the National Council of Applied Economic Research (NCAER) in collaboration with the University of Maryland.

in 2019, the share of rural Marathas was only marginally less than 2004, at 67 per cent.[10] NES data also indicates the internal economic stratification within Marathas. As per the 2004 NES data, more than 50 per cent of Marathas were engaged in agricultural activities. Among them, around 20 per cent worked as landless labourers. In 2019, the share of agriculturist Marathas remained the same. However, the per centage of agricultural labourers among them went up to 35 per cent. The rural rich Marathas accounted for hardly 3 per cent of the sampled families. These realities resonate with the IHDS data in pointing to a possible skew within the community which makes it more difficult for the Marathas to claim a cohesive community identity.[11]

Micro-level studies in two Maratha-dominant villages in Maharashtra confirm these trends. A socio-economic household study was conducted in two villages from Marathwada and western Maharashtra region in 2013. The study shows internal economic divisions among Marathas. The land ownership pattern in these villages suggests that nearly two-thirds of the Maratha families are poor. 12 per cent families were landless. Hardly 5 per cent could be classified as rich farmers with more than 20 acres of land. 40 per cent of the Maratha families in villages under study owned less than 5 acres of land, and this was in addition to another 20 per cent of them who had less than 2 acres of land under their possession. Landless agricultural labourers constituted 10 per cent of the total number of Maratha families engaged in agriculture (for details, see Ghotale, 2017; 83–121; also see Deshpande and Palshikar, 2017; 89). These details underline the deep economic divisions between poor and rich Marathas in rural Maharashtra. The village studies also indicate regional disparities of Maratha existence. One of the villages we studied is located in western Maharashtra, while the other one is from Marathwada. While both villages replicate the internal economic stratification within the community, Maratha families in the village from Marathwada (Khuntegaon) are poorer than those from Randhe in western Maharashtra. Around 10 per cent of Maratha families in Randhe do not own any agricultural

[10] The number of Maratha respondents in the sample was 486 in 2004 and 315 in 2019.

[11] Although N is smaller, we mention this data since it helps gauge how much things have changed between 2004 and 2019.

land, whereas in Khuntegaon around a quarter of the Maratha families were landless. The two villages show significantly different patterns in terms of land ownership, tenancy relations and also access to urban resources.

Access to higher education has always remained an important pathway for a possible shift from rural to urban settings. Marathas developed a sense of relative deprivation as they competed with the OBCs and Dalits in the field of education. As per the IHDS data, 31 per cent of Marathas belonged to the salariat as against 23 per cent of the OBCs and 28 per cent of the Dalits (Jaffrelot and Kalaiyarasan, 2017). Dalits and OBCs could enjoy the benefits of reservation policy though. Marathas could neither claim these benefits nor could they compete with the Brahmans because of their low levels of education. In 2011–2012, only around 8 per cent of Marathas were graduates as against 24 per cent of Brahmans.[12] Naturally, when the service sector expanded in the post-liberalization phase, Brahmans could monopolize the lucrative IT sector job opportunities and Marathas felt deprived.

It is this larger narrative within which the electoral politics unfolded and presented the Marathas with a predicament of being in power and yet being ineffectual. While one response emerging from this consisted of political fragmentation, the community also responded through other strategies, all of which simultaneously indicate the weakening of its hegemony.

THE MARATHA RESPONSE

As the community increasingly faced political and economic challenges, it resorted to internal mobilizations more than consolidating

---

[12] Our studies of patterns of intergenerational occupational mobility across caste groups in the city of Pune (Deshpande and Palshikar, 2008) reveal how the urban spaces provided unhindered possibilities of consolidation of their position to the generations of Brahmans (and other upper castes), while in the case of the Marathas, there is a movement from (limited) disadvantage to spectacular advantage for some sections coupled with the overall pattern of sharply polarized occupational stratification.

its hegemonic position vis-à-vis to rest of the society. This was in line with the contingent and localized nature that politics was assuming since the 1990s. The initial instrument of the Marathas, thus, was turning back to the mechanism of caste associations. As we shall note below, this strategy did not evolve in isolation because many other castes were also busy mobilizing themselves through caste associations.

A few detailed studies on caste associations from different States including Maharashtra reveal interesting patterns of their politics.[13] Most of these associations were either established or came into prominence in the early 1990s when the new OBC identity was consolidated but also faced challenges from within. Elsewhere, Deshpande (forthcoming) argues how caste associations operated as a crucial local-level hinge in the large-scale social and political churning taking place in the Indian democracy since the 1990s. This was also a period for the Indian democracy in which substantive ideological contestations receded in spite of promises of democratic expansion. The newly revived caste associations operated at these crossroads of democracy. In the absence of substantive democratic contestations, these associations were also forced to resort to 'politics of presence' through symbolic, token gestures. More importantly, as the communities they tried to represent began to disintegrate, the associations were forced to cling to the vacant and (therefore) shrill rhetoric of caste in even more aggressive ways. Besides demands pertaining to symbols and identity, most caste associations often make economic demands related to their traditional occupations and also turn to making demands related to reservations.

The Maratha caste organizations were no exception to this trend. As opportunities within mainstream party politics stagnated for them and as their political frustrations grew, Marathas resorted to politics

---

[13] We refer here to studies conducted by Rajeshwari Deshpande (Deshpande, 2009, 2010, 2014b, forthcoming) with the help of three of her research students conducted in the States of Maharashtra, Karnataka, Madhya Pradesh and UP. We studied politics of an erstwhile 'dominant' caste of Lingayats in the adjoining regions of Maharashtra and Karnataka (Deshmukh, 2006), the OBC community of shepherds in the states of Maharashtra and Madhya Pradesh (Gholwe, 2013) and that of a Dalit caste of Charmakars in UP and Maharashtra (Agwane, 2019).

of caste associations (Pawar, 1996; Pawar, 2009). The identity politics of Marathas initially led them to the forces of Hindutva during the 1990s. Here, the Maratha notions of caste pride fitted well in the framework of communal pride. We have mentioned this in Chapter 3. However, the attempts by both the SHS and BJP to also attract the OBCs implied that Marathas could not rely on these parties as their exclusive vehicles for furthering the community's interests. The formation of the NCP in 1999 presented them with yet another political option (Birmal, 1999). NCP became a party of the Marathas during this period when most of its seats in the subsequent assemblies were from western Maharashtra, a Maratha bastion. The social base of the party also mainly came from the Marathas in certain regions. However, the NCP could not represent the Marathas successfully. Because by this time, the arena of party politics had become intensely competitive and just as other parties were trying to attract Marathas, the NCP was also forced to bring OBCs on board in order to expand. In particular, throughout post-1999, there has been an intense competition between the SHS and NCP for Maratha support (Palshikar and Birmal, 2003).

It is in this context that sections of Maratha youths moved out of the official democratic realm of party politics and indulged in violent politics of outrage (Deshpande, 2006). During the 1980s, Maratha Mahasangh was the only prominent non-party platform for Maratha politics. This organization, closely linked to a union for the migrant Maratha workers (mainly head loaders) in Mumbai, maintained a close connection with the mainstream politics of the Congress party. In the 1990s, however, many alternative caste platforms emerged. Maratha Seva Sangh was formed in 1990 when Kunbis were included in the list of OBCs and a possible politics around Maratha demands of reservations was unveiled. Later on, especially in the economically backward Marathwada region of the State, more militant youth organizations such as the Sambhaji Brigade and Chhava (literally, cub—a lion's cub) Sanghatana were established.

These youth organizations tried to pressurize party political domain in several ways. They initiated violent contestations over issues of cultural pride of the caste. As a result, Maharashtra witnessed a series of violent outbursts by the angry and frustrated Maratha youth over trivial issues (Deshpande, 2006). As we discussed briefly in Chapter 5, the James Laine–Bhandarkar Oriental Research Institute controversy over a book on Chhatrapati Shivaji in 2004 was perhaps the first major instance of this kind. It was followed by several other instances where sections of masses straightaway resorted to violent politics (for details, see Deshpande, 2004). These public outbursts were sporadic and unorganized and were not always orchestrated by any particular Maratha organization. However, the Maratha youth participated in these activities on a large scale as the protests were essentially about the symbolic cultural pride of the community either as a caste group or as a religious group.

QUESTION OF RESERVATIONS

It is in the context of dual deprivations in the economic and political fields that the Maratha politics of reservations shaped after 1990. This politics was woven around narratives of deprivations of the community. Historically, Marathas have been very proud of their Kshatriya status, but the writings of the Maratha caste organizations in the post-1990 period reversed this logic and drew attention to the Shudra status of the Marathas (Gaikwad, 2005; Khedekar, 2008).[14] It was argued that Marathas and Kunbis were one and the same and that both basically engaged in subsistence agriculture. These narratives used the same historical tools which the Maratha groups had discarded at one time as Brahmanical interpretations of history. The second reversal was about the celebrations of reservation discourse as an emancipatory discourse. The Maratha Mahasangh, in its first meeting in Mumbai in the early 1980s, had vehemently opposed the Mandal report (Pawar, 1996). It had claimed that Marathas could not be equated with Dalits. In fact, such treatment would be suicidal for the Marathas. The recent writings of Maratha leaders, however, celebrate Dr Ambedkar's legacy and approve the idea of caste-based reservations. These writings revisit

[14] In addition to the books mentioned here, the Maratha organizations published a large number of booklets, pamphlets and other related material during the last decade. New publishing houses dedicated to writings on the Maratha history, English and Marathi biographies of Shivaji and his mother, Jijabai, and on the socio-economic plight of the Marathas mushroomed on a large scale during this period. For details, see Ghotale (2017).

and reformulate the Brahman/non-Brahman cultural divide in which the Dalits are now portrayed as allies of the Marathas. In the past, Maharashtra had witnessed violent contestations between Marathas and Dalits, especially during the 1970s when the movement to rename (the then) Marathwada University after Dr Ambedkar had mobilized the Dalits in Marathwada in large numbers (Murugkar, 1991). These memories of the past antagonism between the Dalits and Marathas are covered up and instead Brahmans are projected as (the sole) instigators of those conflicts. Social and material deprivations of Marathas were also discussed in terms of overall indicators of social and economic condition of the State. The argument was that since Maharashtra was poor and Marathas constituted majority in Maharashtra, Marathas too were poor and needed benefits of reservations. In other words, the contemporary narratives of Maratha deprivation denoted ways in which this dominant caste tried to manipulate the reservation discourse in the times of crisis. The Maratha appropriations of the reservation discourse contained simultaneous registers of deprivation and domination. In their agitations and protests that continued throughout the decade of the 2010s, the Marathas pleaded social, economic and educational backwardness. However, the State's recognition of the claims of backwardness was posited as an entitlement of the community—a legitimate right—which the community was willing to assert at any cost (Deshpande, 2014a).

As the political and material gap between the Maratha leaders and the masses continued to increase, the demand for reservations to the entire Maratha community became the main agenda of Maratha politics. As we discussed earlier, despite (and also because of) the dispersal of their support, Marathas remained an indispensable force in Maharashtra politics. As a result, none of the mainstream political parties could antagonize Marathas. On the contrary, since the early 2000s there emerged a kind of consensus across political parties to support the Maratha demand for reservations. This consensus was also facilitated by the overall nature of politics of reservations in the post-Mandal phase.[15]

[15] The ideological project of Mandal was about democratization of caste and contained possibilities of mobilizations in the form of collective resistance to caste-based discriminations. However, the project was ripped off its anti-caste content when the

Both the Congress parties had supported the Maratha demand in their election manifestoes in the 2004 and 2009 elections. However, the State Backward Class Commission consistently opposed it and refused to accept the claim that all Marathas might be considered Kunbis.[16] The State Backward Class Commission—headed by Justice Bapat—was given a special mandate to study the socio-economic situation of the Marathas. The commission conducted studies in 30 districts of the State to conclude that Marathas only from two districts of the Marathwada region might be considered backward and denied the Maratha claims of backwardness. This decision came in 2008.[17] The disgruntled Maratha groups pressurized the government to appoint yet another committee for investigations into their social and economic backwardness. This time it was a special committee under the chairmanship of the then State Cabinet Minister of Industries Mr Narayan Rane, himself a prominent Maratha leader from the Konkan region. The committee travelled across the State and talked to activists and sociologists. A sample survey of 4lakh families was done, while in all, 18 lakh people were contacted by the committee to understand the socio-economic condition of the Marathas. The committee claimed that in its work, for the first time, a quantitative analysis of the question was taken up. The committee submitted its report in February 2014, just ahead of the LS elections, and recommended reservations to Marathas over and above the OBC quota.[18]

idea of affirmative action was rapidly reduced to a near complete quota system for caste (like) communities. These developments created possibilities for the state to manipulate the affirmative action discourse at various levels (Deshpande, 2005).

[16] For relevant details of recommendations by various State Backward Classes Commission, see Buddhiwant (2009); also see *The Indian Express*, Reading Maratha Quota Verdict, 1 July 2019, https://indianexpress.com/article/explained/explained-reading-maratha-quota-verdict-5807983/ (accessed on 15 June 2020).

[17] *The Hindu*, Will You Table Bapat Commission Report, the Court Asks the Government, 2 July 2014, https://www.thehindu.com/news/cities/mumbai/will-you-table-bapat-committee-report-court-asks-government/article6169496.ece (accessed on 15 June 2020).

[18] Although the Rane committee report was not made public, the GoM ordinance refers to its details. See https://www.maharashtra.gov.in/Site/Upload/Acts%20Rules/English/esbc_13_11072014.pdf (accessed on 17 June 2020).

After their defeat in the LS elections in 2014 but before the Assembly election that same year, the State government led by the two Congress parties approved a proposal to grant 16 per cent reservations to Marathas along with special reservation of 5 per cent to the Muslims in education and employment. The decision was challenged in the Bombay High Court. The court ordered a stay to the reservations provision in its decision in November 2014. In the meantime, the State Legislative Assembly elections of 2014 had brought in a new government in power. The newly formed BJP–SHS government was faced with the wrath of the Maratha youth because the issue of reservations was continuing to remain elusive. During the hearing challenging the decision of the previous Congress–NCP government, the High Court in 2015 pointed out to discrepancies and inadequacies in the government's decision. Following that, the BJP–SHS government appointed yet another commission, under Justice (Retd) Gaikwad in June 2017 with a special mandate to look into the Maratha claims of backwardness. This appointment, however, was preceded by large-scale state-wide agitation by the Marathas.

The issue of Maratha reservations kept recurring around almost every election since 2004. However, after the refusal of the Court to approve the 2014 decision of giving reservations to Marathas, the community became all the more restless and launched a massive State-wide agitation in the year 2016. The agitation consisted of huge Maratha gatherings that were *mook morchas* (silent marches). These were named as the Maratha Kranti Morchas or Maratha Revolutionary Marches. The marches were coordinated by a committee of Maratha leaders who claimed to be non-political since they were not affiliated to any political party. Along with reservations, the rallies had two more specific demands. The first was about swift justice in a rape case in Kopardi, Ahmadnagar—in which a Maratha girl was the victim of sexual assault. The other demand proposed amendments to the anti-atrocity Act—officially the Scheduled Castes and Scheduled Tribes (Prevention of Atrocities) Act, 1989—in order to avoid its alleged misuse (by the Dalits). Since its enactment way back in 1989, the anti-atrocity Act has remained a major bone of contention between the Marathas and the Dalits. The Act was implemented in the context of increasing atrocities against Dalits in the decades of the 1970s and 1980s and was viewed by the Dalits as an empowering Act despite its dubious execution. Controversies surrounding the Act had subsided since the time when Marathas claimed a backward status and sought camaraderie with Dalits. However, they resurfaced during the renewed Maratha agitation of 2016, when Maratha men saw it as their 'duty' to protect 'their' women—women from the Maratha community.[19]

During a period of hardly six months, between July and December 2016, Maratha groups had organized 57 massive silent rallies in every nook and corner of the State. Each rally attracted hundreds of thousands of Maratha youth who vouched for an assertive yet disciplined, silent and non-political protest against the government and against the elite Marathas. No political leader was allowed to lead and hijack the mass protests. Instead, the rallies saw women, especially young women, at the forefront—perhaps as representing the benign 'non-political' elements of the community in Maratha men's patriarchal imaginations of the community. There were loud proclamations of community solidarity in slogans like 'Ek Maratha Lakh Maratha' (literally, hundreds of thousands of Marathas will be there for each and every Maratha). The visible symbols of the marches contained multiple subtexts of deprivations, desperations and domination. During the heydays of Maratha protests in 2016, fancy luxurious cars with the Maratha morcha stickers could be seen frequenting the streets of major cities in Maharashtra.[20] Banners and posters put up at every possible place threatened the rulers of dire consequences if Marathas were not recognized as a backward community. Many Maratha youth

[19] Many Maratha women, especially young women, were at the forefront of the Maratha morchas. Their leadership and their (newly acquired) political agency in this otherwise socially conservative community was much celebrated by the Maratha groups as a new progressive turn of the community and as an indicator of the social transformation within. On the other hand, some women leaders of the morchas complained of their instrumental role in these mobilizations, challenged the claims of women's empowerment made by the Maratha men and floated a separate front of Maratha women—Maratha Mahila Kranti Morcha (Loksatta, Pune, 7 September 2018).

[20] A few (among many) such images can be seen at https://amp.reddit.com/r/india/comments/6sl3x5/lshabby_vehicle_of_a_poor_protester_at_mumbai/ (accessed on 1 June 2020); https://images.app.goo.gl/j1tWCrEtyKGi31bm6 (accessed on 1 June 2020).

had migrated to cities and towns and worked in sundry jobs like the courier delivery, cab services, etc. They made it a point to wear designated jackets, hoodies and bags that flashed images of Shivaji Maharaj besides other symbols of Maratha cultural pride in order to ensure a visible presence of the community as an extension of their more organized street politics. There were all kinds of efforts to maintain a visible presence of the community on the streets—out in the open. A Maratha member of the Legislative Assembly appeared in his office dressed as Shivaji, a full length feature film woven around the Maratha agitation was planned, and ballads and songs conveying the angry and desperate messages of the Marathas were penned and widely circulated on social media.[21] In other words, Marathas left no stone unturned to communicate their plight to the rulers and the Maratha elites. In the background of growing economic and political divisions within the community, there were all sorts of efforts of loud and aggressive appropriations of caste identity.

It is in response to these developments that the State government appointed the Gaikwad Commission. However, it is also important to decipher why the Maratha youth chose to march silent in *mook morchas* across the State. As a politically vocal community, street politics was not new to the Marathas. In the past, however, it had always been noisy and stormy where leaders and the followers invoked their legacies as warriors and raised metaphorical swords against the opponents. The anger persisted in the *mook morchas*, but Marathas vouched to make it a 'silent' revolution as they came together in massive rallies. What prompted the Marathas to go silent in 2016? The answer probably lies in the configuration of electoral and party politics in Maharashtra at that time.

As we discussed earlier, the 2014 elections (LS and VS) saw more than half of Marathas supporting the BJP–SHS alliance. Between the

---

[21] The Facebook page of Maratha KrantiMorcha gives interesting details of such efforts. This page has viewership of over 250,000 people. See https://www.facebook.com/Sakalmarathakrantimorchamaharashtra/ (accessed on 16 June 2020). The *morcha* also has its Instagram account which is followed by over 50,000 people. See https://instagram.com/marathakrantimorcha?igshid=11cym4vyu5 jbm (accessed on 17 June 2020).

two alliance partners, Maratha vote went in favour of the SHS rather than the BJP. However, in these elections, the BJP had also successfully advanced a new social equation in the State consisting of the urban, upper-caste and OBC voters. A significant section of Dalits had also voted for the ruling alliance. With this new social equation, the BJP had not only cornered its partner, the SHS, and the Congress-led opposition but had also neutralized the Maratha dominance and their potential discontent. BJP's victory in 2014 at both national and State levels had seriously weakened the space for anti-establishment politics. The Marathas, who are too used to be part of the political establishment, could not afford to antagonize the reigning establishment and in fact would very much want to be a part of it. As a desperate attempt to prove their worth in these confusing political circumstances, Marathas chose the path of tactical silence, so as not to antagonize the new establishment altogether. Of course, during the course of the agitation, when the establishment seemed less than responsive, Maratha groups changed their course once again to go from *mook morchas* to *thok morchas* (where *thok* in Marathi means to hit, strike or rough up). This was by the end of 2018 when once again the parliamentary elections were around the corner.

The Gaikwad Commission submitted its detailed report to the government in November 2018. In its report, the commission acknowledged the Maratha demands for recognition as a socially and economically backward community. Immediately after that, the State government extended reservations to Marathas through legislation. The Maharashtra State Reservation (of seats for admission in educational institutions in the State and for appointments in the public services and posts under the State) for Educationally and Socially Backward Category (ESBC) Act, 2018[22] declared Marathas as a socially and educationally backward class and awarded 16 per cent reservations to them in public employment and in education. This was over and above the existing provisions of reservations in the State. A number of petitions were filed in Bombay High Court, challenging the decision of the government as violative of the Supreme Court

---

[22] The Act is available at https://indiacode.nic.in/bitstream/123456789/6131/1/sebc_act.pdf (accessed on 17 June 2020).

orders regarding the ceiling of 50 per cent for reserved seats. In its decision in July 2019, the High Court upheld the validity of the Act but ordered the government to reduce the quota for Marathas to 12 or 13 per cent.[23] The decision of the High Court was challenged in the Supreme Court, where it is still under consideration (June 2020). While the court battles continued to further assuage the frayed tempers of the Maratha youth and, more than that, to win over the support of the community, the BJP-led government also established an autonomous research, training and human development institute dedicated exclusively for the socio-economic and educational development of the Marathas.[24]

Even as the judicial scrutiny of Maratha reservation policy is pending, the entire episode over the demand for reservations suggests both the dominance and desperation of the Maratha community. If the agitation symbolized desperation, the response of parties and governments indicated the dominance of the community. Like Lingayats in Karnataka, the Marathas could get the State to appoint commissions, reject or accept their reports and act rapidly on recommendations irrespective of possible constitutional issues involved or social consequences that may have long-term ramifications.[25] Besides the constitutional issues, however, the crucial issue is how the separate arrangement for one community would unfold in terms of both demands from other communities and inter-community relations in the State. While this aspect would have long-term implications for the politics of the State, the victory of the Maratha community in

[23] The ruling of Bombay High Court is available at https://indiankanoon.org/doc/165879409/ (accessed on 16 June 2020).

[24] Chhatrapati Shahu Maharaj Research Training and Human Development Institute, Pune, was established by the GoM as a non-profit government company for research, policy advocacy, training, etc., for socio-economic and educational development of Maratha, Maratha-Kunbi, Kunbi-Maratha, Kunbi community and the families dependent of agriculture in Maharashtra State.

[25] For various constitutional issues involved, see Mustafa, F., Explained: Reading the Maratha Quota Verdict, *The Indian Express*, 1 July 2019, https://indianexpress.com/article/explained/explained-reading-maratha-quota-verdict-5807983/ (accessed on 17 June 2020); Ajaz, A., Why the Bombay HC Judgment on Maratha Reservation Is Inherently Flawed, *The Wire*, 3 July 2019, https://thewire.in/law/bombay-high-court-maratha-reservation (accessed on 17 June 2020).

achieving a separate quota, though testifying to electoral might of the community, has most probably dented its much weakened hegemony over politics and society in the State.

As we discussed in the previous chapter, these manoeuvres helped the BJP (and the SHS) in a substantial manner during the 2019 elections. Not only did they get handsome support from Maratha voters, but they could also encourage large numbers of Maratha leaders to join the ruling coalition. Moreover, having pacified the community, the government could keep the rebellious Marathas in check without really granting any leadership to them. The fragmentation of the Maratha vote continued even in these elections (2019) but more Marathas voted for the BJP and SHS than the Congress parties in parliamentary as well as State Assembly elections. These elections also witnessed an accelerated dispersal of Maratha elites as many of them defected from the Congress parties to the BJP in an exodus ahead of the Legislative Assembly elections. Throughout the period of its ascendance in State politics, the BJP has tried to contain Maratha dominance in its aspirations to create a larger social coalition that would include Marathas along with the OBCs and the upper castes but would not be steered by them. As the trajectory of politics of Maratha reservations suggests, these aspirations of the BJP could not be completely fulfilled as yet both because of the indispensability of the Marathas in Maharashtra politics and because of the tentative nature of social coalitions. Both these factors impacted the political prospects of the BJP in the Legislative Assembly elections in 2019 when a significant section of the Maratha voters moved back in the Congress fold and helped the NCP win a sizeable number of seats, especially in the western Maharashtra region.

What have been the more long-term implications of the long-drawn crisis emerging out of the hegemonic position of a dominant community?

TRUCE OVER CASTE QUESTION?

While the legal battle over the issue of 'Maratha reservations' had not been settled at the time of writing this, two things seem quite clear.

One is the ultimate culmination of crisis of the Maratha community in its concerted effort to focus attention on the issue of reservations. The other is that in the politics of the State, the issue has ceased to be contentious. This consensus over Maratha reservations takes us back to two sets of issues which we mentioned at the beginning of this chapter.

The first is about the nature of social coalitions in Maharashtra's politics and its implications for the structuring of the regional party system. The other is a more general issue regarding the nature of caste–politics interaction in the post-Mandal phase and the predicament of the erstwhile dominant castes like Marathas.

Let us consider the more general issue first because it provides a broader backdrop for State-level dynamics to unfold. The situation of crisis we have discussed in this chapter is not unique to the Marathas. Many other similarly placed, regionally dominant castes in other States also share analogous trajectories of loss and (partial) recovery of their dominance of the yesteryears. As the case of Marathas shows, most of these castes have used claims of backwardness as a successful political strategy to negotiate with the changing nature of party-political competition and to compensate for the loss of their entrenched status. In the case of Jats in Rajasthan, the elite backlash of this dominant community precedes the very subaltern challenge that in theory should trigger it as expected in the logic of Mandal (Jenkins, 2004). In Karnataka, the dominant castes of Lingayats and Vokkaligas lead and subsume the potential subaltern challenge and even when it rises, they are successful in diffusing it as has been witnessed by the rise and fall of Urs model subsequently followed by Siddaramaiah.

In Maharashtra, on the other hand, the Marathas initially opposed the weakly articulated challenge of OBC politics but later joined in their discourse in order to compensate for their crumbling dominance under the new political configurations but, interestingly, also to assert their indispensable position under the new political regime. In all the States like Maharashtra, Karnataka, Rajasthan and Andhra Pradesh, where the congress system survived for a long time, the OBC challenge remained only weakly articulated and remained largely confined to the demands for reservations. Instead, the politics of backwardness was mostly hijacked by the erstwhile dominant castes in all these States. This may be seen as an important strategic success of the dominant castes in appropriating the reservation discourse as their assertive claims of backwardness seriously undermined the potentiality of reservation discourse as a text of social justice.

The trajectories of OBCization of the Marathas also take us back to the larger discussion of the nature of caste dominance in contemporary Indian politics and the ways in which caste politics interaction shapes in the more recent times. In the post-Mandal moment of caste politics, almost all castes, but larger and more powerful castes particularly, had to negotiate the discursive space called Mandal. This logic recognizes the fact of caste-based backwardness and the need to rectify that. It provides institutional space for this through the constitutional provisions and a discourse of anti-caste search for equality and social justice. Simultaneously, this logic incorporates spaces for group mobilization, formation of group identities, differential definitions of groups and actual mobilizations. But this democratic logic and the institutional appropriation of it has a wider implication. While 'caste' became the more or less officially recognized space for 'doing politics', it got redefined through the logic of democracy.

While democratic politics redefined caste, other developments in the material field intervened in the traditional caste hierarchy and caste system. Capitalist development played an important role in these new definitions. However, even the routine changes such as urbanization, (limited) spread of education and formal access to freedom of occupation reinforced the effects of the logic of capitalist development. This development also led to the fragmentation of caste in terms of material status of its members. While politics makes it viable to converse in the language of caste, for that to be possible it is necessary that strategies of overcoming this fragmentation are employed.

While distortions produced by capitalist development and globalization make it possible to claim material deprivation and backwardness, reservation became the only discursive space available within the democratic institutional set-up that different castes and communities were bound to occupy. On the one hand, the discursive space of

Mandal facilitated a suitable construction of caste ideology that covered up material deprivations at least in a tokenist manner and also kept intact the consensus around the theme of social justice. On the other hand, the Mandal discourse legitimized caste as a political category and created small openings within practices of democracy, for assertions of traditional caste dominance. This is what the Marathas attempted in recent times—despite, but also because of, their dominant political position in the State politics.

Returning to the more specific concerns pertaining to State politics, we may ask how and why the Maratha crisis looms large as an overall crisis for the post-Congress regional polity in Maharashtra. There are two answers. The first is about the indispensability of the Marathas in Maharashtra's politics. The indispensability is a combination of factors such as their numerical presence, the lingering remnants of their earlier political dominance and the shifting social support bases of political parties in the post-Congress polity. The second answer to this question takes us back to the material anxieties of the Marathas and to the unresolved issues of development. Beyond the dynamics of electoral competition, the developmental issues require effective political control over the regional political economy and civil society. The Congress of yesteryears in Maharashtra could manage it in a reasonable way as it presided over a well-knit social coalition and a thriving regional economy. However, in the post-Congress scenario, neither the BJP nor the two Congress parties have been able to establish such control. If the BJP–SHS government was somewhat successful in pacifying the Marathas with the award of benefits of reservations, the Dhangars (shepherds who constitute another influential group among the OBCs) and many other small communities were angry with the government for postponing their issues of identity and of material interests.[26] Similarly, the inability of the ruling parties to address the distress of farmers also led to frustrations among not

---

[26] *The Indian Express,* Who are Dhangars, Why Demand for ST Status Is a Challenge for Maharashtra? 31 July 2018, https://indianexpress.com/article/explained/who-are-dhangars-why-demand-for-st-status-is-a-challenge-for-maharashtra-5283820/ (accessed on 17 June 2020).

only the Marathas but also many other social groups. In other words, the Maratha crisis alerts us to the fact of failure of ruling parties in Maharashtra to effectively address the material anxieties of different social groups in terms of effective policy interventions. Instead, parties have mostly resorted to temporary, knee-jerk policy responses to the demands of various social groups—as amply shown in the case of Maratha reservations. In that sense, the Maratha question discussed in this chapter becomes a part of the larger questions related to the regional political economy of Maharashtra. We will discuss these issues in the next chapter.

Political Economy of Maharashtra

Electoral and party politics do have autonomy of their own in the sense that they shape on the basis of their internal dynamics as much as on the basis of the context in which they operate. However, a better understanding of the political process has to be situated in political economy. In the case of Maharashtra, this was brought out sharply long ago by Kamat (1983), who early on pointed out that policy and governance in the State were shaped by the nature of capitalist development and the relationship of the ruling sections with the established industrial and agrarian interests in the State. Our discussion in the previous chapter on Maratha question shows how, along with the routine political processes and politicking, electoral politics in Maharashtra is firmly rooted in the interplay of social forces and therefore connects with the politics of material domination.

To put it differently, political economy provides a context to voter choices and a context for policy choices for rulers. It also helps the analysts make sense of voter choices and policy choices. On the one hand, electoral politics becomes a battlefield for the elites, such as the Marathas, as they contest for a better share in dominance. On the other hand, this politics also subsumes confrontations between the dominant interests and the dominated masses. In both cases, elections provide a crucial opportunity for the contending sections to assert themselves. The dominant sections seek continuation of their dominant position through elections. On the other hand, the dominated masses—the 'people'—look upon elections as a leveller, as an opportunity to intervene in the process of domination. In this chapter, our review of Maharashtra's political economy of development over the past six decades is informed by this understanding that elections combine the democratic expression and the expression of domination and therefore need to be studied in the context of political economy.

Unfortunately, the idea of elections as an expression of democratic aspirations of the people mostly remains subdued in the current practices of democracy. Instead, electoral politics largely becomes an elite game and reinforces the patterns of domination. Politics in Maharashtra is no exception to this trend. In the earlier chapters, we passingly mentioned how Maharashtra today sits on various distortions and inadequacies. The origin of these distortions can be located in the political economy of the State. Increasingly, it appears that the political process is unable to intervene and rupture the chain of distortions, and this inability is becoming a central character of the politics and governance in Maharashtra. In fact, as Palshikar (2013) argues, it seems that contemporary politics draws its sustenance from these distortions rather than intervene in them.

These distortions are manifested in Maharashtra's politics in the (im)balance between agriculture and non-agrarian sector of the economy, in the continuing agrarian crisis, in skewed urban growth, in regional imbalance of development and in the ad hoc handling of the issue of well-being. They overlap and intersect each other to create a fragmented regional party system on the one hand and also seriously compromise the possibility of democratic policymaking on the other.

Policy choices at the State level are often dictated by the overall development policy of the country. States can only rarely depart from the development policy adopted at the national level and Maharashtra is no exception. The prolonged and successful inning of the Congress party at the State level ensured a better synchronized existence for Maharashtra within Indian federalism. Also, leaders of the Congress party in the State often played an important role in policymaking at the national level. All these factors ensured that the developmental policy agenda of Maharashtra never deviated much from the national model. In fact, both during the pre- and post-liberalization phase of the Indian economy, Maharashtra always remained a poster boy of the dominant development discourse. In Kohli's work on the 'ideal types' of sub-national regimes in India (Kohli, 2012), he considers Maharashtra to be a 'developmental' State—along with Gujarat, Andhra Pradesh, Karnataka and Punjab—where the government works closely with business in order to promote private sector-led economic development. These States, according to Kohli, tend to have a clear public purpose defined more narrowly in terms of the pursuit of growth and can see more volatile or exclusionary politics and have a mixed record on poverty reduction (Kohli, 2012; 46–55).

QUESTION OF SECTORAL (IM)BALANCE

Since its establishment in 1960, the State of Maharashtra tried to combine both these aspects in its developmental agenda, albeit with distinctive regional flavour. There were attempts to combine strategies of urban–industrial development with various poverty-alleviation programmes. At the same time, the regional ruling elite were also keen to invest a great deal in the agrarian sector of the economy. These investments along with the accommodative political strategies of the State Congress leadership helped Maharashtra create a more inclusionary rather than exclusionary developmental agenda in its early career. As discussed in the first chapter, the congress system in Maharashtra in the 1960s successfully presided over a complex set of entrenched interests in which the competing claims on resources could be kept under control. As a result, the State government of that time managed to establish a fairly good record of urban–industrial development and welfare strategies during the initial period. However, as one study comparing political economy of Maharashtra with Andhra Pradesh has argued, the roots of later distortions existed in this same strategy (Vamsi, 2010). Besides, these legacies were seriously jeopardized when the congress system declined and anew framework of party-political competition was established in the State. As a result, since the 1990s, the State has witnessed an increasing asymmetry in the arena of political economy.

Maharashtra was fortunate to inherit a robust industrial base at the time of its establishment, thanks to its acquisition of Mumbai. Considering the predominantly agrarian nature of Indian economy at that time, this was a rare advantage for the State elite. Over the years, the State could successfully expand its industrial/economic base and could maintain its reputation as one of the top-five economically advanced States of the country. The average share of the State's contribution to national GDP is 14.3 per cent, making it the largest State economy in India. During 1960–1961, Maharashtra had State income of ₹2,249 crore. After 60 years, it has increased to ₹2,332,992 crore—evidently indicative of the scale of expansion of the State's economic base. Maharashtra boasts of one of the highest per capita incomes among the States of the country (₹191,736; approximately 1.5 times higher than the national average of ₹126,521 for 2018–2019; GoM, 2020; 9–10).

In the first phase of post-liberalization economy, Maharashtra recorded a steep growth rate of 7.3 per cent during the Eighth Plan period. It dwindled considerably in the later years to an average growth rate of 4.2 per cent during 1995–2002 (Planning Commission, 2007; 72). But this was the case with economy of most States during that time. Maharashtra's economy recovered again during the 2010s to register a growth rate of 6.9 per cent, higher than most States in the country. As a highly industrialized State, Maharashtra contributes nearly 20 per cent of the country's industrial output (GoM, 2020; 13). From 1991 to 2019, more than 20,000 industrial proposals with proposed investment of ₹1,302,518 crore were approved in the State. Maharashtra was also able to attract 29 per cent of total foreign direct investment (FDI) inflows at all-India level during the past two decades (GoM, 2020; 14).

The service sector contributes nearly 60 per cent of the gross state domestic product (GSDP) in Maharashtra and is one of the fastest-growing economic sectors (GoM, 2020; 27). In the year 2018–2019, this sector recorded a more than 8 per cent growth as against over 6 per cent for the industrial sector and just above 2 per cent for the agriculture. According to a recent NASSCOM–AT Kearney report, 90 per cent of the IT–BPO industry in India is concentrated in and around seven cities in India, including Mumbai and Pune in Maharashtra (Kopardekar, 2020; 13). Maharashtra government has encouraged growth of the IT sector since 1998 when its first Information Technology Policy was enacted. Since its second IT Policy implemented in 2003, IT exports from Maharashtra have increased by 135 per cent, positioning Maharashtra among the top three States along with Karnataka and Tamil Nadu (GoM, 2008; 193). The IT sector accounts for more than 30 per cent of the total capital investment in the State. Maharashtra's success story as one of the richest States in the country is offset by the existence of several entrenched inequalities and disparities. The Planning Commission of India published *Maharashtra Development Report* in 2007. One of the main findings of the report was that Maharashtra's success in achieving high rates of growth was tarnished by its inability to reduce poverty, ignorance and disease (Planning Commission, 2007; 41).

The Planning Commission report notes a distinctive skew in the sectoral development of Maharashtra's economy. In tune with the national trajectories of economic development in the post-liberalization era, Maharashtra also followed the East Asian rather than the Western model of sectoral change as the tertiary sector grew ahead of the secondary. The share of the primary sector in Maharashtra's economy decreased from about 28 per cent in the decade of the 1980s to 10 per cent in 2018–2019. Similarly, the share of the manufacturing sector marginally declined from 32 to 30 per cent with some upward trends in between. On the other hand, as noted above, the tertiary sector grew disproportionately during the three decades from the 1980s to 2010s from 40 to 60 per cent (GoM, 2020; 27). Despite the rapidly declining share of the primary sector in the economy, a large number of workers remain engaged in agriculture even today. As per the latest estimates of 2018–2019, more than 50 per cent of the State's workforce depended on agriculture as their primary source of income (GoM, 2020; 93).

AGRARIAN CRISIS

The crisis pertaining to agriculture in the State is multi-pronged and has technical and economic dimensions to it. Droughts of the early 1970s almost neutralized the gains of the Green Revolution of the late 1960s. From then on, two broad characteristics can be witnessed in the State's agriculture: One is a very slow growth of irrigation (17.7% of agricultural land is currently under irrigation; GoM, 2011; 3) and the other is a very unimpressive rate of per-hectare yield (1,074 kg in contrast to the national average of 1,798 kg; GoM, 2011; 79). The three factors—proneness to droughts, limited irrigation and low per-hectare yield—produce the context in which the 'agrarian crisis' of Maharashtra needs to be understood. To these, one might add the fourth factor of decline of sugar cooperatives having a cascading effect on the rural economy in general.

The decline of cooperatives in a way symbolized the failure of strategic devices used by the State and the ruling elite to ensure a sectoral and social balance in the regional political economy. Gradual privatization of the assets of cooperatives since 2000 marked a new phase of commercialization of agriculture in which the role of the State was considerably reduced (Birmal, 2010). According to one estimate, sugar factories run by private companies contributed to nearly 30 per cent of sugar production in the State in 2011.[1] The share of State's expenditure on agriculture was 5.6 per cent in the Seventh Plan. It declined to 3.5 per cent in the Tenth Plan. Between 1994–1995 and 2010–2011, the percentage of non-agricultural land use to the total geographical area of the State increased from 3.9 to 4.7 per cent, whereas the share of small and marginal farmers increased by 17 per cent during the 2001–2005 period (GoM, 2013; 480). In the year 2019, small and marginal holdings constituted 79.5 per cent of the total number of operational holdings in the state (GoM, 2020; 95). As per the First Agricultural Census of 1970–1971, the average size of agricultural holding in Maharashtra was 4.28 hectares. This was reduced to 1.34 hectares in 2015–2016 as per the Tenth Agricultural Census (GoM, 2020; 95).

The post-liberalization agenda of commercialization of agriculture under the auspices of the urban industrial capitalist sector was operationalized with the help of new strategic devices such as land reforms, reforms in the power sector, irrigation and most importantly through the financial sector reforms in banking and marketing of agricultural produce (Mohanty, 2019; 47). The government implemented several

---

[1] *The Times of India*, Private Sugar Factories to Make Their Presence Felt, 25 May 2011, https://timesofindia.indiatimes.com/city/pune/Private-sugar-factories-to-make-their-presence-felt/articleshow/8561048.cms (accessed on 19 June 2020).

programmes to promote horticulture. The ambition was to declare Maharashtra as a leading horticultural State. It was in tune with the Central government's National Horticulture Mission of 2005. The State established a similar body, namely the Maharashtra State Horticulture and Medicinal Plants Board, in the same year. The board encouraged contract farming as a viable method of procurement. Initially, many multinational companies such as Hindustan Unilever, PepsiCo, Marico Ltd and Reliance Retail entered into contract with farmers from Western Maharashtra as well as from Marathwada and Vidarbh region and by 2008 over a hundred such partnerships were established (Mohanty, 2019; 48). However, as per a report, contract farming was a completely disappointing experience for the farmers, particularly those from Vidarbh where the essential infrastructural support for their agricultural activities was lacking.[2]

The main idea behind these initiatives was to allow the urban material interests to have a free hand not only in urban development but in the field of rural development as well. The arrangement implied that urban interests would play a decisive role in controlling the regional political economy. The rural rich would participate in the implementation of these decisions and would also benefit in this arrangement. However, they were marginalized in the economic and policy-level decision-making process and therefore in the framing of material relations (Palshikar and Deshpande, 2003; 15).

The Maharashtra Agricultural Produce Marketing (Regulation) Act of 1963 was amended in 2005 to facilitate direct and private marketing of agricultural produce. Immediately, as many as 101 direct marketing licenses were issued including 24 private market licenses. Nearly half of them were for purchase of cotton (GoM, 2014; 94). Agribusiness Infrastructure Development Investment Program was launched with the assistance of the Asian Development Bank in 2012. This was a public–private partnership scheme in which private investors were

---

[2] *India Today*, Contract Farming Not Helping Farmers in Maharashtra, 1 December 2011, https://www.indiatoday.in/india/west/story/contract-farming-helping-farmers-maharashtra-147429-2011-12-01 (accessed on 17 May 2020).

allowed to invest up to 60 per cent of the project cost.[3] Many corporates such as Reliance, Godrej and ITC entered the agricultural market in the State for processing, marketing and export of agricultural products. The flow of agricultural credit increased considerably in the post-2000 period. This was because of the more active role played by the commercial banks in the system. Chavan (2015) shows how significant changes were made in the definition of agricultural credit during this period to accommodate financing commercial, export-oriented and capital-intensive agriculture. She also reports that much of the increase in the total advances to agriculture was due to the increase in the number of loans with a credit limit of ₹100 'million' and above (Chavan, 2015; 55). Between 1995 and 2005, the share of agricultural credit supplied by urban and metropolitan branches increased, whereas the share of rural and semi-urban branches declined. In 2008, the metropolitan branches of commercial banks provided nearly half of the agricultural credit, and Mumbai alone covered 43 per cent of it (Mohanty, 2019; 50).

These developments permitted deep penetrations of urban capital into the agrarian economy. As expected, the penetrations reinforced existing adversities in Maharashtra's agrarian economy. One such glaring adversity was the continued overburdening of agriculture despite the decline of its share in the economy. For most farmers, the small size of their holdings makes the occupation unviable; the absence of alternative livelihood strategies makes them cling to those sparse resources. An additional dimension of this crisis is the shift in cropping patterns. With the State's drive to commercialize agriculture, there is an increasing tendency to opt for commodity cropping or cash crops; alternatively, there is also a pressure to commoditize the existing cereal production. However, the overburdening of agriculture does not allow the practice of cash crops to actually benefit small and marginal farmers, leading to a further polarization within the farming community.

---

[3] *The Hindu, Business Line,* $85 from ADB for Maharashtra Agri Infra Project, 29 February 2012 (updated 15 November 2017), https://www.thehindubusinessline.com/economy/agri-business/85-m-from-ADB-for-Maharashtra-agri-infra-project/article20403371.ece (accessed on 17 May 2020).

The two main contentious issues which brought into focus the sharp divides between the farming community and urban interests were water resource management and land acquisition. Given that Maharashtra has more than 80 per cent of rain-fed area, irrigation has always remained at the centre stage of agricultural planning. Even when the State's investment in agriculture declined considerably in the post-liberalization phase, the allocation for irrigation in fact increased substantially (Mohanty, 2019; 47). During the first SHS–BJP government, between 1996 and 1998, five irrigation development corporations were created for different regions in Maharashtra and a major part of their funds came from the private sector. According to a government report, these corporations raised funds of more than ₹120 billion' from open market which was more than the paid-up share capital of the State government (Mohanty, 2019; 47).

The GoM declared 'Water Policy of the State' in July 2003. It was recognized as one of the progressive water policies. Integrated development and management of water resources was the focal point of this policy. The policy recommended mandatory public participation in the management of water use and transfer of water from 'water-abundant' regions to 'water-deficit' regions of the State. For effective management of water use, it recommended establishment of legally entitled Water Users Associations (WUA; GoM, 2013; 304). Accordingly, more than 10,000 such associations were formed till December 2019 in the State. A total number of 3,877 big and small irrigation projects were completed till June 2019 (GoM, 2020; 99). However, activists and NGOs working in the water sector complain of total absence of water governance in the State.[4] The Kelkar committee,[5] in its report on issues of regional imbalances, developed a detailed comment on Maharashtra's water governance. The committee reported how data on region-wise water use indicated sizable disparity in the use of available

[4] For detailed commentaries on Maharashtra's failure in the field of water governance, see Purandare (2013, 2017), Desai (1987).

[5] The GoM appointed a committee to study the developmental issues related to regional imbalances in 2011, 'High Level Committee on Balanced Regional Development Issues in Maharashtra' known as the Kelkar committee after its chairperson Dr Vijay Kelkar. The committee submitted its detailed report to the government in 2013.

water.[6] Most importantly, the committee concluded that compared to the earlier period, the irrigation gap between three regions considerably widened during the period of 1980–2010. The Kelkar committee, in tune with the Maharashtra Water and Irrigation Commission of 1996, recommended a nuanced, multidimensional approach to water governance in the State with an emphasis on micro and participatory management. The State policies so far, however, have been contingent, callous and corrupt,[7] treating water as a market commodity available for purchase of the select few. Over the three decades since the 1990s, a large number of localized protests took place over issues related to water management. The protests took up issues of unequal distribution of water at the inter- and intra-state levels, lack of planning,

[6] The report stated that western Maharashtra with 36 per cent crop area used 47 per cent of the water, whereas Vidarbh with 30 per cent crop area used 28 per cent water. Marathwada with 31 per cent crop area used 14 per cent water and Konkan with 3 per cent crop area used 11 per cent water. Similarly, utilization of irrigation potential created in rest of Maharashtra region was 76.4 per cent, 38.3 per cent in Marathwada and 47.4 per cent in Vidarbh. Thus, utilization of irrigation potential created was very poor in the backward regions of Marathwada and Vidarbh.

[7] The irrigation scam of 2012 rocked Maharashtra politics when allegations of irregularities in irrigation projects surfaced against the then water resource minister. Between 2001–2002 and 2011–2012, various reports of the Comptroller and Auditor General (CAG) of India on Water Resources Department projects highlighted the absence of long-term plans, non-prioritization of projects, delays in completion, commencement of work without forest/environmental clearances, etc. The annual Economic Survey report tabled in the Assembly in 2012 said that the department had spent about ₹70,000 crore over a decade on dam projects that had added a mere 0.1 per cent to area under irrigation. (In subsequent years' Economic Survey reports, the mention of 'increase in area under irrigation' was simply dropped.) In August 2012, the ruling Congress–NCP government ordered a white paper to be prepared. The opposition insisted on an impartial probe, following which the government constituted a special investigation team chaired by Dr Madhav Chitale, former Union Water Resources Secretary. In June 2014, the Chitale committee report was tabled in the Assembly. It gave a clean chit to Water Resources minister and instead accused the officials for callousness. It said that the irrigation potential in the State had grown by 20 per cent, not 0.1 per cent, over 10 years. See, *The Indian Express*, Explained: Maharashtra's Irrigation Scam and How NCP Leader Ajit Pawar Figures in It, 28 November 2019, https://indianexpress.com/article/explained/maharashtras-irrigation-scam-ajit-pawar-sharad-pawar-anti-corruption-bureau-6138598/ (accessed on 17 May 2020).

political interference and flawed priorities of the State government as Maharashtra faced frequent droughts during 2016–2019.[8]

In January 2015, the BJP–SHS government introduced a new ambitious ground water conservation scheme called Jalyukt Shivar Yojana. In the next four years, the government spent around ₹7,000 crore on this scheme. It was claimed that 20,000 villages in the State benefited under the scheme.[9] The scheme became controversial when the water crisis in the State became severe during the drought in 2019 and when the ruling BJP's alliance partner SHS levelled charges of corruption in the implementation of the scheme against its own government (Gholwe, 2020)![10] When the scheme failed, the State proposed yet another ambitious scheme of creating a water grid by linking 11 big dams in drought-prone Marathwada region with a budget of ₹16,000 crore (Purandare, 2020). A large part of the budget would be in the form of private sector capitalist investment.

In tune with the BJP's national-level pro-welfare discourse of the post-2014 period, the BJP–SHS government in Maharashtra also

---

[8] For detailed coverage of these disputes, see Purandare (2017) and also reports in popular media such as, *The Week*, Water Conflicts on the Rise in Maharashtra, Say Experts, 23 November 2018, https://www.theweek.in/news/india/2018/11/23/water-conflicts-on-the-rise-in-maharashtra-say-experts.html, (accessed on 17 May 2020); *Outlook*, Modi's Pet River-Linking Project Is a Reason Why Maharashtra Farmers Are Protesting, 12 March 2018, https://www.outlookindia.com/website/story/modis-pet-river-linking-project-is-a-reason-why-maharashtra-farmers-are-protesti/309398, (accessed on 17 May 2020); *First post*, Mumbai's Burgeoning Water Needs Leave Nearby Villages Parched; City's Wasted and Free Supply More Than Nagpur's Daily Need, 23 March 2020, https://www.firstpost.com/india/mumbais-burgeoning-water-needs-leave-nearby-villages-parched-citys-wasted-and-free-supply-more-than-nagpurs-daily-need-8127461.html (accessed on 17 May 2020); and *The Hindu Business Line*, Maharashtra's Water Scarcity Hits Crisis Level, 31 May 2019, https://www.thehindubusinessline.com/news/national/maharashtras-water-scarcity-hits-crisis-level/article27393500.ece# (accessed on 19 June 2020).

[9] For a detailed assessment of this scheme, which involves local projects for water conservation at the village level, see Bhadbhade et al. (2019).

[10] Also see BBC.com, The Ambitious Water Project That Failed to Prevent Drought, 19 March 2019, https://www.bbc.com/news/world-asia-india-46341433 (accessed on 19 June 2020).

implemented many welfare schemes for farmers.[11] Among these, the PM crop insurance scheme announced by the Central government in 2016[12] was much publicized by the government during the LS and VS election campaigns in 2019. Maharashtra was touted as the top-ranking State in implementing the scheme. As per the government record, a large number of farmers, especially from the backward region of Marathwada (close to 75%), had availed it (Kulkarni and Deshmukh, 2020; 360). As is well known, the crop insurance schemes existed even earlier. However, the new scheme launched in 2016 was lauded as better, incorporating the best features of earlier crop insurance schemes while removing all their shortcomings. Contrary to these claims, studies revealed that rather than ensuring relief for suffering farmers, the scheme worked through and for the benefit of private sector intermediaries who could use the public infrastructure for their own benefits with the help of the government.[13] Studies of this scheme conducted at the State level also documented how the insurance company and the government conspired to deny the expected benefits of crop insurance to the farmers (Kulkarni and Deshmukh, 2020). As a result, there was an interesting twist in the 2019 election campaign when not only the communists but the SHS also led protest marches against the farm insurance companies in the State (Kulkarni and Deshmukh, 2020; 366).

LIMITS OF URBANIZATION

As we shall discuss further, State's development is deeply skewed regionally. Industry thrives in the Mumbai–Pune–Nashik triangle and so does urbanization. As per the 2011 Census, more than 45 per cent of Maharashtra's population lived in urban areas (GoM,

---

[11] Our studies listed more than 15 welfare schemes implemented by the State government either under the directive of the Centre or independently. For details, see Pandkar (2020).

[12] For a concise and critical review of the scheme, see Rai (2019).

[13] Scroll.in, How Modi's Crop Insurance Scheme Benefits Private Insurers Far More Than It Does Farmers? 1 February 2019, https://scroll.in/article/910611/heres-how-modis-crop-insurance-scheme-profits-private-insurers-far-more-than-it-does-farmers (accessed on 20 May 2020).

2020; 3). Maharashtra is one of the highly urbanized States in the country—second only to Tamil Nadu among the larger Indian States. It is estimated that by 2020, the share of urban population must have crossed the halfway mark and more than 50 per cent of Maharashtra was urban by the end of the 2010s. According to the Kelkar committee, the State is more urban than the official figures suggest because there appears to be concerted effort to underestimate the process of urbanization (for political reasons; GoM, 2013; 141). Urban development of Maharashtra is extremely uneven. On the one hand, about a quarter of total number of million-plus cities in the country are located in the Mumbai–Pune–Nashik triangle. But on the other hand, there are around 130 talukas or blocks in the State that have no city-town or urban space within them. These blocks overwhelmingly belong to the backward regions like Vidarbh and Marathwada (GoM, 2013; 142). The extent of urbanization correlates well with district-wise per capita income. On the other hand, the overall instance of urban poverty remains very high with around a quarter of the urban population of the State living in slums (GoM, 2020; 18).

The accelerated rates of migration to cities in the past three decades tell us only one part of the story of urban transformations in Maharashtra. The other part of the story consists of the city's spread into villages to create what Gupta (2015) describes as the 'rurban' realities for a large number of citizens of the State.

The latest Census data for migration is available for 2001. At that time, nearly half of Mumbai's population was categorized as migrant population, and among the migrants nearly 40 per cent came from within Maharashtra (Jha and Kumar, 2016; 69). But then, Mumbai is an exceptional city that has always been a hub of migrants. The rest of Maharashtra typically did not see much movement of the population prior to the 1970s. It was the severe drought of 1972 which compelled many families in Marathwada to migrate to cities like Mumbai and Pune (Brahme and Upadhayay, 1979). The more routine patterns of migration in Maharashtra consisted of seasonal migration of the labour, especially the sugarcane cutters who travelled form districts like Beed and Osmanabad in Marathwada to the prosperous sugarcane-growing areas of western Maharashtra (Guru, 1999). Since the 1990s, a distinctive change was visible when more and more people drifted to the cities. As per a GoM report published in 2010 (GoM, 2010), the share of migrants for reasons of employment and education had considerably increased in Maharashtra between 1991 and 2007. The report also indicated higher rates of migration for the manual labourers.

The rural population growth rate in the State during 1991–2001 was 15.25 per cent. It was reduced to 10.36 per cent during 2001–2011. The urban growth rate also declined—coming down from 34.57 per cent in 1991–2001 to 23.64 per cent in 2001–2011. However, the population growth rate was higher in certain districts than the average rate of growth in the State. The highly urban districts of Thane and Pune along with Aurangabad in Marathwada recorded much higher population growth rate during the 2001–2011 period (GoM, 2020; 24). As a result, Maharashtra became one of the most urbanized States in the country as per the 2011 Census. As Kelkar committee noted, Maharashtra is more urban than what the official records suggest because of the rapid expansion of the urban fringe around its emerging urban centres.

In 1993, the Sharad Pawar government had issued an ordinance to change the provisions in the Maharashtra Agricultural Lands (Ceiling and Holdings) Act to enable certain categories of individuals and companies to hold land on lease beyond the prescribed ceiling limit. The ordinance was rejected by the Central government, but the strategic moves to relax the ceiling limits for private players continued. The industrial policy of the State implemented in the same year provided for acquisition of land beyond ceiling limits for a certain type of industries. Subsequently, the Maharashtra Industrial Development Corporation (MIDC) acquired more than 30,000 hectares of land for purposes other than setting up its own industrial estates (Jenkins, 1999; 105). The Special Economic Zone (SEZ) Act was passed in 2005. Since then, the State received 251 SEZ proposals till 2019 of which 30 SEZs with total investment of ₹36,352 crore and employment of about 5.94 lakh were executed on an area of 4,231 hectares (GoM, 2020; 137). The Economic Survey of the State for the year 2019–2020 reported that the MIDC has one of the largest industrial land banks among all the industrial development corporations in India (GoM, 2020; 139). The land was used to build industrial areas, SEZs, silver zone and specialized parks for IT, biotechnology, wine (grape processing) and gems.[14] In other words, industrial development was invariably linked to acquisition of land, and the attempts of acquisition invariably led to contestations in a number of villages. This is not an uncommon phenomenon and, in many States, CMs have attempted to keep control of such land issues under their direct control but in the case of Maharashtra, NCP, having strong roots in rural and semi-urban areas, has always tried to intervene in the process. As a result, many times, NCP leadership is seen as being more partisan towards land dealers and intermediaries than local public, thus inviting criticism and local anger as in the case of Maan (see below). Thus, while the macro-level debates revolve around questions of livelihood of locals, environment and development perspectives, micro-level processes are more directly involved in the chain of corporate interests, interme-diaries and compulsions of the party leadership to balance corporate interests and their local base.

We have already mentioned the politics of Enron project in the third chapter. A similar controversy took shape in the village of Jaitapur in Konkan since 2007 when a (world's largest) nuclear power station was planned there in collaboration with France. The project was to occupy around 1,000 acres of land in five villages which affected livelihoods of over 40,000 people (Parihar, 2017). People's protests against this nuclear power plant touched upon many controversial issues ranging from environmental depletion to the risky uncertainties involved in the use of nuclear power. Acquisition of land for the project was an important issue among these. Throughout these struggles, the State government, all the mainstream political parties and even expert

---

[14] As on December 2019, the MIDC had built 289 industrial areas of which 143 were major industrial areas, 95 were minor industrial areas and 51 were growth centres. As on December 2019, there were 50,788 units having investment of ₹194,011 crore with potential employment of 15.08 lakh. About 72 per cent of 96,637 developed plots were allotted to entrepreneurs (GoM, 2020; 139).

groups remained indecisive and frequently changed their positions, leading to a policy chaos.[15]

Village Maan, near Pune, also became the site of a major struggle over land acquisition when the government established an IT park in the adjacent village of Hinjewadi (Sathe, 2017). The decades of the 2000s and 2010s witnessed growing opposition to such land transfers not only because of tardy record of compensation and rehabilitation but also because of the lack of alternative livelihood strategies designed for this purpose. The political process in the State was unable to mediate between urban/industrial and agrarian interests. Instead, the manipulative strategies of the government in alliance with the capitalist interests invariably led to lumpenization of farmers and accentuated their material and social deprivations.

Conflicts over issues of land acquisition became more and more intense when the idea of industrial development became more and more capital intensive. In 1995, when the BJP–SHS government first came into power, it launched the Pune–Mumbai Expressway project as a communication highway and an infrastructural corridor for industries[16] (Dandekar and Mahajan, 2001). The State has implemented Mega Project Policy since 2005. As a part of this policy, 643 mega projects with an investment of ₹479,950 crore and proposed employment of 5.23 lakh were approved till December 2019 (GoM, 2020; 135). In 2006, the Government of India in collaboration with

---

[15] Partly due to the protests, but also because of funding and technology issues, the project, though technically alive, is almost on the backburner. The official website of Nuclear Power Corporation of India Limited (NPCIL) is silent as to the current status of the project. See https://www.npcil.nic.in/content/425_1_JaitapurNuclearPowerProject.aspx (accessed on 27 June 2020). See also *The Indian Express*, No Point of Setting Up Lab, if Local People Have Reservations: BARC Chief, 31 October 2018, https://indianexpress.com/article/cities/mumbai/nuclear-power-plant-no-point-of-setting-up-lab-if-local-people-have-reservation-barc-chief-5426305/ (accessed on 27 June 2020).

[16] The concentration of the State's industrial activity in Mumbai and Pune was vividly highlighted by data which showed that the two cities and the corridor between them, the Mumbai–Thane–Pune urban belt as it is sometimes referred to, contained 72 per cent of factories, provided 77 per cent of industrial employment, controlled 88 per cent of working capital and yielded 86 per cent of total state industrial output (Dandekar and Mahajan, 2001; 552).

Japan launched the Delhi–Mumbai Industrial Corridor (DMIC), a planned industrial development project that covered six States along with Maharashtra.[17] The project would develop new industrial cities as 'smart cities' by converging next-generation technologies across infrastructure sectors. One of these cities will be Aurangabad Industrial City in the Marathwada region, spread across an area of over 4,000 hectares with an investment of more than ₹5,000 crore (GoM, 2020; 137). Sai Balkrishnan (2019) shows how such large-scale land use changes are being driven, negotiated and contested in Maharashtra as policymakers search for decentralized and market-oriented means for the transfer of land from agrarian constituencies to infrastructural promoters and urban developers and how the reallocation of property control is erupting into volatile land-based social conflicts.

As we discuss in the following section on regional imbalance, a related dimension of development policy involves the question of regional spread of projects. (In a sense, besides reasons of locational advantage, projects like Enron or Jaitapur also take into consideration this dimension since Konkan is seen as being less developed industrially beyond Raigad district.) Despite the State's assurances to the contrary, most of the mega-scale industrial projects remained confined to the western Maharashtra region even in 2019, leading to an extremely uneven process of urbanization. On the other hand, the only mega-scale infrastructural project of Multi-modal International Cargo Hub and Airport at Nagpur (MIHAN) in the Vidarbh region failed to attract

---

[17] The six States covered under this project are Delhi, Rajasthan, Haryana, Gujarat, Maharashtra and Madhya Pradesh. For details of the project, see http://delhimumbaiindustrialcorridor.com/index.html (accessed on 22 May 2020). The catchment of DMIC includes 22 industrial estates, 9 freight destinations, 6 airports and 3 seaports of 7 States. Out of the total area covered under DMIC, Rajasthan covers 39 per cent, Gujarat covers 38 per cent and Maharashtra and Haryana cover 10 per cent each. Dhule, Aurangabad, Nashik and Pune are the beneficiary destinations of DMIC in Maharashtra. This corridor covers two industrial areas, namely Shendra-Bidkin and Dighi port in the State. The Shendra-Bidkin Industrial Area is envisioned as a very large-scale industrial cluster and the Dighi Port Industrial Area is intended to be a port as well as a trade and industrial hub that will augment the port of Mumbai. Perspective planning for the entire DMIC has been completed and the master planning and preliminary engineering have been undertaken for the cities identified as part of Phase I of DMIC.

investments.[18] Out of 350 mega projects sanctioned by the State, 85 per cent were located in and around cities like Mumbai, Thane, Pune and Nagpur, and 60 per cent of the employment generated was in Thane, Pune, Nagpur and Kolhapur (GoM, 2013; 270). From the 200 private IT parks established in the State, less than 10 units were located beyond the Mumbai–Thane–Pune–Nashik privileged industrial belt (GoM, 2020; 137). As per the Industrial Entrepreneurs Memorandum data of 2012, the four districts Pune, Raigad, Ratnagiri and Thane accounted for more than 50 per cent investments in Maharashtra and three regions of Pune, Mumbai–Thane and Nashik accounted for more than 80 per cent of the entire investment. Thus, in spite of fiscal incentives announced by the government from time to time,[19] private investment flows remained heavily concentrated in the Mumbai, Pune and Nashik areas, while the eastern, backward regions received minuscule capital investment (GoM, 2013; 270).[20] Small-scale industries employed nearly half of the industrial workforce. Nearly two-thirds of it was in six districts of Mumbai, Thane, Pune, Nashik, Nagpur and Aurangabad (GoM, 2013; 270). No wonder that only one out of the eight districts of Marathwada, Aurangabad, came close to

---

[18] The GoM formed a special purpose entity in the name of Maharashtra Airport Development Company for development of MIHAN. The project is financed by multiple Indian banks with total loan amount of ₹30,000 crore along with investment from State government and Airports Authority of India. The estimated capital cost of the project is ₹2,581 crore (by year 2035) and is supposed to generate revenues of ₹5,280 crore.

[19] Industrial policies of the State in 1993,1995, 2001, 2006, 2013 and 2019 have all emphasized the government's efforts in the form of ease of doing business and financial incentives to spread industrialization to the backward regions. For details, see Kopardekar (2020).

[20] Out of the total number of industrial units setup in the MIDC, industrial area was 33,355 hectares of which 74.3 per cent was located in the rest of Maharashtra region while the proportions of industrial units setup in Marathwada and Vidarbha were 13.4 per cent and 12.3 per cent respectively. The total amount of investment made in these industrial units was ₹53,792 crore. Of these total investments, the shares of the three regions were as follows: rest of Maharashtra (74.6%), Marathwada (8.0%) and Vidarbh (17.4%). As regards employment created in these industrial units, it was found that of the total employment created (8.80 lakh), the maximum employment (83.8%) was created in the rest of Maharashtra region. The shares of Marathwada and Vidarbh were 6 per cent and 10.2 per cent, respectively (GoM, 2013; 271).

the State's average per capita income and Human Development Index of Maharashtra (GoM, 2013; 288).

In other words, Maharashtra's urbanization remained top heavy and spatially skewed. As per the 2011 population Census, metropolitan cities of Mumbai and Pune subsumed half of the urban population within them. The emerging regional urban centres like Nashik, Aurangabad and Nagpur accommodated another 10 per cent of the urban residents. It means that around 40 per cent of the State's urban population resided in towns which were only notionally urban— administratively categorized as urban centres. Economically, these remained semi-urban areas where the employment in non-agricultural sector was growing only in bits and pieces. Such stunted urban growth especially in the economically backward regions of the State led to migration of the aspirational youth to metropolitan centres and also to emerging second-grade cities near home. However, there too, the shrinking opportunities of employment in the industries and in the organized sector of economy[21] pushed them to the margins of city life and added to their relative deprivations (Deshpande, 2013). Even the bigger cities of the State have a very weak economic base of their own and could boast large populations as perhaps their only asset. A large number of workers in these cities were employed in the informal sector economy and took up sundry, odd jobs on temporary basis.[22]

---

[21] Between 2014 and 2019, the public sector employment in the State reduced from 22.41 lakh to 22.25 lakh (Pandkar, 2020). Most of the private sector employment in cities was in the unorganized service sector. As per the sixth economic census (2013), manufacturing sector was the largest employer providing employment to 20 per cent workers. The average employment per establishment at the State level had reduced from 2.68 in 2005 to 2.36 in 2013. In the case of agricultural establishments, average employment per establishment declined from 1.74 in 2005 to 1.66 in 2013. However, the average employment per establishment in non-agricultural establishments declined from 2.83 (2005) to 2.61 (2013). The percentage share of smaller establishment with employment size class of 1–5 workers in total number of establishments in the State had a rising trend over the period 2005–2013 with a consequent decline in the share of establishment having employment in the range of 6–9 workers and also in the range of 10 and above workers (GoM, 2016; 23–25).

[22] For details on the informal sector economy in urban Maharashtra, see Patel (2013) and Deshpande (2003). Government statistics revealed that the number of auto-rickshaws in Mumbai, for example, increased by 8 per cent between 2017–2018 and 2018–2019 (GoM, 2020; 135). According to one estimate, in 2018, around 25,000 cabs

Vora (1996) noted the 'urban turn' in Maharashtra's politics and argued how the BJP–SHS's electoral victory in 1995 elections symbolized the moment of arrival of the 'urban'. Since then, the BJP and SHS—independently as well as in alliance—have been trying to carve out a new urban constituency for themselves. At the same time, the arrival of the urban in the State's politics does signify the arrival of a new policy discourse which is exclusionary rather than inclusionary in nature; it is rooted in populism rather than institutional networks and encourages manipulative state practices. As a result, politics becomes an extractive activity for the regional ruling elite. With the rapid loss of their control over material resources, the regional ruling elite and the new politics often resort to populist and knee-jerk policy measures for both urban and rural constituencies. A large number of ad hoc welfare schemes implemented by the GoM during 2014–2019 for every possible social group and community is a case in point. Studies of these schemes reveal their very limited spread among the beneficiaries, making Maharashtra only a weak welfare regime compared to many other States in the country (Deshpande and Birmal, forthcoming; Deshpande et al., 2019).

REGIONAL IMBALANCE

One of the long-standing issues related to spatial skew was that of uneven regional development. As we discussed in the first chapter, the politics of regionalism was central to the formation of the State of Maharashtra. The leadership of the State, from various regions, was aware of the possibility of a regional imbalance because, for various historical reasons, Marathwada and Vidarbh were already backward in comparison to the region of western Maharashtra. The formation of the State was based on an explicit understanding that attempts would be made to arrive at balanced development and sharing (of resources and power). The Nagpur Pact—an agreement reached between leaders

were attached with Uber—the app-based aggregator company—in just one city, Pune. *Hindustan Times*, Pune Commuters Left Stranded as Ola, Uber Go on Strike, 24 October 2018, https://www.hindustantimes.com/pune-news/pune-commuters-left-stranded-as-ola-uber-go-on-strike/story-6iDZYK5WnSxCt5tILVlN9O.html (accessed on 23 May 2020).

of Vidarbh, Marathwada and rest of Maharashtra in 1953—served as the basis for this vision of balanced growth and equitable sharing of power and resources.

The pact did two things. One, it framed the issues of regional imbalance within the framework of governance rather than politics. Two, consequently, it introduced an element of administrative ad hocism in the decision-making on issues of regional imbalance. Besides, the pact was sidestepped during the 1960s and 1970s when the district rather than region became the unit of planning and development. District Planning and Development Committees and separate District Annual Plans were formed to take resources closer to the people (GoM, 2013; 207). The idea of district-level plans fitted well within the dominant developmental framework of that time and also delegitimized the politics of regionalism. As we discussed earlier in Chapter 2, regionalist sentiments were articulated in terms of rivalries among the Maratha leaders when Congress factionalism erupted in the 1970s. The fact that the 1974 agitation for regional development in Marathwada happened under the official banner of a non-party platform once again reaffirmed the dominant logic of situating regional imbalance as an issue of governance rather than politics. The logic continued till 1984 when the government appointed a committee to look into the issue of regional imbalance under the chairmanship of V.M. Dandekar (1983). The appointment of the committee and its report (1984) brought forward the issue of regional imbalance in its substantive details. (For the history of this committee and the discussion of the backwardness of Marathwada, see Kulkarni, 1998.)

Although the report of the committee did not satisfy most stakeholders, a structural solution was adopted by the government to address the issues of regional development. This was known as 'development boards' which functioned directly under the purview of the governor. While the State legislature adopted a resolution in favour of this arrangement in 1984 itself, the Parliament passed a legislation to that effect only in the next decade in 1993. Accordingly, development boards came into being in 1994 (on the role of development boards, see Kadukar, 2006; Kurulkar, 2009). As a result of the political dynamics, three development boards came into existence—one each for the Vidarbh and Marathwada regions and one for the 'rest of Maharashtra'.[23] The creation of development boards raised an issue related to the State-level political equilibrium as designed by the Constitution. This concern was raised by S.B. Chavan, though he himself hailed from a backward region—Marathwada (Palshikar, 2013). Development boards reported directly to the governor and functioned under the governor's direct stewardship. While this was potentially an area of conflict between the CM and the governor, this arrangement also problematized the role of the legislature since resources were made available directly to the boards with no legislative control.

Besides these issues, none of the stakeholders have been happy with the experience of development boards. The leaders from 'rest of Maharashtra' saw this as an unreasonable encroachment in the democratic process, while in the regions of Vidarbh and Marathwada there was a feeling that these boards were notional. The budget allocated to the developmental boards remained inadequate, thus giving effective control of the regional finances to the State government. The mechanism of developmental boards once again underlined the logic in which issues of regional development were depoliticized.

The issues of regional imbalance became important again when the agrarian crisis in the State deepened in the 2000s and many farmers, especially in the backward region of Vidarbh, committed suicide. As one of its policy responses, the State government under the leadership of Prithviraj Chavan appointed yet another high-level committee on balanced regional development issues in the State (Kelkar committee, see Note 5). In its detailed report submitted to the government in 2013, the committee highlighted the multidimensional and overlapping existence of regional as well as socio-economic inequalities in the

[23] The creation of a separate board for rest of Maharashtra was questioned. Development boards were expected to address the issue of regional imbalance and, so, ideally there should have been only two boards for the two comparatively less developed regions. While Vidarbh and Marathwada are more well recognized 'regions' with specific regional identities and region-based issues of development, 'rest of Maharashtra' is neither a regional category nor a territorial grouping since it includes Konkan, North Maharashtra, South Maharashtra and western Maharashtra areas of the State and these areas do not have a common development trajectory.

State. One of the most important observations of the committee was the continued and increased presence of inequalities across regions and within regions in contemporary, post-liberalization Maharashtra. The committee observed a gradual decline in disparity of district-level per capita income during the years 1993–1994 and 1999–2000. However, this trend reversed in the latter period of 2000–2001 to 2009–2010 (GoM, 2013; 38). Thus, the per capita income of Marathwada was 40 per cent lower than that of 'rest of Maharashtra' in 2009–2010. Similarly, per capita income of Vidarbh was 27 per cent lower than that of the 'rest of Maharashtra'. This ratio had gradually deteriorated in Marathwada and Vidarbh during the decade of 2001–2010, as a result of which the pre-existing disparity among these regions further worsened.

The report identified agrarian crisis, water resource management and lack of industrial capital as three critical issues in addressing regional imbalance. It also underlined the interconnected nature of these issues. Most importantly, the committee observed how agglomerates breed regional (spatial) imbalance in the State's economy. Generally, all economic activities have an inherent propensity to agglomerate to reap the benefits arising out of being closer to 'parent industry' which generates demand and assures supplies of various resources. Hence, the incentive to co-locate with others generates agglomeration and location-based specialization. According to the committee, the imbalanced growth pattern across the rest of Maharashtra, Marathwada and Vidarbh was the result of this process (GoM, 2013; 84). However, it is one of the essential aspects of functioning of the State and the political institutions to break this capitalist logic and to ensure balanced growth. This is precisely what the Kelkar committee expected when it considered political power sharing as an important strategy to ensure balanced regional development (GoM, 2013; 116).

So far, none of the mainstream political parties in Maharashtra have engaged in any substantial politics over the issues of regional imbalance. There has been no consistent support by political parties to the occasional demands of separate statehood in both the backward regions. Although the BJP and SHS operated as alliance partners since

1989, they had different positions on issues of regional imbalance—
especially vis-à-vis the demand for a separate statehood to Vidarbh.
While the formal position of the BJP was in favour of reorganization
of the large States and hence more favourable to separate Vidarbh, this
did not help the party in that region. Also, the BJP could not overem-
phasize its pro-Vidarbh stand for fear of losing support in the other
regions of the State. The SHS, on the other hand, was always most
strongly opposed to separate statehood for Vidarbh. The Congress
party did not have a clear stand on this issue because of the fear of
adverse effect in the rest of the State and because of the cascading
effect it may have in other States. Ever since the Telangana agitation
became prominent since 2009, in Vidarbh too, the Statehood demand
had gathered some momentum.

However, the region never had a strong leadership either wedded to
statehood or focusing on region's development. The sporadic demand
for statehood attracted a small section in the region and also became
relevant as a protest against what the region perceives as injustice to
it. In a post-election survey conducted by us at the time of Assembly
election of 2004, it was found that overall, not more than one in three
persons in the entire State was aware of the demand for a separate
State of Vidarbh. In the region itself, this awareness was naturally
greater—51 per cent. However, support to the demand was much less
in the State as a whole.[24] Most notably, there was no specific party
character to the support. Thus, statehood demand did not muster critical political support to be strong enough to occupy the political agenda
in the region. This lukewarm response perhaps captures the complex
situation in the region of Vidarbh—disappointment with backwardness, uncertainty about the demand for statehood and an absence of
a political vehicle to push either for development or for statehood
or both. The deepening agrarian crisis and the sheer desperations of
suicides of farmers in the 2010s capture these complexities, albeit in
a rather cruel manner.

---

[24] Maharashtra Assembly Election Studies 2004 were coordinated by Suhas Palshikar
and Nitin Birmal for Lokniti-CSDS, Delhi. The studies involved a voters' survey (with a
sample of 1,448), studies of social profile of candidates and constituency-level studies.

In the case of Marathwada too, politics inflicted its own cruelties once the demands of regionalism died down quickly with the disintegration of Maratha leadership. As discussed in the chapter on Maratha politics, the youth in Marathwada have been looking for an appropriate political vehicle to register their anger and disappointment since then. Their search culminated in politics of reservations and of caste organizations as frustrations grew both against the material disparities and against the political elite. In the meantime, just as Vidarbh, Marathwada also continued to experience acute agrarian crisis and water shortage throughout the first two decades of the new millennium.

QUESTION OF POVERTY/WELL-BEING

Maharashtra does not have a very impressive record of poverty alleviation. Although the percentage of population living below poverty line has halved during the last quarter of the 20th century (from 53.24% in 1973–1974 to 25.02% in 1999–2000), according to the Planning Commission, Maharashtra's performance in this area came closer to many of the less-developed States in the country (Planning Commission, 2007; 64). Like many other Indian States, the pace of poverty reduction was faster in Maharashtra in the second phase of economic reforms after 2005. Poverty declined more rapidly in both urban and rural areas in this period. And yet a significant share of India's poor live in Maharashtra (World Bank, 2017).

Among the highly developed States like Gujarat, Tamil Nadu, Punjab and Kerala, Maharashtra ranked low on infrastructural development as per a composite comparative State-level index developed by the Government of India (Planning Commission, 2007; 63). The same was the case with human development indicators. Despite its reputation as a socially progressive State, so far, Maharashtra has had only a moderate performance in terms of social sector attainments. As per the Human Development Index of 2011, Maharashtra hung somewhere in the middle among the major States—slightly better than Gujarat and Karnataka but much worse than Kerala, Punjab and Himachal Pradesh.

Also, the human development levels significantly differed across districts indicating the internal spatial disparities within the State. Except Nagpur, districts with very-high and high levels of human development indicators belonged to the western—that too south-western—part of the State. On the other hand, the deprived districts belong to the East and the North (GoM, 2020; 259). The same is the case with sex ratio. Compared to the all-India average of 943, the State recorded an adverse sex ratio of 929, depicting deep-rooted patterns of gender inequality against women. Even fewer women are present in highly urbanized and industrial districts in and around Mumbai mainly due to the male-heavy patterns of inter-district migration in the State.[25] Obviously, far more number of men than women are registered as regular workers in the State's workforce. Maharashtra was placed on a par with Tamil Nadu and Punjab (at around 7.5%) in terms of rate of unemployment in 2017–2018 and did much better than Kerala. At the same time, States like Gujarat, Karnataka and even West Bengal could keep the rate of unemployment much lower than Maharashtra (GoM, 2020; 213). Despite the overall reduction in the extent of poverty, economic inequalities slightly increased rather than decreased in the post-liberalization Maharashtra.

In other words, even a cursory glance at the macro-level development indicators of Maharashtra's economy over the past few years directs our attention to the distortions and inequalities present in it. It also underlines the intersecting nature of these distortions resulting in overlaps and reinforcements of economic and social inequalities along multiple axes. The existence of intersecting inequalities led to numerous and complex narratives of deprivation and anxieties in the States' politics over the years. In some assessments, this was an inevitable outcome of the development strategy adopted at both all-India and State levels (Desai, 2011; Kamat, 1983).

However, as we mentioned earlier, in the initial stages of development, these distortions could be kept under control as a result

---

[25] https://www.census2011.co.in/census/state/districtlist/maharashtra.html (accessed on 6 May 2020).

of a combination of factors working in favour of the ruling elite. The encouragement to cooperativization, state intervention in agrarian economy and the formation of Panchayati Raj institutions proved to be helpful strategies in initial years after the formation of Maharashtra.

The first was the rise of the cooperatives. The State's strategy of pumping resources in the cooperative sector paid off in the decades of the 1950s and 1960s and a somewhat balanced picture of robust economic development could be projected. The cooperative institutions became critical conduits for the flow of development resources to the rural areas as the political centre of gravity rested in the countryside (Kale, 2014). State support was a crucial element in the success of the cooperatives. Damodaran (2008) estimates that the Maharashtra government had cumulatively invested roughly ₹1,200 crore as share capital alone in the State's cooperative sugar factories during the half-century of their functioning. But state patronage to cooperatives came in many forms ranging from policies such as land reforms to non-financial interventions through the practices of Licence Raj. Kale (2014) calls it the policy of 'selective rural developmentalism' that had important implications for the emerging politics in the State.

Success of cooperative sugar factories brought the Marathas into industrial mainstream and transformed them into one of 'India's new capitalists' (Damodaran, 2008). Besides, it created the possibility of what Lele (1982b) calls a civilized competition among the various elite fractions—the industrial capitalists of Mumbai and the Maratha political elites having control over the rural masses. Also, cooperatives institutionalized the congress system as they became an important part of the inclusionary developmental discourse of the State. On the other hand, a shift in the social character of the rulers after independence also helped significantly in legitimizing the policies of the State which were designed to protect the interests of the industrial capital along with those of the rural elites. In fact, as Vora (1994) argues, the Congress rule could protect agrarian interests only by accommodating Brahman interests as well as those of the industrial capitalists and thus imposed certain inherent limitations to the Maratha dominance. Rosenthal (1977) suggested that the role of the expansive Maratha elite of Maharashtra's countryside was more reactive than initiatory and although they could exercise significant veto power over policies detrimental to their interests, they were forced to compromise with the urban/industrial capitalist interests.

Second, the policy shift at the national level prioritizing agriculture during the mid-1960s also boosted agricultural development in Maharashtra. Maharashtra's Third Five-Year Plan—the first such exercise in the newly created State—established the goal of planned development to be an agro-industrial economy (Kale, 2014). During both the Chavan and the Naik regimes, efforts were made to enhance agricultural productivity. Naik ushered in the Green Revolution in Maharashtra to promote commercial production of high-yielding varieties—mainly of cotton along with sugarcane. The Green Revolution policies provided institutional support to cooperatives and other agro-industries as they spread to regions beyond western Maharashtra during Naik's tenure. In order to regulate the marketing of agricultural produce, the Maharashtra Agricultural Produce Marketing (Regulation) Act was passed in 1963. The Act ensured higher returns to farmers, minimized the role of the middlemen and institutionalized an expanding agrarian market with benefits trickling to small and marginal farmers along with the rich. It is estimated that about 45 per cent of the total plan expenditure of the State was diverted to the development of agriculture and irrigation during this period (Mohanty, 2019; 39).

The State government's efforts to modernize and transform agriculture received a major setback due to drought in 1972. The output of food grains declined in many districts during this period and a large number of rural masses were pauperized after the drought (Brahme, 1983). In order to counter these adversities, the Maharashtra government instituted the EGS in 1972. The EGS came as a political masterstroke that distinguished the State governance from many other States and was appreciated at the national level. The EGS also became a link between the rural elite and the masses when it facilitated at least a thin distribution of resources. However, after an initial success of a few years, the EGS coverage declined sharply. Moreover, the poor and chronically unemployed were rarely covered under the scheme (Dev, 1995; Mohanty, 2019). The EGS functioned more as a relief programme rather than an employment guarantee scheme and failed to arrest the migration of rural labour to urban centres that began in the aftermath of the 1972 drought.

In order to make it a more inclusive agenda, the State government established a network of primary agricultural credit societies and rural development banks to meet the growing credit need of the farmers. The government's initial efforts to extend the agricultural revolution to the backward regions of the State rapidly faltered in the later decades and became one of the most controversial issues in State politics, especially in the politics of the regionalist movements. Similarly, the politics of rural/agrarian subsidies continued in Maharashtra for a long time.

Irrigation was used as a related strategic device by the State to ensure a more balanced distribution of resources between the rural and urban sectors. However, the long history of water resource (mis) management in Maharashtra so far (mentioned earlier in this chapter) conveys a rather different story. Besides, irrigation potential of the State always remained rather limited with its location in an agro-climatic zone that is drought prone. In her study of the politics of power sector in Maharashtra, Kale (2014) notes how irrigation schemes along with rural subsidies for electricity, fertilizers and prices had become increasingly important as the glue that bound the State government to the larger commercial farmers and agro-industrialists.

Finally, it was the creation and consolidation of the Panchayat Raj institutions that helped the congress system and the ruling elites in presenting a more inclusive political and economic agenda during the early decades of their functioning. Maharashtra was considered a pioneer State in developing the institutional mechanisms of decentralized democracy. These mechanisms ensured enhanced opportunities of political recruitment for the local elites as a further advancement of the inclusionary agenda of the State. More importantly, the local self-government institutions also became a major political arena for securing privileged access to the newly consolidated resources of development administration of the State (Lele, 1990a). The expansion of local self-government along with the recognition of district as a basic unit of developmental planning thus prominently contributed to the intricate arrangements of balance of power between the rural and urban and political and economic interests.

These intricate arrangements were disturbed a great deal during the 1970s and 1980s as the congress system in the State received its initial shocks. Agricultural growth during the Green Revolution produced a section among the agricultural classes that drew its material power from agriculture but increasingly aligned with the non-agricultural interests. That helped resolve the tension between agricultural and non-agricultural elites. However, tensions did not dissolve for the rural (and the urban) subalterns. Also, the rural-agrarian elite, who aligned with non-agrarian interests, had to depend upon rural subalterns for their political sustenance. This situation necessitated that politics would only nominally determine and control the economy and political elites would try to separate 'electoral support' from policy preferences as far as possible (Palshikar and Deshpande, 2003). Much of the politics of post-1980 phase can be explained in terms of this new arrangement and the roots of the Congress's decline in the State can also be located in this development.

Even the moderate development of secondary and tertiary sectors had some problems. First, it did not keep pace with the rising levels of education and expectations.[26] As a result, the number of persons on live register of employment exchange increased by three times from the mid-1970s to the mid-1980s (GoM, 1996; 137). Despite the increase in the number of industrial units, employment did not increase much and actually declined between 1981 and 1986 (GoM, 1996; 132). While economic growth showed signs of a slump during

[26] This period recorded a rapid increase in educational enrollment at various levels. Between 1975–1976 and 1985–1986, enrollment in primary schools rose by 42 per cent. In secondary and higher-secondary schools, it rose by almost 84 per cent and for higher education the rise was 37 per cent (GoM, 1996; 160).

this period, the State continued to pump its resources generously into capitalist development. Financial assistance disbursed by financial institutions rose from ₹372 crore in 1980–1981 to ₹7,871 crore in 1995–1996 (GoM, 1996; 160). And yet, industrial growth happened at a dismally slow pace. Besides, it was concentrated only in certain districts of the State. Mumbai, Thane and Pune districts from western Maharashtra continued to be major sites of growth during this period. Of the total number of factory workers in the State in 1986–1987, 66 per cent were employed in these three districts (GoM, 1987; 38–39). This suggests that industrial growth in other districts was very slow. They experienced growth mainly through the spread of the tertiary sector, which mainly consisted of petty businesses and offered sundry jobs. While the manufacturing sector grew only at a limited pace, the importance of the tertiary sector in the State's economy rapidly increased in this decade. As a result, petty contractors, hoteliers, speculators and traders became increasingly important in the economy of the State. It also led to informalization of the labour force in the cities.

POLITICS IN THE MIDST OF DISTORTIONS

The foregoing discussion brings forward two issues: One is the limited success of the State in handling issues of well-being and development and the other is the inability of the political elite to balance political and economic compulsions. This is where the process of disjunction between politics and economy was evident. The State-level political leadership continued to derive their political support from the rural/agrarian masses. At the same time, they chose to cater to the ascendant material interests of the urban-industrial and service sectors. As a result, the agrarian interests became less effective vis-à-vis urban capitalist interests. This created a problem for the State-level political leadership, which for the most part remained rooted in rural Maharashtra. Although they nurtured an ambition to ally with the industrial capitalist interests, the political elite did not wish to do so at the cost of their own rural empires and votes.

The three contentious issues before State's political economy have been regional imbalances, agrarian crisis and urban–rural divide. There is a recurring overlap among them. As we argued in the third chapter, politics over these contentious issues did not lead to emergence of large-scale and long-standing mass movements. There were only sporadic attempts of mass mobilizations. Instead, as we discussed in the case of Marathas in Chapter 7, the issues of material disparities and deprivations were mainly articulated in the form of politics of identities and, thus, remained vulnerable to manipulations by the ruling elite. On their part, the ruling elite and the mainstream political parties always saw these issues in isolation. They refused to pay attention to the implicit connection among most of these critical issues facing the regional political economy. The interconnectedness of the critical issues was often missed in policymaking, public debates and competitive politics. As a result, politics in the State failed to develop a holistic understanding of these issues, whereby policies for larger issue-clusters rather than for individual issues could be framed. Questions of economic inequalities and economic policy had not been central to electoral or party competition in the State since the 1990s.

As we discussed in the fourth chapter, the strategy of adopting rapid liberalization did not pay off. It partially benefited the ruling elite, but it also scared locally based Maratha political workers as well as rural masses. Both the first SHS–BJP government of 1995 and their second government in 2014 aggressively pursued the urban–industrial–capitalist agenda and contributed to the spatial and sectoral skews in Maharashtra's political economy. Policies of Congress–NCP coalition governments have been no different. This indicates a consensus on the question of approach to political economy, it represents the stalemate on the question balancing development and well-being, and it also signals the continuing chasm between political power and economic power. The reading of political economy of Maharashtra over the past 60 years reveals how Maharashtra graduated to fit well into Kohli's ideal type of a developmental State regime, where public purpose is defined narrowly in terms of growth and where the state promotes capitalist development at the expense of welfare.

The electoral politics that we discussed in Chapters 4–6 needs to be seen in this broader context of distortions and compulsions. This context also draws attention to the limits of politics and the ways in which politics may respond to the compulsions. When politics is not able to keep the reigns of economy, it is more likely to turn to socio-cultural issues in order to search for legitimacy of the political elite. We return to this predicament of politics in the next chapter.

CONCLUSION
Footprints of a New Dominance?

This book has attempted to look at the political process in Maharashtra mainly through the prism of party politics and electoral competition. However, our argument is not confined to electoral ups and downs alone. Electoral politics is the peg to hang discussions of broader socio-political processes because there is a relation of mutuality between broader processes and electoral politics. Together these shape the phenomenon of what is often understood as 'State politics'. In that sense, the book belongs more to the subfield of State politics, which in turn throws light on dynamics of Indian politics. This link between State politics and all-India politics has been noticed for quite long.

'State politics' always holds the ability to tell us in great detail about the State under discussion. But besides that, State politics also tells us about politics more generally because even before the rising salience of States in Indian politics became noticeable,[1] most States evolved distinct and yet comparable patterns of democratic politics through their foundational struggles and subsequently their interface with

---

[1] In the 1990s, States suddenly occupied place of prominence in Indian politics and analyses of India's competitive politics, though comparative State politics was understood as the key area of study much earlier by scholars such as Myron Weiner, Francine Frankel and M.S. A. Rao. For a discussion of this point and the argument as to how States emerged as important foci of the 'Indian politics', see Yadav and Palshikar (2008, especially 14–16). However, beyond arguing about the emergence of States as the centre of the all-India, Yadav–Palshikar have presented an agenda for the study of State politics.

competitive politics. Thus, while States appear to be distinctive, they also hold many possibilities of comparisons and yield many common patterns. We have argued earlier that the exceptional features of politics of a given State resurface in the study of many other States and this allows for meaningful comparisons (Deshpande and Palshikar, 2009). Therefore, any study of the politics of a State is situated in both State specificity and cross-State comparability.

This more general point applies to this book as well. We aim at deciphering the State-level processes, but we also hope that this discussion will lead students of comparative politics to raise questions of comparison, and what looks at the first glance as rather 'unique' to Maharashtra may appear more comparable from the comparative perspective.

A NEW PARTY SYSTEM

Therefore, Maharashtra is no exception to this broader pattern of uniqueness and comparability. For decades, Maharashtra has always been held as the fortress of Congress party, and therefore this book appears to be constantly referring to the Congress party and the congress system. But we are aware that Congress party's electoral dominance was by no means exceptional to Maharashtra. Thus, a discussion of rise and fall of Congress dominance in Maharashtra holds comparative lessons for studying politics of the States like Rajasthan, Karnataka and Andhra Pradesh. Interestingly, these three States have thrown up different patterns of competitive politics in the aftermath of the congress system in each State. From bipolarity in Rajasthan to State-level parties becoming crucial in Andhra (and subsequently even in Telangana) to Karnataka passing through the phase of regionalism and making way for an emergent BJP, we witness varying patterns. Does Maharashtra come close to Karnataka—though with a difference? The State party and its regionalism has been part of the coalition politics of the State. But is it now turning towards making way for BJP's dominance?

Similarly, an engagement with the congress system and its trajectory in Maharashtra holds lessons about the nuances of functioning of the congress system in general. It draws attention to the fact that the 'congress system' was more powerful—and diverse—in its State-level manifestation than the all-India appearance. This realization about the Congress party and the congress system leads us to two further points beyond Maharashtra. One, other States also witnessed prolonged spells of Congress dominance, and two, dominance of Congress always had many cracks which ultimately led to the demise of the Congress party. Also, even before the decline of the Congress party set in, the congress system met with debilitating challenges in each of the States. This happened sooner in some States, later in some others. This led to a new party system in some States, while in others there was a prolonged and messy interregnum before some semblance of a new party system could shape. This supposition has spurred us to address the question of congress system and trajectory of Congress party in the post-1990 period as the central theme through which to weave the larger story of party politics in Maharashtra.

This holds a larger lesson just as much as it throws light on politics in Maharashtra. We believe that only through a critical analysis of the downfall of congress system one can comprehend the new phase/s of competitive politics at the State level. This book has attempted that exercise with respect to Maharashtra.

A student of Maharashtra's politics from the 1990s might be at a loss to distinguish between State-specific aspects of contemporary politics of Maharashtra and the all-India factors that resurfaced in the State in post-2014 phase. Once a Congress bastion, Maharashtra's politics decisively entered a post-Congress phase and a new regime in 2014. This change aligned State's politics completely with the all-India trend that emerged in that year. Arguments as to whether this change was only an extension of the rise of the BJP in parliamentary elections that year (and subsequently in 2019) or whether the State-specific factors shaped this change will continue among observers and students of State politics. What is more intriguing is the question whether the rise of the BJP in 2014 was strong enough to change politics at the State level. This question suddenly became urgent in the immediate aftermath of the Assembly elections of 2019. Even as the BJP appeared set to dominate the politics of the State following its parliamentary victory in 2019, the two Congress parties managed to forge a post-election alliance with the SHS and keep the BJP out of power after the Assembly elections of 2019 (more about this alliance discussed further).

As our chapter on these two elections (Chapter 6) has shown, the driving factors behind BJP's victories were the all-India developments and, at the same time, the rejuvenation of the BJP in 2014 was rooted in the State-level dynamics of social and political developments. As a result, the changes from 2014 have affected State's politics almost beyond recognition. Will this change be reversed because the BJP was kept out of power in the State following 2019 Assembly election?

In terms of party competition, it may be appropriate to say that like at the all-India level, Maharashtra has also entered a phase of 'second dominant party system' (Palshikar, 2017b). Nevertheless, there are a few limiting factors to the narrative of BJP's dominance at the State level as pointed out by Palshikar and Birmal (2019). It is necessary to note that the BJP has not emerged as the dominant party on its own—in both parliamentary elections where it recorded handsome victories, it was in alliance with the SHS and while the BJP itself may believe that the victories were entirely made possible because of its leadership, strategy and organization, the fact of alliance puts a question mark on the extent of dominance. If one goes by the outcomes of Assembly elections, the BJP came very close to winning a majority on its own in 2014 but had to finally get the support of the SHS to form the government, whereas in 2019, despite its reasonable success in terms of seats, the party was unable to form a government in the State.

The outcome of these elections indicates that in spite of BJP's new-found dominance, competitiveness is still a crucial characteristic of State politics. The BJP indeed emerged as a potentially dominant force since 2014, but its dominance has remained shaky at least till the time of writing this. Since 2014, the BJP repeatedly resorted to inducting members of the Congress and NCP into its fold. As late as in July–August 2019, on the eve of the Assembly election, a large number of MLAs from the Congress and NCP migrated to the BJP.

While this clearly indicates the growing sense of frustration within the then opposition parties, it also suggests that the BJP is building its dominance mainly with the help of such defections, and its project of achieving full-fledged dominance over State politics is yet in the making. Above all, in a comparative context, the electoral ascendance of the BJP in Maharashtra (around 2019) was much different from its complete control of polity and civil society in Gujarat (or, for that matter, MP and to an extent Rajasthan).

Thus, the emerging 'second dominant party system' in the State is still somewhat contingent, groping, lacking in clear social base and quite derivative in being dependent on national leadership.

STATE-SPECIFIC CONTEXT

This trajectory of BJP's halting march towards dominance since 2014 reiterates the fact that party competition and electoral politics shape in a larger State-specific context beyond the national one. To expand on the argument of 'second dominant party system', we might say that while it would have a particular all-India character, this new party system is also going to have State-specific expressions. As mentioned earlier, the BJP has had a long and deep-rooted existence in some States and has probably consolidated its hegemony there (Gujarat, for instance). In a State like UP, it has been trying hard since 2017 to similarly shape a more lasting influence on the civil society. On the other hand, Karnataka is a State where it is mainly striving to keep its electoral dominance intact. Maharashtra may also be in this same category where the urgent task before the BJP would be to situate itself electorally as a dominant player.

This book has implicitly argued, therefore, that the shift away from the congress system needs to be situated in this State-specific context. This context consists of (a) the historical legacy, (b) intertwining of regional and sub-regional identities, (c) the arena of movements, agitations, protests, etc., and (d) the asymmetry of competing claims over public policy. Therefore, our narrative of party competition is situated in the discussion of how these factors unfold in the political process of Maharashtra.

History and memory: As mentioned in the first chapter, Maharashtra's contemporary public discourse engages with history through some deeply entrenched ideas: the rise of Maratha rule with the advent of Shivaji Maharaj in the 17th century; the Bhakti sampradaya and its varied assessments during the nationalist movement; social churning occasioned by both non-Brahman movement and the awakening among the oppressed castes; and the movement for the formation of Marathi-speaking State—the Samyukta Maharashtra Movement. Needless to say, there is no single way in which each of these ideas or moments can be understood or appropriated. But their diverse appropriations have contributed to the language of politics in the State, the ways in which mass mobilizations occur, the way in which political competition is framed and the ways in which the idea of public (and therefore public policy) is comprehended. These legacies continue to occupy public attention, albeit with constantly renewed emphases and connotations. They provide ideological and emotive resources to incumbents and opponents; they supply ammunition to protest movements and radical activists, just as they are appropriated for legitimation of dominance and justification of the established order. While the Congress used these skilfully for shaping its hegemony, the SHS too, right from its inception, engaged with the memory of Shivaji and the legacy of the movement for State formation. The Left and other more radical groups also always went back to these moments in history/ memory to construct counter-hegemony. No wonder, the BJP has emerged in more recent times as the claimant and interpreter of history and linking that to its narrative of Hindutva. The success of the BJP in shaping a more durable dominance in the State will depend much on its ability to weave a cultural narrative connecting this historical memory with its broader Hindutva claims. In that task, the party has already made an advance in that its narrative has long ceased to be confined only to the upper-caste, middle-class urban constituency. As we have noted, long since the 1990s, the reconstruction of State's historical memory consistent with Hindutva has been taking place and the post-2014 popularity of the party does indeed expand the scope of this cultural initiative into rural hinterland beyond the upper and intermediate castes.

Region/regions within region: While history in general and the memory of the Samyukta Maharashtra Movement in particular sustain the Maharashtrian identity, this regional identity based on a common language, from the time of its formation, Maharashtra has always been a story of regions within region. Alongside regional identity, the claims of sub-regional identities have also resonated with politics in different parts of the State. While its non-colonial context and anti-Nizam struggles have often contributed to a muted sense of regional identity in the case of Marathwada region, the political economy of backwardness and a continuous experience of droughts have given a bitter political tinge to this identity. Vidarbh has also always nurtured a separate identity within the State even after more than six decades of its joining rest of the Marathi-speaking areas. While backwardness is the key factor in Marathwada, a sense of injury and betrayal mark politics of Vidarbh region where statehood beckons many regionalists. Yet it is remarkable that in both Marathwada and Vidarbh, regional sentiment has not produced any strong regional political vehicles for fighting backwardness. The movement for the formation of a separate State of Vidarbh has often failed to convert itself into a party of that part of the State. Instead, this regional identity claim has remained within the confines of existing party politics of the State—and played out mainly in terms of intra-party factionalism. Probably, this is the single most critical reason why Maharashtra has not witnessed an agitation like the Telangana agitation. As we saw in Chapter 8, the question of regional imbalance is an important issue in the State, but it has often remained subdued and within the confines of the existing party system rather than giving birth to new political processes or new parties.

This regional dynamics has two implications. One is that among the four major parties, no party can exclusively rely on any single region if it wants to sustain itself in the State-wide competitive politics. This is borne out in the case of the SHS, which, in order to expand beyond Mumbai and Konkan, had to diversify its nativist ideology, talk of Hindutva and also take up issues of Marathwada's agriculture. Similarly, the BJP, though having a robust base in Vidarbh and in principle wedded to the idea of small States, nevertheless, cannot overplay that issue lest it loses its support in rest of the State. The other implication, and following from the former, is that sub-regionalism will play out mainly in the realm of political economy and public policy. Politics in each region can, from time to time, turn to questions of development, allocations and share in power and resources.

Mass mobilizations: Movements and agitations on small scale have often dotted the politics of the State. But seldom have they assumed such proportions to force a change in the politics of the State either in terms of nature of competition or in terms of policy options. For a State that emerged from a long-drawn movement which mobilized large sections, this is a particularly strange feature. Besides the movement for a linguistic State, the movement of landless labourers led by Dadasaheb Gaikwad and then the Dalit Panthers Movement were important agitations that drew attention in terms of both distributive policy and equitable social relations. The 1970s also witnessed the slow evolution of the organization of informal sector workers gradually intervening in policy discourse (Deshpande, 2003). But as mentioned in Chapter 3, the State witnessed a major large-scale movement in the form of Shetkari Sanghatana in the 1980s. While the Sanghatana did convert itself into a party at a later stage, the party was a miserable failure, though the Sanghatana was able to make a deep impact on State's politics.

Besides the hugely evocative agitations of the Shetkari Sanghatana, the 2010s witnessed another similar State-wide movement in the form of the leaderless and loosely organized agitation by Maratha youth for the demand for reservations. Chapter 7 has contextualized this agitation within the larger framework of crisis faced by the Maratha community and its leadership. Although widespread, this agitation was a caste-based mobilization and, thus, opens up many new possibilities for politics of mass mobilizations in the State. The after-effects of the Maratha agitation have not exhausted yet nor has the agitation so far given rise to any particular political vehicle of the Maratha community. Unlike Karnataka or Gujarat, where the intermediate caste of the State has remained loyal to a particular party, Maharashtra's intermediate caste seems to be continuing its search for a political vehicle for more than two decades and over, and this prevarication of the Maratha elite seems the key factor in keeping State's party politics in a flux for a long time.

Policy universe: As Chapter 8 on political economy has brought out, politics of the State coexists with many asymmetries of competing claims over public resources. At one time, the State was known for the disproportionate patronage enjoyed by the 'sugar lobby'— which broadly included both the sugarcane cultivators and the political entrepreneurs engaged in managing sugar cooperatives. The overlap between the bosses of sugar cooperatives and influential party functionaries of the Congress party ensured that this sector would exercise greater control over state resources. As our discussion on political economy has argued, however, this asymmetry was easily overshadowed by the extent of influence exercised by industrial interests (and subsequently the interests of service sector which often overlapped with industrial interests) even while the sugar lobby was seen as the centre of political power. In fact, the two had an uneasy sharing of influence over making of public policy and over resource allocation. As Maharashtra became more and more urbanized, the asymmetry also took an urban–rural shape, pushing to margins the interests of middle and small farmers as also weakening of possibilities of either infrastructure development of rural areas or the robust growth of agro-industry as visualized at the time of founding of the State.

It might not be an exaggeration to say that over time, and particularly since the 1990s, this asymmetry in the arena of political economy has silently set aside most other factors in shaping not just policy but also nature of competitive politics; it has dominated all parties and eclipsed or redefined many other contradictions and cleavages in the society and politics of the State. This might appear paradoxical because as we discussed in Chapter 8, main political parties do not have very different visions of State's development, and they all share the broader idea of privately driven growth. In spite of that, the nature of distortions in the political economy is such that it throws up issues that occupy the realm of party politics—from SEZs to Maratha agitation, to demands by various castes for a better deal and the frequently emerging agrarian protests. Although not taking the shape of demands for a different set of public policy, the political economy of Maharashtra keeps shaping politics.

THE 1990s AS THE NEW PHASE

This book has identified the 1990s as the critical moment of departure in the politics of the State. Periodization of the ongoing political processes and their link to the past are always tricky issues.

Let us first take a long shot of the historical transformations. If one looks at the overall character of the politics of Marathi-speaking areas for the past century, Maharashtra has witnessed many key transformations or phases. Beginning with the advent of Lokmanya Tilak, who represented a combination of nationalist assertion and claims to power by the upper sections of the society around the end of the 19th century, past 130 years (1890s–2010s) have witnessed (a) rise of Brahmanetar politics that combined social reform, contestations over pre-existing social hierarchies and claims to power (1900–1930); (b) consolidation of Maratha domination within the framework of the congress system (1930–1960s); (c) stagnation and decaying of both Maratha dominance and the congress system accompanied by a long interregnum of bipolar competition (1970s–2000s); and finally (d) the first footprint of a new dominant party system (2014 onwards).

However, within the confines of post-independence competitive politics, it is fruitful to identify the 1990s as demarcating a major phase in State politics. In a specific sense, 'State politics' begins shaping only in the late 1950s when the uneasy management of the big bilingual State produced the politics of contemporary Maharashtra. In this sense, the six decades of the Marathi State (in 2020, Maharashtra completed 60 years of existence) can be clearly demarcated around 1990, as that point in time represents the coincidence of the decline of the Congress party and fall of the congress system in the State. Although all the features outlined above dominating the State politics (history/memory, regional identity, social churning and movement for State formation) did not undergo a transformation in this phase, their salience and relative importance in State politics changed in post-1990 period and, thus, the 1990s mark a major departure. Electoral politics brings out this departure even more sharply.

Chapters 3 and 4 have discussed the developments that led to this change. It is quite instructive that ups and downs in political fortunes do not immediately give a complete picture of what course politics is taking. Such fluctuations and indeed, seemingly stable patterns too, only contribute to the larger change that becomes perceptible more by hindsight. When the election of 1995 pushed the Congress aside, the political outcome was mainly understood in terms of the contemporary happenings such as the rise in popularity of Bal Thackeray, who became the nemesis of the Congress in that election, or the internal factionalism within the Congress party. When the SHS–BJP alliance failed to retain power in 1999, it looked as if the Congress had managed to turn the tide. Nevertheless, the analyses of 1995 even at that time indicated towards a more long-term impact. Overshadowed by the comeback of the Congress (along with the NCP), that long-term impact is something that ultimately characterizes the change brought about by 1995. In retrospect, therefore, 1995 becomes the most critical moment in the politics of the State since its formation in 1960. That election pushed to the forefront trends that were emerging since the late 1980s. Chapter 4 has identified that election as the first critical election in Maharashtra's politics. This characterization does not change just because the Congress was able to stage a comeback subsequently.

During the three decades (since 1990) that this book focuses upon, the Congress party was in power for 20 years. This begs the question about resilience of the Congress party. The networks it evolved over the years must have stood in good stead even during this critical period. In fact, writing in the 1980s, Lele (1984) had drawn attention to Congress party's resilience as far as Maharashtra was concerned. The outcome of 1990 Assembly election could also be seen as continuation of that resilience, but at the same time, that election also symbolically represented an initial crack in Maratha hegemony (Lele, 1990b). At the same time, the non-electoral trends that were identified by Vora and Palshikar (1990) and also subsequently by Hansen (1996) and Lele himself (1996), all directed attention to the nature of the impending change. It was not merely a change in the incumbent party; it was a party system change that also incorporated a change in the nature of State politics. Therefore, the comeback of the two Congress parties in 1999 and their ability to remain in power even in times of post-Congress polity at the all-India level needed to be situated partly in the resilience of the system that Congress domination had put in place and partly in the fact that there was no single party or political force in the State that could replace the Congress entirely. This interregnum of a departing congress system and an uncertain rise of a new system marked the two decades of 1995–2014. The old order was unable to restore itself, while a new order was unable to shape and stabilize.

WHAT CHANGED IN THE 1990s?

But in order to make sense of State politics in the post-2014 phase, we need to identify four factors that have dominated the three decades which constitute the core period discussed in this book. This would give us an idea as to what has changed and what is likely to change further.

- *Party system change:* Chapters 4–6 have brought forward the change in the nature of the party competition in Maharashtra. While we have repeatedly called this a shift away from the congress system, it is useful to further elaborate on this change. In an electoral democracy, the shifting and fluctuating fortunes of political parties should normally not be the centre of analytical attention. But in the case of Maharashtra, something peculiar marked the political process since the 1990s. While the Congress party declined, and while politics became more competitive, no single political force could replace the Congress. The alliance between the BJP and SHS was able to place a challenge before the Congress, but neither of these two parties could singly take the place of the Congress party. So much so that when a leader as strong as Sharad Pawar formed a separate party (both in the 1980s and then again in the late 1990s), that party could also not take the place of the Congress, nor could that split facilitate replacement of the Congress by the SHS or BJP.

In the 2014 Assembly election, the BJP came close to that. For the first time, the 2014 election signified the possibility of the Congress being replaced by another single contender. But the BJP again entered into an alliance with the SHS during the parliamentary election of 2019. This scenario has given rise to a number of smaller players since the 1990s (various RPI factions, Bahujan Mahasangh and its later incarnation, VBA, MNS, Jan Surajya Paksha, Swabhimani Shetkari Paksha, RSP, etc.). They entered the arena of party competition and in turn further ensured that no single party would easily replace the Congress. Rise of these parties also meant that political competition would remain within the confines of coalition politics.

In addition to this, party competition in the State also came to be marked by localization. While the smaller parties are more inevitably localized in terms of their respective spheres of influence, even the four larger players have for long operated in a somewhat regionalized context of political competition. Till 2014, thus, the two Congress parties were main contenders in western Maharashtra, while the SHS and BJP shared the political space of the Mumbai–Thane region and also the Konkan region. In Vidarbh, the competition was more between the Congress and the BJP. The small parties have also mostly been confined to narrow spaces of influence in terms of caste-group support or locale or both. Even the AIMIM, which entered State politics before the 2014 elections, has been able to muster support among Muslims of only the Marathwada region. The VBA led by Prakash Ambedkar aspired to play an important role across the State in 2019 LS elections, but while it polled an overall 7 per cent vote share at the State level, it performed much better in the Vidarbh and Marathwada regions only (Deshpande and Birmal, 2019; 30). The MNS also does not have reliable base beyond the Mumbai–Thane region.

This situation suggests that while smaller parties would continue to claim their pound of flesh, the larger parties have an opportunity to expand in order to gain a central position in the State politics. This also means a certain amount of tentativeness in the politics of the State in the near future until spatial and community-wise alignment with parties stabilizes. As Chapters 1 and 2 have shown, Congress's dominance was linked to specific socio-economic factors and demise of the Congress meant both that the forces aligned with the Congress moved away from that party (ordinarily understood as the process of de-alignment) and also the possibility of reconfiguration of those socio-economic forces. Chapter 7 has explained in detail how the de-alignment process has taken place in the case of the Maratha community and how a new configuration was awaited when the 2019 elections took place.

This somewhat contingent nature of the emergent party system is manifest also from the inability of the BJP to forge any clearly definable social coalition; rather, the success of the party so far depended on adding various social sections on an ad hoc and somewhat emotive basis to its electoral fold. Thus, electorally, while 2014–2019 signify clear indications of an emerging party system, in more substantive political terms, it was not certain what shape that party system would take and what would be the extent of dominance the BJP may acquire. Loss of governmental power in 2019 struck a blow to the party's ambition to gain dominance autonomously from its central leadership.

- *Social bases of parties:* This takes us to the question about the social bases of different parties. Through the 1990s, not only did the social bases of Congress changed, but the social bases of politics themselves underwent changes. To begin with, as we have elaborated, the Congress began to lose the support of Maratha voters. This section of 'drifting Marathas' was subsequently unable to identify with any single political vehicle for its political dominance. This is unlike Karnataka, where the BJP has anchored itself in steadfast support it receives from Lingayat community ever since disintegration of the JD in the State. Around the same time, the traditional base of Hindutva political platform broadened. Instead of only the upper castes and urban sections, Hindutva began to appeal to semi-urban, non-Brahman castes including the OBCs, much as it has in States like Madhya Pradesh and UP.

  The 1990s also witnessed the somewhat muted rise of OBCs, but this happened without any strong party affiliation. The SHS initially reaped the dividends of OBC aspirations and JD also momentarily sought to benefit from the reflected glory of being a party once led by V.P. Singh. Both these developments were effectively overshadowed by the BJP's adroit appropriation of the OBC constituency without adopting the rhetoric of social justice that was associated with it. During the same time, the SCs also continued to be fragmented between the Buddhists and non-Buddhists. The latter were attracted to the SHS and BJP, while the former were splintered among the RPI factions.

But beyond the caste–community considerations, the post-1990 period also saw the emergence of urban voters and middle classes as important drivers of electoral victories. While caste groups did remain relevant to party choices of voters, this development meant that the democratic upsurge (Yadav, 2000), noted in the North, was not able to make much dent in the State. Since 1995, the assertion of urban interests was noted and even during the three terms when the Congress was in power, rather than being able to reverse that trend, the party itself sought to enter the urban arena. In one sense, this is only a natural fallout of the urbanization seen by the State. It would have been unrealistic to expect that rural interests kept dominating, while the State and its economy were turning urban in composition. As we discussed in Chapter 8, around the same time, rural distress became acute, and the imbalance between urban and rural became quite pronounced. Thus, both politics and political competition hinged more on the urban sector in spite of the critical situation obtaining in rural areas. The SHS and BJP were able to make the most of this confusion by garnering greater support among rural voters and effectively breaching the long-standing characteristic of the Congress of being a party of rural voters. This change further ruptured the settled patterns of politics prior to the 1990s.

- *Policy orientation:* The changes in the overall policy framework witnessed by the State are not entirely different from what has happened elsewhere in India. Broadly known as liberalization, the economic policies during the 1990s shifted more in favour of private investments and encouragement to globalization in most of the States. Of course, the direction, speed and timing were different in each State.[2] As already noted, this shift took place in Maharashtra slightly earlier than in most States, with the process beginning in the late 1980s itself. There has been some discussion about the political fallout of changes in economic policies where ruling parties are supposed to be punished by voters used to more protectionist economic policies (Suri, 2003, 2004). In Maharashtra, that took the shape of fragmentation of Maratha vote and de-alignment of Maratha elite from the Congress and NCP.

In the case of Maharashtra, the trajectory of new economic policies also needs to be situated more in a somewhat State-specific context. As our discussion in Chapter 8 has shown, the political economy of the State was rooted in a combination of welfare-oriented capitalist development under State supervision and the less capitalistic initiative of cooperativization of the rural economy. During the 1980s, the crisis of cooperative sector had come to the forefront. This spurred the government around the end of that decade to incentivize private initiatives in the agricultural sector through support to marketization of rural economy. Since the cooperatives in rural areas were partly performing the task of protecting and enhancing private interests of the Maratha elite, the shift to privatization in rural areas went politically more or less unopposed. But soon this had adverse impact on rural economy as far as the poor were concerned. Therefore, since the 1990s, we find a certain amount of contingent public policymaking in the State. Policies have frequently responded to the immediate pressures and are often casually withdrawn and re-introduced. As was the case with Enron (Dabhol power project), whenever the State government was unable to convince local populations or ensure fair rehabilitation, decisions regarding industrial projects as also decisions about SEZs (or later, about the Nanar project) were withdrawn but without changing the overall direction of the policy. The other response has been characterized by the casual relief given by the government to various social sections which is often known

---

[2] On the changes in economic policies at the State level, see Jenkins (1999) and Sinha (2005).

as special packages. The recourse to packages simultaneously represents a hesitant populism and also the contingent nature of public policy. The idea of such packages predates actual coming of the new economic policy because Antulay, when he was the CM, resorted to this technique in order to assuage different aggrieved sections and buy peace with the voters as well as his detractors from the Maratha elite. The post-1990 governments have more frequently taken recourse to such packaged reliefs instead of any well thought-out policy measures whether it be natural disasters or grievances emerging from various policies of liberalization.

As Chapter 8 has shown, the ability of the State government to regulate corporate interests has considerably declined and, at the same time, the service sector has not only grown but also spread into rural areas. This development has meant a setback to rural interests and also shrinking of the cooperative sector. Thus, both the balancing acts that the State was initially intending to undertake—between private capital and cooperatives network on the one hand and between agro-industry and other industrial and trade interests on the other—became unmanageable for the State throughout the period since the 1990s.

- *Social fabric:* In the backdrop of the above changes, it was inevitable that the societal relations and equilibrium would change. When the agitation for the formation of a linguistic State was nearing fruition, there were questions asked about the nature of the new State that was most likely going to be dominated by the Maratha community. The legendry answer given by Y.B. Chavan was that Maharashtra would be ruled by the *bahujan samaj*. While this could literally be translated as the 'majority community' and hence interpreted as the rule of the most numerous Maratha community, this response also had three more connotations. First, as befitting democracy, it could simply mean the preponderance of the lay citizens, or in other words, a fair balance between the elites and the non-elite. Second, this claim also resonated with a much older formulation by V.R. Shinde, wherein he argues that *bahujans* include all labourers, working persons, artisans, etc., thus lifting the discourse beyond calculations of caste numbers. This was obviously a more potent ideological component of the term *bahujan samaj*. Third,

as probably Chavan's critics would argue, this term implied a pat-
rimonial relationship between the dominant Maratha community
and the rest of the society.

In either case, the idea of rule by *bahujan samaj* symbolized the
objective of turning societal domination into a somewhat benign and
legitimate project, a social contract. It also referred to a possibility of
employing caste into public discourse without necessarily turning
the discourse into a casteist argument. This ideological and political project also allowed the construction of multi-caste blocs rather
than restricting social mobilizations to any one caste alone. While
this project was never really very strong or successful (because the
late 1960s saw a series of atrocities against SCs in rural Maharashtra
leading to the formation of Dalit Panthers as a response and the mid-
1970s witnessed an even more severe backlash against the decision to
name a university after Dr Ambedkar), the limited achievement was
to contain fierce social contestations between Marathas and OBCs
on the one hand and the taming of Maratha-Brahman conflict on the
other. Even the post-Mandal mobilization of OBCs and non-inclusion
of Marathas in the list of backward communities did not rupture this
equation very much.

In contrast, since the 1990s, the social fabric began to disintegrate
more explicitly. Last two chapters, discussing the predicament of
Maratha politics and the trajectory of political economy hold an answer
to this. As the capacity of the political elite to negotiate an equilibrium
among competing social claims declined and as the ability of the political economy to contain challenges related to livelihood also became
limited, the ideological social contract that accompanied formation of
the State also began to wear out in more than one way.

First was the snapping of Marathi identity and the rising complaints
of regional imbalance that marked the fragility of the new social relations. As already mentioned, backwardness of Marathwada emerged
as a key issue in the 1970s, but it was handled through a political
balancing among the Congress elite. In the 1980s, another political
response came in the form of a committee to study and recommend
on the issue of regional imbalance. But subsequently, the failure of

political parties to truly represent the entire State symbolized the overall failure of retaining the social unity of a large State comprising of different regions with varying political histories. Two, as the State became more and more urbanized, a sharply polarized spatial division took over. The metropolises such as Mumbai, Thane and Pune saw a turn towards unmanageable urban agglomeration, with many other large cities following in tow, while rural neglect and distress took the form of a crisis. This division makes it extremely difficult to describe Maharashtra as one political community. The only connect between rural hinterlands and the urban centres happen to be the continuous migration of rural poor into the category or urban poor.

Three, as discussed in Chapter 3, since the late 1980s, tensions between Hindus and Muslims took the form of a Hindu political constituency that was first represented by the SHS and was later taken over by the BJP. Although the State did not experience large-scale religious conflicts after 1993, the Mumbai riots and violence of 1992–1993 deeply divided the society without taking the form of direct confrontation. Till the late 1990s, the bitter rhetoric of the SHS continued to reap political benefits and after the re-emergence of the BJP in 2014, a much more consolidated Hindu constituency came into being.

Fourth, and paradoxically, while the Hindu constituency amalgamates most non-Dalit castes (and even some sections of the SCs), the greatest damage to the social fabric has come about through the mobilization of each caste and community as a single unit. Contrary to the project of building social blocs and despite the coming together of many sections on Hindutva platform, the period since the 1990s witnessed single-caste mobilizations as prudent and viable political formations. In other words, not only the various groups (castes) do not believe in aligning with other horizontally located groups in terms of socio-economic hierarchy, but they also do not expect the State to attend to their demands unless they organize as independent political groups. This symbolizes both the torn social fabric of the State and the bankruptcy of the State government to extend well-being in a non-sectarian fashion.

The high-voltage agitation by the Maratha community around 2016–2018 represented this trend in the most expressive manner. In response, the State government not only legislated reservations for a single caste for the first time, but it also went on to devise a number of other caste-specific measures such as scholarships. This policy recognized the deeply fragmented social fabric of the Marathi society and implicitly legitimized mobilizations and policymaking on caste basis.

Where do all these changes take the State? In terms of both electoral politics and sociopolitical dominance, what new patterns might shape on the basis of these developments since the 1990s?

THE POWER TRIANGLE

Three different registers of power constitute the power triangle that determines the course of sociopolitical developments. When two of these three overlap, elite domination is likely to easily shape into hegemony (or at least become durable and broadly accepted dominance beyond electoral successes). Therefore, when one talks of the loss of 'Maratha hegemony', there is an implicit awareness of the collapse of these registers.

During the 1960s, democratic politics and the social composition of the State produced a well-organized structure of political (governmental) power of the Maratha elite, who also happened to have reasonably close linkages below—among the Maratha community—and hence legitimacy deriving from it. This ensured their superiority in one register of power. The skilful interventions in the political economy facilitated the growth of an entrepreneur class among the Maratha farmers who went on to control agrarian resources and public policy, thus making their entry into the second register of power—the economy. Their claim as natural leaders of the Bahujan Samaj and their adroit neutralization of Brahman antipathy allowed the Maratha elite a toehold in the third register of power—the social–cultural realm. As Chapter 7 has shown, this arrangement crumbled in course of time.

As we have argued earlier, from the 1970s onwards, the deep-seated incongruence between power exercised by the political elite and the power of the industrial-economic interests had begun to weaken the hold of the political elite. The political elite, dependent as they were on rural interests and rural votes, could not afford to allow the material interests of the urban-industrial sector to dominate the sphere of public policy completely; but they could also not adequately regulate those interests in public interest. This led to duality of power centres, instability, weakening of the legitimacy of the elite and a disjunction between political power and material power. All governments since then, and particularly from the 1990s, have faced this crisis. If they succumb to the material interests of the urban-industrial sections, they tend to lose both legitimacy and hegemony and become only contingent rulers with vacuous electoral victories. On the other hand, if they seek to counter the material interests, they are unlikely to enjoy governmental power.

The only way to survive in times of this disjunction could be by the way of invoking societal power. But during the period under discussion, this dimension of power was fast eluding the political elite. Both the congress system and the hegemony of the Marathas met with their nemesis because of the erosion of social power during the post-1990 period. This was more than merely losing their electoral base; it pertained to a disjunction between political power and social power. It is not entirely paradoxical that in electoral democracies, governmental power can be won despite the hollowness of social claims and inability to build durable social coalitions. In fact, this broader story of the power triangle is not uncommon. Many States of India have gone through this from time to time. Communities and caste blocs that began as projects of societal power tumbled to remain only electorally successful—the great experiments of OBC politics in both UP and Bihar are instances from the same period that is discussed in this book.

In a similar fashion, much of the inability of Sharad Pawar to replace and remake the Congress, and also his inability to win the goodwill despite being the most durable and fairly popular leader in the State, can be explained by the disjunction between societal and political power. In such a situation, claims to societal power through populism, demagoguery and personality cults temporarily give an appearance of combining the two. Maharashtra experienced this during the 1990s, when Bal Thackeray was riding on the wave of popularity. Once that temporary moment had passed, politics remained fractured into the three registers separately.

When the three registers of power operate independently, two things happen. One is that there is a move towards resource management devoid of much reference to public interest. The other is a social universe made of suspicions and angular identities that appear irreconcilable. We have already discussed the latter above and the former in the preceding chapter.

With the rise of the BJP in 2014, a new narrative had emerged in this process of unfolding of the power triangle. Consistent with its all-India politics, the BJP in Maharashtra also began seeking societal ascendance through the rhetoric of strong leadership and Hindutva (populism and majoritarianism). It may be argued that in Maharashtra, the BJP did not engage much in the Hindutva rhetoric. This is because there is no social counter to it in the State. The SHS claimed to share the societal worldview of the BJP, and the Congress and NCP failed to position themselves as the opponents in the social realm. Even in 1995, a section of Maratha elite migrated to the BJP not merely because of temporary political gains but also because it did not find the Hindutva rhetoric inconsistent with its political and sociocultural universe. Since 2014, when the BJP catapulted itself into the centre of power in the State, it has also been able to neutralize alternative narratives of social power and further marginalize the various 'progressive' movements which upheld a more radical construction of social power.

STRUCTURE AND CHARACTER OF STATE'S POLITICS

But this narrative of an emergent BJP met a challenge in the formation of a non-BJP government in 2019. Does the formation of an 'unlikely' coalition among the Congress, NCP and SHS hold the possibility of changing the course of BJP's ascendance?

First, as we argued above, the BJP will be seeking to emerge as a dominant force in two separate registers—the register of formal/ electoral power and the register of sociocultural dominance. In this sense, the formation of the MVA might have temporarily postponed BJP's consolidation in one arena of power. However, in a somewhat unintended and ironic manner, the formation of the MVA government may signify deeper changes that have occurred in the structure and character of State's politics.

As already noted above, the rise of a new centre in the form of the BJP is sure to change the structure of competition. The formation of the MVA actually testifies to that. Besides that, we have noted the emergence of smaller parties, and this may be the time when their role may become critical more than ever before, because an isolated BJP can strike back only with the help of localized and smaller players. For the MVA partners, the more complicating factor is the challenge of facing next elections together, because that would severely constrain their individual expansion. In this sense, the process of changing the structure of State's politics that got a push in 2014 is only likely to strengthen.

But more than that, the ease with which Ajit Pawar agreed (momen-tarily) to align with the BJP and then the ease with which the SHS chose to align with the Congress parties in exchange of the post of CM need to be seen beyond mere cynical intrigues for power. These developments suggest that the congress system has disappeared and that the *character* of State's politics has almost changed. The SHS as a force represented vigilantism and a popular version of Hindutva politics. Observers will keep debating if it gave up on these two; what is more important is to remember that at least some of its style and content have become the acceptable way of 'doing politics' in the State. In this sense, the SHS represents the new normal in State's politics as earlier hinted by Palshikar (2017c). In other words, there is a meeting ground among the MVA partners beyond their political calculations. Both vigilantism in the sense of mobilizing spontaneous-looking action by party cadres and a broad ethos of political Hindutva have gained acceptability.

This is where the Congress in the State may face deeper challenge than it has ever met with. Having already lost support of the Marathas, who have been willing to turn to Hindutva appeals since 1995, the

Congress does not have a social base just as it does not have an ideological base left to pursue. By aligning with the SHS, it has ensured its survival in the game of power; will it be able to exploit that survival to imagine itself differently in the State? Will it have the initiative and imagination to use this coalition arrangement to re-situate itself in the society and politics of the State? If it does not, and it seems unlikely, then the character of State's politics would change further—and more swiftly.

The electoral victories of the BJP not only meant a momentary upsurge of a party, but it also facilitated ideological and cultural initiatives by the BJP and its sociocultural allies. As a result, the rise in 2014 brought the BJP on the threshold of combining societal and political power. The weakening of cooperatives and the willingness of the urban material interests to align with the BJP nationally suggest that the BJP may also have a comfortable equation with the other register of power, the economy. Notwithstanding the setback in 2019 in not being able to form a government in the State, post-2014 politics has opened up substantive possibilities for the BJP being able to shape and sustain its dominance in all three registers of power and possibly gain reasonable acceptability in the course of time. If that happens, Maharashtra would have truly entered a new phase of politics, aligning with the all-India trend, of a new political dominance sustained by economic and sociocultural registers of power.

REFERENCES

Agwane, R. (2019). *Maharashtra ani Uttar Pradeshatil Charmakar Sanghatananche Rajkaran* [Marathi: Politics of Charmakar associations in Maharashtra and Uttar Pradesh] (Unpublished PhD dissertation). Department of Politics and Public Administration, Savitribai Phule Pune University, Pune.

Anderson, S., Francois, P., Kotwal, A., & Kulkarni, A. (2016). Distress in Marathaland. *Economic & Political Weekly, 2* (51, 17 December), 14–16.

Anubhav. (1996). *Yuti sarkarche ek varsha* [Marathi: One year of the Yuti government]. special issue (March).

Bagchi, S. (2019). Re-evaluating Maratha politics in Maharashtra: 2014 Assembly elections and after. In A. Kumar & Y. Sisodia (Eds.), *How India votes: A state-by-state look* (pp. 270–287). Orient Black Swan.

Balkrishnan, S. (2019). *Shareholder cities: Land transformations along urban corridors in India.* University of Pennsylvania Press.

Bhadbhade, N., Bhagat, S., Joy, K.J., Samuel, A., Lohokare, K. & Adagale, R. (2019). Can Jalyukt Shivar Abhiyan prevent drought in Maharashtra? *Economic & Political Weekly, 54* (25, 22 June), 12–14.

Bhandari, L., & Kale, S. (Eds.). (2007). *Indian states at a glance 2006–2007 Maharashtra: Performance, facts and figures.* Dorling Kindersley.

Bhole, B.L. (2010). *Bharatiya Shetkari Kamgar Paksh* [Marathi: Peasants and Workers Party of India]. Lokvangmaya Griha.

Birmal, N. (1989). *Hindu Ekata Andolan: Maharashtratil Nava-Hindutvavadacha ek abhyas* [Marathi: Hindu Ekata Andolan: A study of Neo-Hinduism in Maharashtra] (Unpublished MPhil dissertation). Department of Politics and Public Administration, Pune University, Pune.

Birmal, N. (1999). Prabal jaticha pradeshik paksha: Rastravadi Congress [Marathi: Regional party of the dominant caste: Nationalist Congress Party]. *Samaj Prabodhan Patrika*, October–November, 221–225.

Birmal, N. (2010). Maharashtrachi badalati rajkiya arthvyavastha (1960 te 2010) [Maharashtra's Changing Political Economy (1960 to 2010)]. *Vichar Shalaka, 23* (89–92), 67–76.

Birmal, N., & Bhoiwar, R. (2020). Lok Sabha ani Vidhan Sabha (2019) Nivadnukantil matdanache sthannihay ani vibhagnihay vishele-shan [Region-wise and locality-wise analysis of the Lok Sabha and Vidhan Sabha (2019) Elections]. In T. Jadhav (Ed.), *Maharashta Varshiki 2020* (pp. 315–322). Unique Academy.

Brahme, S. (1983). *Drought in Maharashtra—1972: A case for irrigation planning.* Orient Longman; Gokhale Institute of Politics and Economics.

Brahme, S., & Upadhayay, A. (1979). *A critical analysis of the social formation and peasant resistance in Maharashtra* (Vol. 1–3; mimeo). Shankar Brahme Samaj Vidynan Granthalaya.

Buddhiwant, A. (2009). *Maratha OBCkaran* [Marathi: Maratha OBCization]. Shramik Pratishthan.

Carras, M. (1972). *The dynamics of Indian political factions: A study of district councils in the state of Maharashtra.* Cambridge University Press.

Carter, A. (1975). *Elite politics in rural India: Political stratification and political alliances in western Maharashtra.* Vikas Publishing House.

Cashman, R. (1975). *Myth of the Lokmanya: Tilak and mass politics in Maharashtra.* University of California Press.

Chavan, P. (2015). Rural credit cooperatives in Maharashtra: A tale of growing divides. *Economic & Political Weekly, 50* (38), 52–60.

Damodaran, H. (2008). *India's new capitalists: Caste, business and industry in a modern nation.* Permanent Black.

Dandekar, H., & Mahajan, S. (2001). MSRDC and Mumbai-Pune expressway: A sustainable model for privatizing construction of physical infrastructure? *Economic & Political Weekly, 36* (7, 17 February), 549–559.

Datar, A. (2007). *The Bharatiya Jan Sangh in Maharashtra* (MPhildissertation). Department of Politics and Public Administration, University of Pune, Pune.

Datar, A., & Ghotale, V. (2013). Maharashtra cabinets: Social and regional profile 1960–2010. *Economic & Political Weekly, 68* (36, 7 September), 37–42.

Desai, D. (1987). *Maharashtratil dushkal* [Marathi: Drought in Maharashtra]. Magoa Prakashan.

Desai, D. (2011). *Maharashtraachya vikasachi disha: Havi navi malvat* [Marathi: The direction of Maharashtra's development: A new pathway needed]. Parivartan Academy.

Deshmukh, A. (2006). *Solapur jillhyatil Lingayat samajyachya sanghatana* [Marathi: Associations of Lingayat community in Solapur district] (Unpublished MPhil dissertation). University of Pune, Pune.

Deshpande, G. P. (Ed.). (2002). *Selected writings of Jotirao Phule.* Left Word Books.

Deshpande, P. (2007). *Creative pasts, historical memory and identity in western India 1700–1960.* Permanent Black.

Deshpande, R. (2000). Balshastri Jambhekar: Paramparik abhijanvargachi patharakhan [Marathi: Balshastri Jambhkear: Case of extending support to traditional elite]. In R. Vora (Ed.), *Adhunikata ani Parampara: Ekonisavya Shatakatil Maharashtra* [Modernity and tradition: Maharashtra of nineteenth century] (pp. 111–141). Pratima Prakashan.

Deshpande, R. (2003). *Informal sector workers in Pune city: Four narratives* (Occasional paper). Pune: Department of Politics and Public Administration, University of Pune.

Deshpande, R. (2004). Reservations to Kunbi-Marathas: Backward journey of a caste. *Economic & Political Weekly, 39* (14 & 15, 3–10 April), 1448–1449.

Deshpande, R. (2005). *State and democracy in India* (Occasional Paper Series III, No. 4), Special Assistance Programme, Department of Politics and Public Administration. Pune: University of Pune.

Deshpande, R. (2006). Maharashtra: Politics of anxieties, frustrations and outrage, *Economic & Political Weekly, 41* (14, 8–14 April), 1304–1307.

Deshpande, R. (2009, September). Breaking free of the post-Mandal deadlock (Seminar No. 601), 76–80.

Deshpande, R. (2010). *Caste associations in the post-Mandal era: Notes from Maharashtra* (CAS Occasional Paper Series, No. 2). Pune: Department of Politics and Public Administration, University of Pune.

Deshpande, R. (2013). Who doesn't want Pune to become Singapore? In I. Shirley & C. Neill (Eds.), *Asian and Pacific cities: Development patterns* (pp. 138–149). Routledge.

Deshpande, R. (2014a). Seeking OBC status: Political strategies of two dominant castes. *Studies in Indian Politics, 2* (2, December), 169–183.

Deshpande, R. (2014b). 'Bhagwangadavarun mala Mumbai disate aahe' : How caste survives amidst democratic politics. In D. Deak & D. Thorner (Eds.), *Rethinking western India: The changing contexts of culture, society and religion* (pp. 91–104). Orient BlackSwan.

Deshpande, R. (forthcoming). Caste associations and the post-Mandal politics of caste. In S. Jodhka & J. Naudet (Eds.), *Oxford handbook of caste*. Oxford University Press.

Deshpande, R., & Birmal, N. (2009). Maharashtra: Congress–NCP manages victory. *Economic & Political Weekly, 44* (39, 26 September), 136–140.

Deshpande, R., & Birmal, N. (2017). Beyond the Congress system in Maharashtra. In S. Palshikar, S. Kumar, & S. Lodha (Eds.), *Electoral politics in India: Resurgence of the Bharatiya Janata Party* (pp. 137–152). Routledge.

Deshpande, R., & Birmal, N. (2019). BJP replaces the Congress in Maharashtra. *Economic & Political Weekly, 54* (32, 10 August), 29–32.

Deshpande, R., & Birmal, N. (forthcoming). Maharashtra: (The pangs of) transitions into a new party system. In S. Shastri, A. Kumar, & Y. Sisodia (Eds.), *Electoral dynamics in the states of India: Return of a second dominant party system*. Routledge.

Deshpande, R., & Palshikar, S. (2008). Occupational mobility: How much does caste matter? *Economic & Political Weekly, 43* (34), 61–70.

Deshpande, R. & Palshikar, S. (2009). Redefining state politics in India: Shift towards comparisons. Lokniti. Retrieved from http://www.lokniti.org/newsletter/theme_note.pdf.

Deshpande, R., & Palshikar, S. (2017). Political economy of a dominant caste. In R. Nagaraj & S. Motiram (Eds.), *Political economy of contemporary India* (pp. 77–97). Cambridge University Press.

Deshpande, R., Tillin, L., & Kailash, K. K. (2019). The BJP's welfare schemes: Did they make a difference in the 2019 elections? *Studies in Indian Politics, 7* (2, January–June), 219–233.

Dev, M. (1995). Alleviating poverty: Maharashtra employment guarantee scheme. *Economic & Political Weekly, 30* (41–42, 14 October), 2663–2676.

Dhanagare, D. N. (1994). The class character and politics of the farmers' movement in Maharashtra during the 1980s. *The Journal of Peasant Studies, 21* (3–4), 72–94.

Gadgil, D. R. (1952). *Poona—A socio-economic survey: Part 2.* Gokhale Institute of Politics and Economics.

Gadgil, D. R. (2011). The Pravara Sahakari Karkhana: An interpretative account (written on the occasion of the visit of Pandit Jawaharlal Nehru to the Karkhana on 15 May 1961). In S. Brahme (Ed.), *Indian economy—Problems and prospects: Selected writings of D. R. Gadgil* (pp. 309–3220). Oxford University Press.

Gadgil, D. R. (1975). *Writings and speeches of Prof. D. R. Gadgil on cooperation.* Gokhale Institute of Politics and Economics.

Gaikwad, P. (2005). *Brahmani dharmanusar Marathe Shudrach* [Marathi: Marathas are Shudra only according to Brahmani religion]. Jijai Prakashan.

Gholwe, S. (2013). *Maharashtra ani Madhya Pradeshatil Dhangar samajache rajkaran: Ek toulanik abhyas* [Marathi: Politics of Dhangar community in Maharashtra and Madhya Pradesh: A comparative study] (Unpublished PhD dissertation). Department of Politics and Public Administration, Savitribai Phule Pune University, Pune.

Gholwe, S. (2020). *Jalayukt Shivar Abhiyanamule gava kharach dushkalmukta zhali ka?* [Marathi: Did villages become drought-free because of Jalayukt Shivar Abhiyan?]. In T. Jadhav (Ed.), *Maharashta Varshiki 2020* (pp. 315–322). Unique Academy.

Ghotale, V. (2017). *Maratha varchaswache badalte akrutibandh* [Marathi: The changing patterns of Maratha dominance] (Unpublished PhD dissertation). Department of Politics and Public Administration, University of Pune, Pune.

Ghotale, V., & Kulkarni, M. (2019). Maharashtra Legislative Assembly elections 2019: Changing social equations. *Economic & Political Weekly, 54* (51, 28 December), 33–39.

Gokhale, P. ([1988] 2006). Lokahitawadi Gopal Hari Deshmukh (1823–1882). In Y. Sumant & D. Punde (Eds.), *Maharashtratil jaatisanstha vishayak vichar* [Marathi: Thinking about Caste system in Maharashtra] (pp. 39–47). Pratima Prakashan.

Gore, M. S. (1989). *Non-Brahman movement in Maharashtra*. Segment Book Distributors.

GoM. (1972). *Economic survey of Maharashtra (1971–72)*. Directorate of Economics and Statistics, Planning Department.

GoM. (1977). *Economic survey of Maharashtra (1976–77)*. Directorate of Economics and Statistics, Planning Department.

GoM. (1987). *Statistical abstract of Maharashtra state (1986–1987)*. Directorate of Economics and Statistics, Planning Department.

GoM. (1996). *Economic survey of Maharashtra (1995–96)*. Directorate of Economics and Statistics, Planning Department.

GoM. (2008). *Economic survey of Maharashtra (2007–08)*. Directorate of Economics and Statistics, Planning Department.

GoM. (2010, April). *Migration particulars: Report based on data collected in state sample of 64th round of national sample survey (July 2007–June 2008)*. Directorate of Economics and Statistics, Planning Department. Retrieved from https://mahades.maharashtra.gov.in/files/report/nss_64_10.2_m.pdf

GoM. (2011). *Economic survey of Maharashtra (2010–11)*. Directorate of Economics and Statistics, Planning Department.

GoM. (2013). *Report of the high-level committee for balanced regional development*. Planning Department.

GoM. (2014). *Economic survey of Maharashtra (2013–14)*. Directorate of Economics and Statistics, Planning Department.

GoM. (2016). *Economic census of Maharashtra (2015–16)*. Directorate of Economics and Statistics, Planning Department.

GoM. (2020). *Economic survey of Maharashtra (2019–20)*. Directorate of Economics and Statistics, Planning Department.

Gupta, D. (1982). *Nativism in a metropolis: Shiv Sena in Bombay.* Manohar Publications.

Gupta, D. (2015). The importance of being 'rurban'. *Economic & Political Weekly*, 50(24, 13 June), 37–43.

Guru, G. (1995). *Gowari tragedy—Crisis of Maratha hegemony. Economic & Political Weekly*, 30 (6, 11 February), 303–304.

Guru, G. (1999). *Sugar workers' radicalism in Maharashtra* (Occasional paper, I (2)). Pune: Department of Politics and Public Administration, University of Pune.

Hansen, T. B. (1996). The vernacularization of Hindutva: The BJP and Shiv Sena in rural Maharashtra. *Contributions to Indian Sociology*, 30 (2), November, 177–214.

Harriss, J. (2001). *Depoliticizing development: The World Bank and social capital.* Left Word Books.

Jaffrelot, C. (2003). *India's silent revolution: The rise of the lower castes in North Indian politics.* Permanent Black.

Jaffrelot, C., & Kalaiyarasan, A. (2019). The political economy of the Jat agitation for other backward class status. *Economic & Political Weekly*, 54 (7, 16 February), 29–36.

Jagzap, H. (2nd edn. 2010). *Republican Paksh* [Marathi: Republican Party]. In S. Palshikar & S. Kulkarni (Eds.), *Maharashtratil satta-sangharsh* [Power play in Maharashtra] (pp. 180–197). Samakaleen Prakashan.

Jasper, D. (2002). *Commemorating Shivaji: Regional and religious identities in Maharashtra, India* (Unpublished PhD dissertation). Graduate Faculty of Political and Social Science, New School University, New York, NY.

Jenkins, R. (1999). *Democratic politics and economic reforms in India.* Cambridge University Press.

Jenkins, R. (2004a). In varying states of decay: Anti-corruption politics in Maharashtra and Rajasthan. In R. Jenkins (Ed.), *Regional reflections comparing politics across India's states* (pp. 219–252). Oxford University Press.

Jenkins, R. (2004b). *Reservation politics in Rajasthan* (Working paper, Crisis States Programme). London: London School of Economics.

Jha, M., & Kumar, P. (2016). Homeless migrants in Mumbai. *Economic & Political Weekly, 51* (26–27, 25 June), 69–75.

Joshi, R. (1968). Maharashtra. In M. Weiner (Ed.), *State politics in India* (pp. 177–214). Princeton University Press.

Kadukar, H. (2006). *Vidarbhache magaslepan aani Vidarbha Vaidhanik Vikas Mandal* [Marathi: Vadarbha's backwardness and Vidarbha Development Board] (Unpublished MPhil dissertation). University of Pune, Pune.

Kale, S. (2014). *Electrifying India: Regional political economies of development.* Stanford University Press.

Kamat, A. R. (1983). *Essays on social change in India.* Somaiyya Prakashan.

Key, V. O., Jr. (1955). A theory of critical elections. *The Journal of Politics, 17* (1), 3–18.

Khedekar, P. (Ed.). (2008). *Maratha aarakshan* [Marathi: Maratha reservations]. Jijai Prakashan.

Khopade, S. (1992). *Bhivandi dangal 1984* [Marathi: Bhivandi riots 1984]. Granthali.

Kohli, A. (2012). *Poverty amid plenty in the new India.* Cambridge University Press.

Kopardekar, G. (2020). *Policy ecosystem for industrial infrastructure in Maharashtra* (unpublished). Report submitted to the Centre for Public Policy and Democratic Governance, Savitribai Phule Pune University, Pune.

Kothari, R. (1964). The congress 'system' in India. *Asian Survey, 4* (12, December), 1161–1173.

Kotwal, A., Kulkarni, A., Francois, P., and Anderson, S. (2015). One Kind of Democracy. *Economic and Political Weekly, 50* (26–27, 27 Jun).

Kshirsagar, R. K. (1979). *Bharatiya Republican Paksha* [Marathi: Republican Party of India]. Kailash Publications.

Kulkarni, A. G. (1968). *A study of political parties in Maharashtra: With special reference to the period 1947–1962* (PhD dissertation). University of Pune, Pune.

Kulkarni, B. (1998). *Marathwadyacha vikas: Abhyas va chintan* [Marathi: Development of Marathwada: Studies and reflections]. Padm Prakashan.

Kulkarni, S. (1991). *Brahmanetar Chalwalicha jaati vishayak drushtikon* [Marathi: The non-Brahmin movement's perspective on caste] (Unpublished MPhil dissertation). University of Pune, Pune.

Kulkarni, S. (1997a, 16 March). *Sthanik swarajya sanstha nivadnuka* [Marathi: Elections to local self-government]. *Loksatta*, pp. 1–5.

Kulkarni, S. (1997b, 26 January). *Nagar palika nivadnukit sarvach paksh parabhut* [Marathi: All parties defeated in the municipal council elections]. *Loksatta*, pp. 6–7.

Kulkarni, S. (2nd edn. 2019). *Maharshi Vitthal Ramji Shinde Samajun ghetana* [Marathi: Understanding Vitthal Ramji Shinde]. Samakaleen Prakashan.

Kulkarni, M., & Deshmukh, K. (2020). *Pantapradhan Peek Vima Yojanechi Maharashtratil kamgiri* [Marathi: Performance of the prime minister's Crop Insurance Scheme in Maharashtra]. In T. Jadhav (Ed.), *Maharashtra Varshiki 2020* (pp. 358–366). Unique Academy.

Kurulkar, R. P. (2009). The problem of regional disparities in Maharashtra state and the role of the regional development boards. *Journal of Indian School of Political Economy, 21* (1–4, January–December), 261–280.

Lele, J. (1982a). Chavan and the political integration of Maharashtra. In Inamdar N., Bapat R., Tawale S., Limay P. Kshire V., & Vora R. (Eds.), *Contemporary India* (pp. 29–54). Continental Prakashan.

Lele, J. (1982b). *Elite pluralism and class rule: Political development in Maharashtra.* Popular Prakashan.

Lele, J. (1984). One party dominance in Maharashtra: Resilience and change. In J. Wood (Ed.), *State politics in contemporary India: Crisis and continuity* (pp. 169–196). Westview Press.

Lele, J. (1990a). Caste, class and dominance: Political mobilization in Maharashtra. In F. Frankel & M.S. A. Rao (Eds.), *Dominance and state power in modern India: Decline of a social order* (Vol. 2; pp. 115–211). Oxford University Press.

Lele, J. (1990b, April–June). *Vidhan Sabha nivadanuk ani Marathyanche dhurinatva* [Marathi: State Assembly elections and Maratha hegemony]. *Samaj Prabodhan Patrika*.

Lele, J. (1996). Saffronization of the Shiv Sena: The political economy of city, state and nation. In S. Patel & A. Thorner (Eds.), *Bombay: Metaphor for modern India* (pp. 185–212). Oxford University Press.

Lele, J. (2015). Indian society in the times of Chavan. In P. Pawar (Ed.), *Yashwantrao Chavan reflects on India—Society and politics* (pp. 14–57). Diamond Publications.

Lenneberg, C. (1988). Sharad Joshi and the farmers: The middle peasant lives. *Pacific Affairs, 61* (3), 446–464.

Maharashtra Assembly Elections: Farewell to Maratha Politics?, *Economic and Political Weekly*, 49 (43–44, 1 November 2014), 10–13.

Manor, J. (1989). Karnataka: Caste, class and dominance and politics in a cohesive society. In F. Frankel & M.S. A. Rao (Eds.), *Dominance and state power in modern India: Decline of a social order* (Vol. 1; pp. 323–360). Oxford University Press.

Mohanty, B. B. (2019). *Agrarian transformation in western India: Economic gains and social costs*. Routledge.

More, S. (2013). *Garja Maharashtra* [Marathi: Hail Maharashtra]. Sakal Prakashan.

Morkhandikar, R. S. (1967). The Shiv Sena: An eruption of sub-nationalism. *Economic & Political Weekly, 2* (42, 21 October), 1903–1906.

Motegaonkar, S. (2012). *Maharashtratil aitihasik pratikanche rajkaran—Chhatrapati Shivaji Maharaj ek vishesh abhyas* [Marathi: Politics of historical symbols in Maharashtra: A study of Chhatrapati Shivaji Maharaj] (Unpublished MPhil dissertation). Department of Politics and Public Administration, University of Pune, Pune.

Murugkar, L. (1991). *Dalit Panther movement in Maharashtra, a sociological appraisal*. Popular Prakashan.

Novetzke, C. L. (2004). The Laine controversy and the study of Hinduism. *International Journal of Hindu Studies, 8* (1–3), 183–201.

O'Hanlon, R. (1985). *Caste, conflict and ideology: Mahatma Jotirao Phule and low caste protest in nineteenth-century western India (Cambridge South Asian Studies)*. Cambridge University Press.

Omvedt, G. (1976). *Cultural revolt in a colonial society*. Scientific Education Trust.

Omvedt, G. (1993). *Reinventing revolution: New social movements and the socialist tradition in India*. M. E. Sharpe.

Palshikar, S. (1996). Capturing the moment of realignment: Maharashtra assembly elections. *Economic & Political Weekly, 31* (2–3, 13 January), 174–178.

Palshikar, S. (1998). *Jaatwa Maharashtratil sattakaran* [Marathi: Caste and power in Maharashtra]. Sugawa.

Palshikar, S. (1999). *Shiv Sena: An assessment* (Occasional paper series II, No. 3[SAP]). Pune: Department of Politics and Public Administration, University of Pune.

Palshikar, S. (2004). Shiv Sena: A tiger with many faces? *Economic & Political Weekly, 39* (14–15, 3 April), 1497–1507.

Palshikar, S. ([2007] 2010). Shiv Sena. In S. Palshikar & S. Kulkarni (Eds.), *Maharashtratil sattasangharsh: Rajkiya pakshanchi vatchal* [Marathi: Power conflict in Maharashtra: Trajectroy of Political Parties] (pp. 76–104). Samakaaleen Prakashan.

Palshikar, S. (2010). In the midst of sub-democratic politics. *Economic & Political Weekly, 45* (7, 13 February), 12–16.

Palshikar, S. (2013). *Reimagining Maharashtra: Moving towards creative politics—Overview and suggestions* (unpublished). Report submitted to the High Level Committee for Balanced Regional Development. Maharashtra: Government of Maharashtra.

Palshikar, S. (2014). Maharashtra Assembly Elections: Farewell to Maratha Politics?, Economic and Political Weekly, *49*, 43–44, November, 1, 10–13.

Palshikar, S. (2017a, October–November). Pawar nawache prakaran [Marathi: The thing called Pawar]. *Maha-Anubhav*, 66–74.

Palshikar, S. (2017b). India's second dominant party system. *Economic & Political Weekly, 52* (12, 18 March), 12–15.

Palshikar, S. (2017c). Third life of the Shiv Sena: Notorious becomes 'normal'. *Economic & Political Weekly, 52* (48, 2 December), 33–36.

Palshikar, S., & Birmal, N. (2003). Maharashtra: Fragmented Marathas retain power. In P. Wallace & R. Roy (Eds.), *India's 1999 elections and 20th century politics* (pp. 206–232). SAGE Publications.

Palshikar, S., & Birmal, N. (2009). Maharashtra: Towards a new party system. In S. Shastri, K. C. Suri, & Y. Yadav (Eds,), *Electoral politics in Indian states: Lok Sabha elections in 2004 and beyond* (pp. 108–129). Oxford University Press.

Palshikar, S., & Birmal, N. (2015). Maharashtra: Congress' dramatic decline. In P. Wallace (Ed.), *India's 2014 elections: A Modi-led sweep* (pp. 284–301). SAGE Publications.

Palshikar, S., & Birmal, N. (2019). Onward march of BJP in Maharashtra. In P. Wallace (Ed.), *India's 2019 election* (pp. 220–234). SAGE Publications.

Palshikar, S., Birmal, N., & Ghotale, V. (2014). Coalitions in Maharashtra: Political fragmentation or social reconfiguration? In E. Sridharan (Ed.), *Coalition politics in India: Select issues at the centre and the states* (pp. 107–172). Academic Foundation.

Palshikar, S., & Deshpande, R. (2003). Maharashtra: Challenges before the congress system. *Journal of Indian School of Political Economy*, 15 (1–2, January–June), 97–122.

Palshikar, S., Deshpande, R., & Birmal, N. (2009). Maharashtra polls: Continuity amidst social volatility. *Economic & Political Weekly*, 44 (48, 28 November–4 December), 42–47.

Palshikar, S., Deshpande, R., & Birmal, N. (2014). Survival in the midst of decline: A decade of Congress rule in Maharashtra—1999–2009. In S. Palshikar, K.C. Suri, & Y. Yadav (Eds.), *Party competition in Indian states: Electoral politics in post-Congress polity* (pp. 431–450). Oxford University Press.

Pandkar, M. (2020). *Maharashtratil krushi, sinchan ani gramin rojgar kshetracha vikas* [Marathi: Development of agriculture, irrigation and rural employment in Maharashtra] (unpublished). Report submitted to the Center for Public Policy and Democratic Governance, Savitribai Phule Pune University, Pune.

Pansare, G. (1988). Shivaji Kon Hota? [Marathi: Who was Shivaji?], Mumbai, Lokvangmay Grih.

Parihar, S. (2017). *Jaitapur Anu Prakalpache rajkaran* [Marathi: Politics of Jaitapur Nuclear Power Plant] (Unpublished MPhil dissertation). Savitribai Phule Pune University, Pune.

Patel, S. (2013). Mumbai. In I. Shirley & C. Neill (Eds.), *Asian and Pacific cities: Development patterns* (pp. 127–137). Routledge.

Pawar, N. (2009). *Maratha Seva Sangh pranit Sambhaji Brigade: Ek chikitsak abhyas* [Marathi: Maratha Seva Sangh directed Sambhaji Brigade: A critical study] (MPhil dissertation). Department of Politics and Public Administration. University of Pune, Pune.

Pawar, P. (1996). *Akhil Bharatiya Maratha Mahasangha: Ek chikitsak abhyas* [Marathi: All India Maratha Confederation: A Critical Study] (Unpublished MPhil dissertation). University of Pune, Pune.

Pendse, L. ([1965]2010). *Maharashtrache mahamanthan* [Marathi: The great churning of Maharashtra]. Lokvangmay Gruha.

Phadke, Y. D. (1979). *Politics and language.* Himalaya.

Phadke, Y. D. (1982). *Keshavrao Jedhe* [Marathi]. Shrividya.

Phadnis, J. (1978). *Shetkari Kamgar Pakshache rajkaran* [Marathi: Politics of Peasants and Workers Party]. Ajab Pustakalay.

Planning Commission of India. (2007). *Maharashtra Development Report.* Academic Foundation.

Purandare, P. (2013). *Water governance and droughts in Marathwada. Economic & Political Weekly, 48* (25, June), 18–21.

Purandare, P. (2017). *Panyashappath* [Marathi: Swear by water]. Lokvangmay Gruha.

Purandare, P. (2020). Marathwadyatil water grid [Marathi: Water grid in Marathwada]. In T. Jadhav (Ed.), *Maharashtra Varshiki 2020* (pp. 311–314). Unique Academy.

Rai, S. (2019, 28 May). *Pradhan mantri Fasal Bima Yojana: An assessment of India's crop insurance scheme* (Issue briefs and special reports). Delhi: Observer Research Foundation. Retrieved from https://www.orfonline.org/research/pradhan-mantri-fasal-bima-yojana-an-assessment-of-indias-crop-insurance-scheme-51370/

Rosenthal, D. (1977). *The expansive elite: District politics and state policy making in India.* University of California Press.

Sathe, D. (2017). Land acquisition and beyond: The farmers' perspective. *Economic & Political Weekly, 52* (13), 59–64.

State Election Commission, Maharashtra. (2014). *Report of local bodies: Elections, 2009–2013.* Author.

State Election Commission, Maharashtra. (2015). *State Election Commission report 2009–2013.* Retrieved from https://mahasec.maharashtra.gov.in/Site/Upload/GR/Report_2009_2013.pdf

Shah, S. (1994). *Indian socialists: Search for identity.* Popular Prakashan.

Shinde B. S. (1988). *Maharashtratil Zilla Parishadnivadnuka* [Marathi: District Council elections in Maharashtra] (MPhil dissertation). Department of Politics and Public Administration, University of Pune, Pune.

Sinha, A. (2005). *The regional roots of development politics in India: A divided leviathan.* Oxford University Press.

Sirsikar, V. M. (1965). *Political behaviour in India.* Manaktalas.

Sumant, Y. (2006). Prastavana [Marathi: Introduction]. In Y. Sumant & D.D. Punde (Eds.), *Maharashtratil jaisansthavishyak vichar* [Thinking in Maharashtra about caste system] (pp. 16–38). Pratima Prakashan.

Suri, K. C. (2003). Andhra Pradesh: From populism to pragmatism. *Journal of Indian School of Political Economy, 15* (1–2, January–June), 45–78.

Suri, K. C. (2004). Democracy, economic reforms and election results in India. *Economic & Political Weekly, 39* (51, 18 December), 5404–5411.

Taagepera, R. R., & Soberg Shugart, M. (1989). *Seats and votes: The effects and determinants of electoralsystems.* Yale University Press.

Vamsi, V. (2010). *Political economy of inequality in Andhra Pradesh and Maharashtra.* Paper read at the international conference on contextualizing Maharashtra at the Department of Politics and Public Administration, University of Pune, Pune.

Vora, R. (1982). Rajkaran. In V. Hardikar & S. Dastane (Eds.), *Maharashtra 1982* (pp. 10–23). Dastane Ramachandra.

Vora, R. (1994). *An agenda for the study of political economy of Maharashtra* (Occasional paper no. 1, SAP). Pune: Department of Politics and Public Administration, University of Pune.

Vora, R. (1996). Shift of power from rural to urban sector. *Economic & Political Weekly, 31* (2–3, January), 13–20, 171–173.

Vora, R. (1999). Maharashtra Dharma and nationalist movement in Maharashtra. In N. K. Wagle (Ed.), *Writers, editors and reformers: Social and political transformations of Maharashtra—1830–1930* (pp. 23–30). Manohar Publishers.

Vora, R. (2009). Maharashtra or Maratha rashtra? In C. Jaffrelot & S. Kumar (Eds.), *Rise of the plebeians? The changing face of Indian Legislative Assemblies* (pp. 215–244). Routledge.

Vora, R., Palshikar, S., & Sumant, Y. (1983, January–June). Sixth Lok Sabha elections: Maharashtra. *Research Abstract Quarterly*, ICSSR, 61–74.

Vora, R., & Palshikar, S. (1990). Neo-Hinduism: A case of distorted consciousness. In J. Lele & R. Vora (Eds.), *State and society in India* (pp. 213–243). Chanakya.

Vora, R., & Palshikar, S. (1996). *Maharashtratil sattantar* [Marathi: Change of regime in Maharashtra]. Granthali.

Wersch, H. V. (1992). *The 1982–83 Bombay textile strike and the unmaking of a labourers' city*. Oxford University Press.

World Bank Group. (2017). *Maharashtra: Poverty, growth and inequality*. Retrieved from http://documents.worldbank.org/curated/en/806671504171811149/pdf/119254-BRI-P157572-Maharashtra-Poverty.pdf

Yadav, Y. (2000). Understanding the second democratic upsurge: Trends in Bahujan participation in electoral politics in the1990s. In F. Frankel, Z. Hasan, R. Bhargava, & B. Arora (Eds.), *Transforming India: Social and political dynamics of democracy* (pp. 120–145). Oxford University Press.

Yadav, V. (2003). Haryana: Social coalitions, political strategies and the capture of power. *Journal of Indian School of Political Economy*, 15 (1–2, January–June), 143–172.

Yadav, Y., & Palshikar, S. (2003). From hegemony to convergence: Party system and electoral politics in the Indian states, 1952–2002. *Journal of Indian School of Political Economy, 15* (1–2), 5–44.

Yadav, Y., & Palshikar, S. (2008, November). *Ten theses on state politics* (Seminarno. 591), 14–22.

ABOUT THE SERIES EDITORS AND AUTHORS

Suhas Palshikar, based in Pune, India, taught political science from 1978 first at SP College, Pune, and later at Savitribai Phule Pune University, Pune (1989–2016). He is co-director of Lokniti, a research programme on comparative democracy, based at CSDS, Delhi, and chief editor of the biannual journal brought out by SAGE, *Studies in Indian Politics*. He was also the editor of *Samaaj Prabodhan Patrika* during 1990–2004.

He is associated with the National Election Study since the 1996 elections. He has also been involved in various research projects of Lokniti, focusing on study of public opinion in India. He was one of the principal investigators of the international project on Democracy in South Asia (Round One and Round Two).

Professor Palshikar writes in English and Marathi on contemporary politics and has also written extensively in academic publications on the theme of democratic politics in India. He has been a frequent contributor to *The Indian Express* and journals such as *Seminar* and *EPW*. His Marathi books include *Maharashtratil Sattasangharsh* (2007), *Rajakarnacha Taleband* (2013) and *Desh Pradesh* (2014). His recent publications include *Indian Democracy* (2017) and co-edited volumes in *Electoral Politics in India: Resurgence of Bharatiya Janata Party* (2017) and *Party Competition in Indian States* (2014). His forthcoming work includes a report on *Politics and Society between Elections* (with Siddharth Swaminathan, 2020).

Besides participating in many international seminars, he has been a visiting fellow at the University of Chicago and Brown University.

Rajeshwari Deshpande is Professor of Politics at Savitribai Phule Pune University, Pune. She was the Indian Council for Cultural Relations visiting professor (Rajiv Gandhi Chair in Contemporary Indian Studies) at the University of Technology, Sydney, in 2014 and UK–India Education and Research Initiative visiting fellow at King's India Institute, London, in 2012.

Her research interests are in areas such as intellectual traditions of Maharashtra, comparative state politics, politics of the urban poor, urban caste–class realities, women's politics and policies related to social welfare.

At present, she is the lead researcher in India for a European Commission-sponsored international research project, 'Cultural Heritage and Identities of Europe's Future' (CHIEF 2018–2021; http://chiefproject.eu/), in which a consortium of eight European universities along with Savitribai Phule Pune University from India are partners. She is also the principal researcher at the Centre for Public Policy and Democratic Governance established by Savitribai Phule Pune University under research grants from RUSA Maharashtra.

Rajeshwari has been a member of the Lokniti network of Indian political scientists that conducts the National Election Studies in India and has worked on the nature of women's vote and the connect between welfare and vote in Indian elections using the NES data. She is a member of the editorial management team of the Lokniti/SAGE journal *Studies in Indian Politics*, where she also coordinates a discussion forum on 'Teaching and Learning Political Science in India'.

Rajeshwari has recently published an intellectual biography of a late colonial Gandhian intellectual from Maharashtra—Acharya Javdekar—in Marathi and has edited in 2015 *Politics of Welfare: Comparisons across Indian States* (with Louise Tillin and K. K. Kailash).

She has also published more than 30 research papers and book chapters in English as well as Marathi during the past 10 years and regularly contributes to the op-ed pages of English and Marathi newspapers.

Professor Palshikar and Professor Deshpande are the series editors of the **SAGE Series on Politics in Indian States**.

INDEX